Acts of Faith

Acts of Faith

A Memoir

Faith Abbott

Introduction by J. P. McFadden

IGNATIUS PRESS   SAN FRANCISCO

© 1994 Ignatius Press, San Francisco
All rights reserved
ISBN 0-87870-527-4
Library of Congress catalogue number 94-76951
Printed in the United States of America

For Jim and our five children,
& Monsignor Eugene V. Clark,
the *sine qua non*.

Contents

Introduction

T HAT RENOWNED CONVERT, G.K. Chesterton, once wrote: "Becoming a Catholic broadens the mind." And to those who charged that, on the contrary, the Church imposed unreasonable demands—that the Faithful must believe only what they were *told* to believe—he replied: "To become a Catholic is not to leave off thinking, but to learn how to think."

In the early 1950s, the young Faith Abbott had not yet discovered Chesterton, but she had broadened her mind into what might be called the quicksand of belief: trying to "find herself," she instead found herself sinking ineluctably into the embrace of a Church which (Chesterton again) "is much larger inside than it is outside." The result was a conflict of allegiance, between her family and the particular creed she had been raised in, and her newly-discovered faith in the Roman Catholic Church. Her answer was to write her way out of the dilemma.

It is fitting that one of the writers who inspired her then was Whittaker Chambers, who wrote his classic *Witness* not only to record his abandonment of a faith (the Communist ideology that had sustained his subversion) but also—if not primarily—to explain to his former comrades, including Alger Hiss himself, *why* he had left them. Perhaps without realizing it, that is precisely what the then Miss Abbott set out to do.

The audience she had first in mind was her own family, who remained in Moral Re-Armament, the "movement" into which Faith had been born and raised. It is doubtful that many Americans today would recognize the initials "MRA," but in the 50s its promotion of "an ideology to change the world" commanded considerable attention, both here and abroad. MRA had certainly commanded Faith's full commitment from her earliest years, and until she discovered the Catholic Church. There were, of course, some Catholics in MRA, but Faith thought of them as "teammates" rather than as members of any particular religion.

So her second audience was those she was leaving behind in the movement. Others had left MRA without giving any reasons; Faith wanted to explain how and why she had come to the realization that her discovery of what she calls "Capital-T Truth" would inevitably separate her from her old comrades. More, she wanted to "share" with them the sense and sanity of Catholicism.

But most of all she wrote for herself, which is what writers do. Putting down on paper what we nowadays call "feelings" came naturally to her. Indeed, she wasn't at all sure that she would let anybody else see what she was determined to write: she would think about that only *after* "the manuscript"—she never thought of it as a "book"—was finished. In the event, except for her immediate family and a very few friends (and the man she later married), no one *has* seen it until now.

Why then should it be published *now*? Simply because, in my judgment, the story you have in your hands is far more timely now than when it was first written, not least for Catholics who never knew what the "old" Church *felt* like. It's also a good story: a few years after the first draft had been completed, Faith decided to get a professional opinion; this was arranged by the then Father Eugene V. Clark, the priest who had instructed her (and also encouraged her to write the story). The professional editor who read it worked for a major publisher which specialized in Catholic books—a major market in those days. He was impressed (I can vouch for that, he described it to me at the time), but accurately gauged its weakness: it was "one more convert story"—and they were a dime a dozen in that era of Bishop Fulton Sheen, whose many converts included such famous people as Henry Ford and the redoubtable Clare Boothe Luce.

Nowadays, needless to say, converts are, well, *news*. True, many people still join the Church each year, but not in the same numbers—nor in the same manner—as in those days. As it happens, I edit a newsletter, *catholic eye*, which has gained a considerable readership not only of "conservative" (read *orthodox*) Catholics but also others who, for whatever reason, are inclined toward the Church. A goodly number who have actually become converts (or are thinking about it) have written to me, on the quite-correct assumption that I would be interested in their stories. Indeed I am—more than they could imagine. For while each story is personal and distinct, taken together they seem to me brush strokes in a portrait of an "updated" Church that bears little resemblance to the one in which I was raised.

For instance, some "searchers" have had to *pursue* what used to be called "instructions"—our clerics can no longer be accused of proselytizing. Even then, virtually every *catechumen* must now endure the so-called "Rite of Christian Initiation of Adults" which, if my correspondents have it right, is stultifyingly long on trendy "feelings" of "community" but woefully short on the kind of thing the *Baltimore Catechism* provided. (One young woman wrote that she didn't realize, until she made her first entry into the Confessional, that nobody had taught her what to *say* when the priest—presumably an old timer—said "Now make your Act of Contrition"!)

What was it like to receive the old one-on-one instructions? You will find the answer, meticulously detailed, in this book. Perhaps the better word is *lovingly*: Father Clark was not your average just-ordained priest; the revelations he imparted were revelations indeed to a young woman who had never dreamed that any one person *knew* all these things, much less how to expound them all with unfailing good humor. It must have seemed an amazing grace, and Faith took copious notes, recording the liberating notions and, yes, the feelings (here the word *applied*) she experienced. They ring true still: if you stumble upon someone who cannot find a priest available for "instructions," just give him (or her, of course) this book.

*   *   *   *   *

AFTER HER MANUSCRIPT WAS at last completed, Faith put it aside and went on with her new life. In 1959 she was married (to me, as it happened), and over the next decade bore five children.* Although always a prodigious writer of letters, she wrote little else until, the children no longer little ones, she began writing and editing (mainly for the *Human Life Review*) professionally. But from time to time during those "wife-and-mother" years she would take out the yellowing typescript and tinker with it, to make sure that what she had written retained the meaning she had intended.

She sent one revised draft to Alan Thornhill, a longtime family friend who was a well-known member of MRA (and one of its most effective apologists as well). A man of many parts, Thornhill was a cleric in the Church of England, an Oxford Don, and a prolific author. He had first encouraged Faith's desire to write when she was not yet in her teens. He wrote her that he had read the draft "with much interest" and encouraged her to complete it. Thornhill did not live to read the final draft, but they remained in touch, not least because Alan had become a Sussex neighbor of Malcolm Muggeridge, who was also Faith's good friend through their association with the *Human Life Review*, of which "St. Mugg" was an editor-at-large until his death in 1990.**

---

*Father Clark said the Wedding Mass, and baptized all five babies; the now-Monsignor Clark is Pastor of St. Agnes Church in mid-Manhattan, which Faith attends, faithfully, on Sundays.

**Muggeridge and Thornhill collaborated on several works, including *Sentenced to Life*, an anti-euthanasia play that was first performed in 1978 at London's Westminster Theatre.

When Faith decided that she would begin putting her manuscript into publishable form, she also thought of asking Clare Boothe Luce to read it: Who better to give an honest opinion on a "convert story"? Mrs. Luce had likewise become Faith's friend (and mine as well) through the *Review*, and they had often talked about the Church they loved which, both agreed, had suffered terribly through the vaunted "Spirit of Vatican II." She too passed away, rather unexpectedly, in 1987, and so never read it. But in one of her last letters to Faith, Clare had written that she often found herself "heartsick" after the ordeal of a "New Mass," and asked: "What can I do to change Her back into the Church to which I was converted 40 years ago?" So I believe Mrs. Luce would have greatly enjoyed this book, which vividly evokes that Church, just as it was, and will always be, *in saeculae saeculorum*.

J. P. McFADDEN

Preface

IN 1948, WHEN I WAS STILL IN HIGH SCHOOL, a middle-aged man stood before a congressional committee in Washington and testified against Communism, and a young Trappist monk in Kentucky published his autobiography. The middle-aged man was Whittaker Chambers, the monk was Thomas Merton. They went on to become famous authors, while I went on to Los Angeles, to work full time for a movement known as Moral Re-Armament.

If there was a connection between us, it was something called "ideology." Moral Re-Armament (MRA for short) was an ideology to remake the world. Communism was also an ideology to change the world and Chambers told the world how the communists planned to do this. Merton's search had brought him into an ideology that had already changed the world, whether the world knew it or not. Back in 1948, neither communism nor ideology were household words—as Frank Buchman, the founder of MRA, predicted they would become. But of course the communists knew what an ideology was: and so did *I*, I thought.

And so, although in the year 1948 I knew nothing of Whittaker Chambers or Thomas Merton, what they did in that year would soon "change" me in a way quite different from, and possibly alarming to, the protagonists of my inherited ideology, Moral Re-Armament.

IN 1950, TWO OF THE UNRELATED PEOPLE made a connection: Thomas Merton (from his monastery in Kentucky) sent to Whittaker Chambers (on his farm in Maryland) a small silver medal of St. Benedict, who is known as the Father of Western Monasticism. At that time, I was at Dellwood—a farm-estate in Mount Kisco, in New York's Westchester County. Grande Dame Emily Vanderbilt Hammond had given all 277 acres of Dellwood to MRA for use as its Eastern headquarters. I was spending many hours daily in the kitchen of Dellwood's main house, helping to cook meals for a hundred or more, and doing some secretarial work too. But I was beginning to think about a lot of things which didn't seem to fit into any sort of framework until some years later, when I read Merton's autobiography and also an essay by Chambers about St. Benedict's meaning for the twentieth century.*

The MRA "family" at Dellwood had read, studied, and discussed Chambers's book *Witness*, as the serialized sections appeared in *The Saturday Evening Post*: Chambers was considered "ideologically relevant" to Moral Re-Armament. We were all "tremendously impressed" (one of our pet phrases) by this man Chambers; and in fact I was impressed in a personal sort of way I couldn't explain. Mostly, MRA people prayed communally for individuals who had something, but not yet enough, to do with "the Work"; but now it was as if, somehow, and all ideology aside, Chambers had become important to *me*. And so, obeying this strange impulse, I prayed (privately) for Whittaker Chambers.

(Of course I never thought I'd actually meet the man, but I did, some years later; I wanted to tell him about my prayers and about how he had affected my life. But we were with a lot of people on someone's fancy motor yacht, sailing around in Long Island Sound; it was very noisy and social, and serious conversation was out of the question. I did however manage to tell him that his essay on St. Benedict had meant a great deal to me. "Oh, that," said Chambers, puffing away on his pipe. "Clare asked a bunch of her friends to write about a saint, for a book she was doing . . .")

By the early 1950s, Moral Re-Armament had produced a generation of young people, like me, who had been brought up in the movement and had gone "full time" after high school—so of course we'd not gone to college, or had jobs, or any self-supporting experience. (In MRA we lived on "faith and prayer.") At some point, our elders began to think that MRA could be enhanced by some of us having experience in the Real World (though that wasn't exactly how it was put) and I wondered if I might be one of these.

Mount Kisco was not far from Manhattan, so we at Dellwood got into the Big City now and then, and I was beginning to feel strangely drawn to the metropolis. Could it be that my next step would be to find a job there? If this was truly God's guidance, would it "check" with my mentors? My mother was also then at Dellwood, and she thought New York City might be "over-stimulating" for me. But parents rarely, if ever, had the final say in "team decisions."

My motives were scrutinized as to purity of intent: I wanted to gain writing experience (writing was considered "extremely relevant" to the Work) so I was cleared and went off to Manhattan with MRA's blessing and my mother's fervent prayers.

---

*A chapter in *Saints for Now*, edited by Clare Booth Luce, published by Sheed & Ward, New York, 1952; San Francisco: Ignatius Press, 1994.

We all thought I should begin with magazines, so I began going to offices and filling out applications. They were a problem because of that "Previous Experience?" question: how to translate important but unworldly experience into something coherent in a worldly context? Nothing happened for awhile, and I was becoming discouraged; but then someone suggested I try the Hearst Corporation, which had a lot of publications. So I went to its huge headquarters on Eighth Avenue and filled out the application and took a typing test which I failed on account of nervousness. Nevertheless, whether it was divine intervention or mere happenstance, it seemed I'd been in the right place at the right time, because one of Hearst's magazines, *Harper's Bazaar*, had recently acquired a new managing editor and he needed a secretary. I was sent over to the *Bazaar* on Madison Avenue and 52nd Street for an interview, and I got the job. And with it, a new identity: New York Working Girl.

Harper's Bazaar ran a regular column in each monthly issue: the "Editor's Guest Book," wherein new authors and new editors were introduced. From that column I learned that my boss, Robert Gerdy, was a friend and former Columbia University classmate of "the famous Trappist monk and best-selling author, Thomas Merton." I didn't know what a Trappist was and I'd never heard of Thomas Merton, but I figured he must be important, so I tucked the name away in the back of my mind.

Whittaker Chambers had also gone to Columbia and had taken the freshman-required course in Contemporary Civilization: later-student Merton had taken the same course, with probably the same instructors; and this course was significant in both men's stories. So there was another connection, and I was the third dot on that 1948 connect-the-dots page, but the connecting lines had been drawn with invisible ink that wouldn't show up till later.

WHITTAKER CHAMBERS AND THOMAS MERTON were *witnesses*. The theme of Chambers's book was "the ordeal of the human soul caught in the twentieth century's conflict of faiths." But Chambers couldn't explain the meaning of the Hiss case and of communism until he had explained himself. Through his book he made it clear, in many different ways, that his "witness" was, essentially, the Christian one. Thomas Merton was also a witness: Clare Booth Luce said of *The Seven Storey Mountain* that "It is to a book like this that men will turn a hundred years from now to find out what went on in the hearts of men in this cruel century."

I feel that I have been called to witness too, for reasons not entirely different from those of Chambers and Merton. Chambers wrote about the people for whom, and the idea for which, he had put his life on the line. Merton wrote for and about his friends "in the world" because what had happened to him could not go *un*said, even in the midst of silence. (And as it turned out, Merton also wrote for people he did not, and would never, know.) What I have written was initially intended for my friends and family—all those with whom I grew up in Moral Re-Armament. We were once a part of one another in a deep and invisible bond which can be understood only in the context of a moral and spiritual movement that believes it has been commissioned by God to renew the face of the earth.

I was "born into" Moral Re-Armament, thus becoming a member of its first generation. Our earliest vocabularies included such phrases as "being guided by God," "sharing guidance," being "changed," "giving up self-will," and "living by the four absolutes" which we knew were the "moral standards of honesty, purity, love and unselfishness." The movement was young, and those who were there at the beginning— who, in the words of the signers of the Declaration of Independence, had pledged "our lives, our fortunes, and our sacred honor"—knew that the future of our movement depended in large part on its inheritors' strength of commitment.

When full-timers went out into the world and got jobs, it was tacitly assumed that after their internship they would return to the fold— perhaps bringing "key people" with them. In my case, things didn't go according to that plan.

When my family and friends began to suspect that I was no longer "fully in the fight" I wanted them to know that I was not one of those who had simply left. Others had left, with no explanation: we would hear that someone was "no longer with us" and it was assumed that he or she had found living by the Four Absolute Standards too *challenging*. The silence in the wake of these defections indicated that *they*, not the ideology, had flaws: these individuals had "given in to moral defeat" and just wanted to live their own lives. When I was in Los Angeles and several of our "youth leaders" had packed up and left, I'd had my first stirrings of doubt; was there some *warning* they should have given us younger ones? If so, they'd been irresponsible. (I thought this, but never said it out loud.)

So it seemed I had an obligation to explain what had happened to me—that what might seem like a *leaving* was actually a *becoming*; that through MRA I had found the Catholic Church. It was more than an obligation I felt, though; I wanted to share, with those I loved, all that had happened. And I knew I had to get it all down before it became, as all intense experiences eventually do become, something remembered rather than felt. This would be difficult, I knew, and by the time I realized just *how* difficult, it was too late to back off.

And so I began writing what turned out to be a sort of autobiography.

In my original Preface, I had some things that were—in the mid-1950s—relevant then but which would become less relevant because Moral Re-Armament would go through some changes and the Catholic Church (which had warned the faithful about "indifferentism" in movements such as Moral Re-Armament) would become more "tolerant"—or so it would *seem* in the aftermath of the Second Vatican Council. In any case, there are some parts of my original Preface which I believe still hold true. I had written:

> Perhaps it is not my business to interpret what broad and universal validity there may be in the story of one person who was born and brought up in Moral Re-Armament and who later became a Catholic. I cannot say: this is what happens. I can only say: this is what happened to me. It may be that there is a pattern. I cannot fully define my witness and I do not presume to set down a message. I can only tell my story, and hope that the people who knew and loved me in Moral Re-Armament will draw from it whatever meaning it has for them: not for them collectively, as a movement, but for them as individuals who love God and who want to serve Him.

Acts of Faith

A tattered scrapbook print of the pre-teen Faith Abbott (typically, in pigtails) and friends, grating away ardently in the kitchen at Mackinac; the "Minute Maids and Men" spent all day cooking dinner for a hundred. MRA was a pioneer in family "togetherness"—every age could pitch in for the "movement"—which greatly impressed the many visitors.

Moral Re-Armament

Growing up with the Four Absolutes

IN A VERY LITERAL WAY, I owe my existence to Moral Re-Armament. When, in 1929, my mother and father met "the Oxford Group" (the newspapers were beginning to notice this new movement and had to give it some kind of name, and there was an Oxford University connection) they had two daughters and considered their family complete. The Group believed that God directed the destinies of nations and of individuals as well: "When man listens, God speaks." My parents had always been on friendly terms with God, but their friends in the Group taught them how to *really* listen to God; and it wasn't long before He told my parents that they should have a third child.

After that phrase "When man listens, God speaks" came "When man obeys, God acts." Whether it was God acting and my parents cooperating, or the other way around, the fact is that I came into the world. It was a world full of Depression and anxiety and forebodings, but the Oxford Group had the answers to all these things.

My father, Ernest Spencer Abbott, had gone to war in 1917, but before he was sent overseas he married Ruth Wenzlick, on Christmas Day. When my father was under his first shell-fire in France, he promised God that if he got out alive he'd give his life to Him. No doubt God often heard that from the trenches, but my father felt he'd made a *vow*, so when he got back home he began to study for the ministry. Young "Ernie" had to quit high school at sixteen to go to work; now he was up at five every morning to study ministerial courses before he went to his job at a bank. Before long he was assisting the pastor of

3

his church and even doing some preaching. In due course he got a diploma, *cum laude*, from the seminary.

By the time I was born, he was pastor of a small white Presbyterian church in Woodbridge, New Jersey. The church had been built when America was very new. *I* was still rather new, too, when my father got tubercular meningitis. He was sent to a government hospital in Texas; he died there when I was two, and my sisters, Nancy and Marjie, were nine and twelve.

Both sides of my family had roots in St. Louis, so we moved back there. My mother got a job and managed to support us. There was never any extra money—just enough to get by—so for recreation we enjoyed what we called "The Simple Pleasures of the Poor." One of these was spending Sunday afternoons (other families might be at the movies) reading aloud from the various Winnie-the-Pooh books. Pooh and Piglet and Owl, Rabbit and all his friends-and-relations, became a part of us, and they still are. I don't remember ever feeling impoverished or insecure or deprived in those days, and in fact I felt sorry for my friends who didn't have the kind of family *I* had. I knew we were somewhat "different" but this didn't bother me in those pre-adolescent years. My mother rarely knew how she'd pay the next bill, or where someone's new winter coat would come from, but we never had any sense of crisis—of being all alone in the world. It was my mother's mountain-moving faith that sustained us when there was good reason to feel insecure: God would provide, we had each other, and we had Daddy on the other side.

And we had the St. Louis team.

Though it was true that we had roots in St. Louis, and still had relatives there, it was the local team in St. Louis that was, for all practical (and spiritual) purposes, our extended family. I would occasionally visit aunts and uncles and cousins, but they had distanced themselves from "this Oxford Group business" and didn't seem to be a real part of our lives.

The team in St. Louis, as in many other cities, was made up of individuals and couples who were part-time Oxford Groupers. Though they were certainly "full time" in spirit and commitment, they were not full time in the literal sense of those who had given up homes and salaries and positions so that they could be completely free to work twenty-four hours a day for the movement.

Local teams, in those early years, were very earnest and their members sounded rather pious—people would talk about "making a surrender" and "witnessing" and "receiving direction." (Later on, these would become "change" and "sharing" and "guidance"— phrases were always being sharpened up.) But even in those days of stilted language, local teams had an air of gaiety and adventure, and the team in St. Louis calmly and naturally accepted as its responsibility the physical and material needs of Ruth Abbott and her daughters.

There was no doubt about the fact that "God was the boss" in my family. This was not mere rhetoric: it was a fact made practical by the act of sitting down every morning with pencil and paper and writing down the thoughts that came into our heads. This was called "listening to God" and our sessions were called "Quiet Times." (To my young ears, these two words merged into a single noun: *Kwy-ett-tyme* and I was always being asked "What did you get in your Kwyetyme this morning?") That was of course before I could read or write, but very young children were told they could listen to God, and they would then tell an Older Person what God had said, and that person would write down the youngsters' "thoughts" in his or her very own "Guidance Book." My sisters were very faithful about that.

We all had to make sure that our "thoughts" were from God, not from our own wills or imagination, so we would have to ask ourselves if these thoughts measured up to the Four Absolutes: "Is this absolutely honest, absolutely pure, absolutely unselfish and absolutely loving?" It was a kind of litmus test.

So that's the way it was in my family, and in all the families in the early days of the movement. Quiet times, and the four standards, made child-rearing (and family unity) a lot easier. When the kids were stubborn or disobedient, the thing was *not* for the parents to give orders, but for everyone to sit down together to "find out what *God* wants." This put authority in the right place: kids who would say NO to their parents would hesitate about saying NO to God. The emphasis was on pleasing God, not just on being good—and pleasing God (which had to do with His counting on us to change the world) became very specific when a child began each day by writing down what God said and then "sharing" it with the others. If the child got "off the track" later in the day, someone was sure to ask: Now, what was it God told you this morning?

So God became, in the child's mind, "that good voice down inside." The problem was that God sort of merged with parents. As I grew up, I felt that I was being guided by God and pleasing Him only if I felt the approval of my mother and sisters; as the youngest, surely *I* was culpable if something I thought or did was not in conformity with what they took to be God's will. If I had a "conflict" (a word we used a lot) it was—inevitably— because of my self-will. It's not that they ever accused me of self-will—that's not the way it worked. *This* is how it worked: my mother and sisters would bend over backwards to acknowledge where *they* had been wrong, thereby creating a context in which I could see, for myself, where I had been "unguided." That was the strategy, though I don't think that my mother and sisters ever thought of themselves as strategists.

As a family, the Abbotts were inclined to be excessively introspective and emotional. Or anyway my mother and sisters were, I thought, embarrassingly emotional. They felt everything deeply and were very "open" and the more honest and open and contrite and teary they became, the more I closed up. I was all tangled up in guilt complexes and often felt miserable, but I tried not to show it. They called me The Stoic.

IN THOSE EARLY YEARS of the movement, during which the Oxford Group had become officially known as Moral Re-Armament, the people who were full time were always on the move. They traveled because that was the way to spread the message and because they had no place to settle down anyway. With no property or permanent headquarters, any large-scale gatherings of the full-time team with the various local teams took the form of weekend "houseparties" in someone's home, or on some estate, or in a rented lodge or hall. I went to some of those houseparties when I was too young to know what they were all about, but my awareness of the size and power and spirit of this thing I'd been born into came when MRA took over and began to transform several dilapidated old hotels on Mackinac Island, in Michigan, and— to the bewilderment of the Islanders—established in the summer of 1942 the first American Training Center for Moral Re-Armament.

Mackinac: a beautiful gem of an island where the Great Lakes come together, where there are no automobiles, where in spite of all the summer tourists there is a sense of remoteness and of history, for the flags of Britain, France and the United States have all flown over the Old Fort which was built by the British in 1780. There is the lingering aura of the days of the Indians and of Father Marquette, and the ghost of John Jacob Astor and his fur trade.

In 1942 the ferry boats spilled out men, women and children from scattered outposts all over America and Canada and England, and some from Europe too. They had come to Mackinac to live and work together "as a family" and to learn how to take MRA to the nations which were locked in a world war.

I went to Mackinac that first summer, and every summer for many years. I loved the island—not just the life we lived there, but the mystery and magic of the island itself, with its cedar trees and pines and birches, the horses and carriages, the famous homemade fudge you could buy at the store on Main Street, the bicycles you could rent to ride around the island—around *all* of it, nine miles, on the road alongside the lake. There were winding trails in the woods, caves to explore, and the mansion where the Governor of Michigan stayed in the summer, and all the other beautiful homes up on the bluff overlooking the harbor.

My family and I had left St. Louis and moved to Chicago, and I knew we'd be moving again, and with each birthday I'd had a diminished sense of belonging anywhere. I knew that we were supposed to be "above" roots and family-ties and all that, but nevertheless I felt a bit displaced—until Mackinac. The rhythm of the summers there established a feeling of "home base." There was, we were told, an old Indian saying: Whom God loves, He gives a home on Mackinac. Whether or not God had any special love for me, I felt that Mackinac was my home.

It is difficult to describe the euphoria of those first Mackinac summers, the thrill of being among kindred spirits—such as Alice Blake (at age nine we became friends-for-life) and many other children from the U.S., Canada and England who knew about "being changed" and "having guidance" and who used all those MRA phrases without self-consciousness. At Mackinac we could be ourselves. Some of the children, whose parents were in leadership positions, were always speaking (in a superior and knowing way) about "Uncle Frank and the Team." How I envied them.

Our children's group had a name: we were the Minute Maids

and Minute Men, because we were on the alert to fight for our country. We had our morning tasks on the vegetable, laundry, or housekeeping teams and in the afternoons we had sports, and there was always tea time. We wrote and produced a play, "The Thinking Schoolroom," which had such characters as Tommy Teamwork and Whitey Morale. The grown-ups and visitors loved the play because it was not only entertaining but also fit in with the spirit and program of MRA in those years of the war, when the keynote was national defense. Our play was not about national defense *per se*, but it was about how kids could change and find unity in the schoolroom, and from the classroom to the country and the world, or something like that.

MRA's first full-scale musical, "You Can Defend America," had gone on the road in the winter of 1942, and had attracted nationwide attention and the endorsement of people like General Pershing and then-Senator Harry Truman. Sometimes important visitors to Mackinac said they were as impressed with our play (in which I was Messy Molly) as they were with "You Can Defend America" and "The Forgotten Factor," an "industrial" drama produced in 1943.

"Island House" was headquarters, and plays were performed in the "Barn" and there was also the "little red barn" which was where we Minute Maids and Men had our meetings. There we would plan how to take a new spirit back to our homes and schools and how we could make America "sound from within." At summer's end, as we'd leave the island on the ferry boat, those who could stay longer would run out to the end of the dock, waving and singing the chorus from "You Can Defend America" and we on the deck would wave and wave until the island had become a speck.

The teenagers at Mackinac produced a play too. "The Drugstore Revolution" was about how a typical high school gang kept a home from breaking up. "Drugstore" (or "The D.R." as we "insiders" called it) had a potent effect on the grown-ups, because it was—they said—so "real." And it was indeed based on actual experiences of the kids who had written it, and who acted in it. Whatever they lacked in dramatic talent was more than made up for by the passion they brought to their roles. After performances the curtains would open and members of the audience—hard-boiled, worldly labor leaders and industrialists—would go up to the stage, with their wives, and with tears running down their faces they would tell how their lives had just been changed, their marriages saved, because of the play. They were all obviously moved.

"The Drugstore Revolution" had proved to be an effective ideological weapon during those summers, so the decision was made to take it on the road. By then—I think it was around 1945—some of the cast members had graduated from high school; tutors were found for the younger ones, and so MRA had its first full-time teenagers, and they traveled all over the country playing to large audiences in school and civic auditoriums. It was not unusual to hear later, at MRA's Los Angeles headquarters, full-timers beginning their talks (which were never called "speeches") with "I first met MRA when the gang brought 'The Drugstore Revolution' to my high school."

Some of the "Drugstore" teens were in a movie, too—MRA had ventured into film-making—and it was hoped this movie would give American Youth an irresistible challenge. There were four main characters who had designations rather than names. These were (I cringe now, but they didn't sound so corny then) the Handsome Hunk of Heaven, the Brain Trust (guys); the Smooth Operator and Ye Olde Sad Apple (gals). These four archetypes and their friends met "a gang with the throttle wide open . . . they showed us how to fight for a plan that has fun, adventure, and takes guts." The movie showed how you could get out of your rut and *change* if you put God in charge of your life. You could learn to listen to God, live by the Four Standards, and (gulp) "Get honest with Mom and Dad." And then you'd have this wonderful freedom, and adventure: you'd be "Out of the Frying Pan and into the Fight"—this was the movie's title. Great pains were taken to appeal to the "typical American teenager": it had shots of the kids in the corner drugstore, at the beach, in an old jalopy; there were hamburgers and jazz sessions and of course the jukebox, which also provided the musical background.

At the end of the movie, the "challenge" was stated in strong terms. These words rolled down the screen:

> We can swing this country if we want to. Ever stop to think of it? Twenty-eight million kids with a plan. You can be a part of it or you can skip it. But a lot of us are on our way. This idea belongs to us and to you, and it'll go as far and as fast as we do . . . .
> It starts in you today, in your family and gang tonight, in America tomorrow.

I don't know whether "Frying Pan" got MRA many converts, but I do know that we younger kids needed that movie for our own morale, because we were beginning high school, which was the first crucial test of our commitment. The friendships we had made in summers at Mackinac became terribly important, and we would write long letters to one another, telling about the starts we were making toward "the twenty-eight million kids with a plan," and we wrote that we were with each other in spirit, and our letters always ended with: "Keep up the Fight."

High School Heroics

Temptations of a Teen-age Revolutionary

IN HIGH SCHOOL, what matters is to be like everyone else; in high school it became obvious that we MRA kids were . . . different. If there were a number of us in one school, we would form our "gang"—a "cell group." We stuck together not so much to "turn our school upside down" as to feel *identified* with something, to keep that awful *outsideness* away. Some of us may have succeeded in wakening our schools to the challenge of MRA, or at least to an awareness of its existence. But mostly it was a matter of endurance, which was in itself not without a certain positive value.

Looking back, I suspect this may also have been a difficult time for the parents of MRA high school students. It seems likely that—though they couldn't really admit it—they were somewhat divided within themselves, half of them wanting to see us enjoy normal teenage years and the other half wanting us to be "in the fight." And I guess some of us "stuck it out" mainly to justify our parents' faith in us. When they said things like: "I know it will be tough but I know you will be guided by God," what could we do?

My mother and sisters and I had moved to Richmond, Virginia when I was thirteen, and I was enrolled in Thomas Jefferson High School. Springtimes in Virginia were a fairyland of perfume and pastel; they seductively blurred the edges of "crucial issues." During the spring of my junior year, the world-wide ideological struggle misted in a lilac haze, as I became aware of certain endowments of nature which I'd always taken for granted: having blue eyes and long blond hair acquired a new and important value. And I had acquired a boyfriend. He was in the school cadet corps, and I went out with him every Saturday night. I also began to wear (along with his "colors"—blue and gold) a little lipstick, which was called "Tangee"—it was a sort of "training" lipstick, and I can still remember how it smelled, and the memory brings back the dreamworld atmosphere I had begun to live in—which did not, however, obliterate or obscure the fact that I was just slightly "off the ball." I was sixteen, and I had been kissed, and while nothing ever got beyond *that* stage, I knew that I was not living in full conformity with the total commitment demanded by the way of life I still (more or less) professed. Going completely off the ball wasn't even in the realm of possibility because my family and I were "in MRA" and that was that: it was somehow genetically determined. If you were born black you couldn't turn white, and vice-versa.

So I lived a kind of compromise—always with restraint, always with intricate rationalization about how much more "effective" I could be for MRA if I were "popular." But down deep inside I knew I was being what we called "fuzzy" and was "letting down the gang" and disappointing my mother and sisters as well as some of those for whom I was supposed to be an Example.

When the next summer came, I did not want to go to Mackinac. The cultivation of a glorious suntan had become almost a cult with my girlfriends and me, and I wanted to stay home and languish in the sun and dream about all the things I could do, now that I had (as I thought, privately) come out of my shell. The fact that this was perfectly obvious to everyone made it all the more essential that I should not admit the way I felt. I had my pride.

So: I washed off my lipstick and went to Mackinac, with dread like a lump in the pit of my stomach. I was afraid I would be "found out" though I couldn't admit to myself that there was anything to be found out.

The boy at home, Tom, wrote long and clever letters. In one, meaning (I thought) to convey the sentiment "Stay as sweet as you are" he (who loathed clichés) wrote simply: "Don't change." These words came as a jolt, because that was exactly what I hoped I would be able to manage: not to change.

But that was something few people could manage at Mackinac. Even those who were considered quite "changed" would be the first to find themselves in a "change-session." They would be made to see all the places they'd been "fuzzy" and with tears they would change back again.

I got through most of that summer, saying the right things and working hard on one of the cook shifts. With my good friend from California, Barbara Bluejacket, I wrote some songs; Herbie Allen from Seattle worked out a very jazzy piano accompaniment, all the gang learned the songs, and everyone said they were "inspired."

"Inspired" was another word which MRA used in its own special way. Inspiration was a certification of being "on the ball." MRA had a few trained writers then, but even *their* writings— whether simple skits for birthdays or whole ideological revues— had to come through the guidance of the Holy Spirit. If someone, even a professional, was not being honest and pure and loving and unselfish, was "holding back," then God could not "break through" and that person could not be truly "creative." Everyone was supposed to be creative and often people who had never written anything before they met MRA found themselves writing "inspired" poems and songs and producing plays.

Even though I had passed the "inspired" test, I lived in apprehension: any day now, one of the older girls would surely come up to me and say "Oh, Faith, I was wondering if we could have lunch together sometime?" This meant that they had had *guidance* about me, and we would schedule a meal, or a walk, during the course of which I would be "challenged" and I would end up in front of a lot of people, apologizing for not having "pulled my weight." I knew that if I were to be asked point-blank whether or not I'd been "all the way in the fight" I'd have to be honest; so I tried my best to avoid being put in a vulnerable position. Having done something "inspired" helped, for a while.

When the showdown came, it wasn't as I'd expected. One of my role models was Barbara Belk, a full-timer who had gone to my high school in Richmond. "Barbie" invited me to spend some time with her on the lawn by the lake. During the course of that long afternoon, she told me some things she'd had to "face" in herself, and then she said she'd had some guidance about me, and she read it from her guidance book. Her gentleness, and what seemed to be her deep caring for *me*, created an atmosphere in which there was nothing to do but to make a re-commitment: Yes, I would change, and go "all the way." (Not too many years after that, Barbie left the team and married her high school boyfriend.)

Nevertheless, for the first time I thought I understood what was meant by "having an experience of the Cross." I did not *want* to "die to self" so I had to make a "decision of the will." There was an almost physical sensation of tearing up by the roots the things I loved most and wanted to cling to. It had taken me a long time to get a toe-hold in the slippery ascent to the peak, (which in high school is popularity) and I didn't want to give it up. But I *did*; and when the first panic and shock wore off, I felt different: there was a lightness, a dizziness, a detachment from fears and desires, and unconcern with time and place. There was inside me an empty numbness, which wasn't exactly happiness but it was a kind of joy.

And peace. Not the "fire" that "change" sometimes brought, but a peaceful acceptance of a mission seen now in its real dimensions—a mission so staggeringly big that its acceptance was possible only through a rejection. All ambition, even all desire to see the mission accomplished, had to go and in fact had gone. The revolutionary zeal I'd sometimes felt seemed to have given way to something else—the one thing necessary— which was God. Not God as a general in battle crying Onward, Christian Soldiers, but just God, Who knew *me*. And my only desire then was to stay as limp as I felt, for I knew that in this detachment it was inevitable that God would use me as His instrument; everything that had seemed hard would be easy, because all I had to do was to obey Him.

Dante had written (much later I found out about Dante: then, I thought it was an MRA slogan) "In His will is our peace." I understood that, now.

So I embarked on my senior high school year still enveloped in this sense of peace and joy—not the heroic joy of a crusader going into battle but nevertheless a joy, and a detachment. It didn't matter whether I'd still have a boyfriend, whether I'd be going to football games and dances; it didn't matter what my friends thought about the new me or even what *I* thought about me: I had risen above myself. It wasn't that I felt superior to my friends; I just felt somehow *set apart*. It was as though I had made a secret pact with God and only He mattered. In the God/MRA symbiosis, the *God* part had become real.

This liberation from Self, an experience of "unconditional surrender," was something we all went through at one time or another. You *had* to go through a "real change" before you could be considered for full-time work, and this transformation wasn't easy to fake. I do believe that many of my MRA contemporaries and I had a genuine "spiritual experience." But if psychologists had scrutinized these teenagers who said they had given their lives to God so as to build a new world, they might have said we were too young to know what we were talking about; that our so-called "peace and joy" came from the resolution of conflict. They might have pointed out that, since troubled people found liberation from psychoses and neuroses through integration with "normal" society, our peace-and-joy came from conforming to the demands and standards of MRA. Wasn't our basic need *security*? They might have had something there. It was certainly true that our security in MRA was in direct relation to our renunciation of "the world" and of "normal" society.

There *were* "ordinary" parents who displayed varying degrees of distrust and fear about "this thing" that seemed to face their MRA-enamored youngsters with decisions bearing the solemnity of life and death, before they had any real understanding of mind and will. If *MRA* parents had any such worries, though, they would "convict" themselves of being "over-protective."

I can't say there wasn't damage done to young nervous systems—especially at Mackinac, where we were certainly not over-protected from self-styled "soul surgeons" (there was an early MRA book with that title) who, without any training—just their own inner lights—would probe our psyches ("I'm wondering why you aren't giving one-hundred-percent?"). It wasn't that they played God; they were just passing on what He had told them about us, in case due to moral fuzziness we hadn't heard Him clearly. Most of these self-appointed soul surgeons were well-meaning, kind people, and there often did seem to be a grace in these surgery sessions. Or anyway there was an aura of supernatural grace, because you felt the Hound of Heaven had singled you out, was pursuing you, when you were still so young—you must be very special.

But *was* it always the Hound of Heaven? It never seemed to occur to our parents or guardians that what was hounding us down the nights and down the days and down the labyrinthine ways might not have been Francis Thompson's Hound but a mortal who had recently been dissected by a soul surgeon and put back together not quite whole.

WHEN I LOOK BACK on my senior year in high school, the first thing I remember (almost palpably) is: exhaustion. My calm detachment had given way rather soon to feverish activity. There were twelve of us MRA kids at Thomas Jefferson and we met each morning before school in the auditorium, to share our guidance and map our strategy for turning our school into "an arsenal for inspired Democracy." Strategy involved Key Positions. Our high school wanted to demonstrate the ideals of Democracy, so it had a House of Representatives and a Senate: the latter was a distinguished body of twelve, of which I was one. Each senator was chairman of one or several school committees. One such was the Character Building Committee, which sounded Strategic; none of the other senators wanted it, so I became its chairman. The Character Building Committee was made up of one person from each homeroom, and they would come to meetings where the Steering Committee would inspire them to go back to set their homerooms on fire for democracy. I had of course appointed my MRA buddies as my Steering Committee.

The Character Building Committee had been started (in the interest of higher morale and other vague goals) before my time, but we brought it to life in a way that astonished the faculty. We stressed the Positive: what students should *do*, not what they *shouldn't* do. We sent out mimeographed sheets with statements such as "The purpose of this committee is not to make people good so they'll get to heaven, but to take leadership for starting a spirit that can sweep through T.J." and "With the state the world's in, to be 'bad' is stupid and to be 'good' isn't sufficient— the thing is to be Revolutionary." And "Unless you're different yourself, you can't expect the world to be different . . . every problem facing the world today is facing our school on a small scale. If we can find the answer here, we can do it anywhere . . . ."

We bombarded the homerooms with mimeographed quizzes, charts for the committee member to draw on the blackboard to lead a discussion; we broadcast programs over the P.A. system and used all the means at our disposal in a heroic endeavor to show the relationship between the individual, the home, the school, and government. "As I am, so is my nation." "Everybody wants to be important. It would surprise you to know how important you are. How do you tie in with the news you read in the papers? If you don't like things the way they are, where do you have to start to change them? It won't happen in the world unless it happens in you every day. Remember, America is *you* multiplied 155,000 times."

We wrote editorials for the school paper, and I had a weekly "joke column" through which I tried to get across a few ideological nuggets by means of satire and puns, such as "Number One on the Hit Parade: 'I'll Hold You in My Arms While the World Comes Tumbling Down' by I. Don Care." (I can't believe I ever wrote things like that.)

At times I sensed a certain lack of support from my team of twelve: Could it be that Buddy and Jerry and Wimpy and Ann Mason and the others had on their minds things other than drafting plans for revolutionizing our school? If so, it was somewhat disheartening, but I figured they'd eventually have the "Big Change" experience I had had. Maybe next summer at Mackinac.

Meanwhile, our "ideological thinking" became less a product of "team activity" and more a burden on my dedicated family. My mother, after a hard day's work, would turn her creative mind to the Character Building Committee, Margie would do the typing, I would bite my nails and eat many bowls of cornflakes, and we would all end up in a mild state of hysteria. (It was a relief to all of us when that year was over.) I tried to work "communism" into my various programs and articles for the school paper, but I didn't really know much about communism. I *did* know that the youth of America didn't have an ideological counterpart to it, and that we who had The Answer had to fight with the passion a communist would have if he were in our school. My erstwhile boyfriend, Tom Pettigrew, had made a few attempts to "win me back" (as I put it, in my diary) but he was beginning to realize that I was hopelessly lost in something totally absorbing. He was reading books about social psychology (he would go on to get a Ph.D. and become a prominent professor of that subject at Harvard) and one day he said—with an expression of admiration and resignation—"You'd make a good communist." And, so saying, he became a member of the fraternity of young men across the country, unknown to each other but united in a common fate: rejected for a jealous ideological rival. (Anyway, that's the way one of my MRA penpals put it.)

In January of that year, 1948, the team—The Team—came to Richmond. I state this matter-of-factly because words can't accurately convey the exhilaration of those days.

First, there was the rumor (*could* it be true?) and then the confirmation: MRA would indeed be holding a World Assembly in Richmond, and would be bringing "The Good Road"—the International Musical Revue which had evolved from "You Can Defend America."

Statesmen came from all over the world; there were long columns and many pictures in the two Richmond newspapers. One-hundred and twenty teenagers were traveling with "The Good Road" and they came (Oh, euphoria!) to my high school to put on a special program for a school assembly, under the sponsorship of (of course) my Character Building Committee. Our school paper, *The Jeffersonian*, reported on the assembly, and editorialized: "This bunch of teenagers is fighting to build a new world. They believe that the future of America is up to youth and that youth can do something about it whether traveling with it or staying home."

After that assembly (and I'd had my picture in one of the Richmond papers, too—I don't remember the exact context) everyone at school knew that my team and I were not just do-gooders, that we were a part of something really big and revolutionary. Even after the team had left, we were besieged with questions about "the MRA." New kids (mostly girls) would join us in the auditorium before school each morning, announcing that they had decided to "join the MRA." They would throw away their lipstick and walk around with little black Guidance Books. Some of them stuck with us until their parents became alarmed and suspicious of this MRA thing.

We could have gone after those parents and explained what MRA was all about (and what it wasn't: it was not a religious sect, we were not fanatics; it was always somehow easier to explain what we weren't) but that could lead to "being sidetracked" from "the mainstream." Unless, of course, one of these teenagers with apprehensive parents was thought to be "real MRA material," in which case some of the adults on the Richmond team (which included two well-known Protestant ministers) would "take on" the concerned parents. It was, we knew, very important for MRA not to be seen as a family-divider: after all, the theme of United Families ran through all MRA's songs and plays and writings.

I suppose some kids felt we had let them down, but we were "revolutionaries" not "social workers." And I suspect we did have something of an elitist mentality: the Richmond team had just achieved a new status within the global network, so everything we did had to be one-hundred-percent relevant to The Work, as MRA sometimes called itself.

The remainder of my senior year was filled with Relevant Activity and a kind of ideological euphoria. I felt I'd matured, rather suddenly, beyond my seventeen years; that I was already a part of The Future. As June, 1948, drew near, the big subject was: Where are you going to college? It seemed to me that my classmates displayed a bit of awe and possibly a little envy when they would ask "Are you going to go with The MRA?" I would tell them that's what I hoped to do: that I wanted to give my full time *now* so that the world would be saved and future generations would have colleges to *go* to. This sounded noble and self-sacrificing. It wasn't. The fact was, I had no interest in college—I was dying to be "with the gang on the road."

As Graduation Day approached, however, the world got a clutch on me again. Ah, vanity: I was not, after all, totally detached from the teenage milieu: I was having unideological concerns about how I would look—*sans* makeup—in my white cap and gown. There was nothing against having a little "natural color" in the face, so I availed myself of the General Electric Sunlight Bulb we had at home. And I did indeed get a lot of color— on my *chin*. Graduation Exercises are etched forever on my mind: there I sat, on the stage, under the hot lights, with a painfully blistered and oozing chin.

Faith (front left) and the Mackinac Singers performing at a wedding on Mackinac Island; enthusiastic singing was a movement trademark, the precursor of the "Up With People" musical troupe that later became an offshoot of MRA, and now performs around the world.

California, Here I Am

Ups and Downs of an MRA Full-timer

THE HUMILIATION DIDN'T LAST LONG, though, because I *was* invited, in the important and official way, to join the full-time team. And to join it in the new headquarters in the noisy heart of Los Angeles.

The building, at 833 South Flower Street, with its Florentine walls and archways and balconies and a small central patio, had once been the Women's Athletic Club, so MRA had nicknamed it "the club," but the vision was that this building would be a "new-world embassy." There was plenty of work involved in transforming the enormous building into an "embassy" which would be not only gracious and homelike but also manageable— not by a large staff of cooks and clerks and receptionists and plumbers—but by *us*. There were the long-range projects of re-piping the whole place, getting offices ready for the Finance team and the Press team, remodeling and painting; there were the daily jobs of feeding one hundred or more people, running elevators, answering telephones, and keeping the bedrooms on the third, fourth and fifth floors clean. There was always the danger of bogging down in the physical details and thus forgetting to "think creatively and fearlessly" about what God had in mind for the club in relation to the whole international program.

I learned how to operate the switchboard, run the elevator, plan and cook meals for the multitude, and enlist the ladies who came from their homes in Pasadena and Glendale to help us for a day, or an afternoon. It was a load for a seventeen-year-old, but I embraced each new challenge enthusiastically—and none of the elders (looking back, I wonder why they didn't worry about "burn-out") imposed any limitations on us new recruits.

One of the popular songs then in the MRA repertoire was about California: "Land of Sun and Sea." I didn't see much of either in those first few months. The job of running the club was so intense and all-consuming that most of us spent 24 hours a day, week after week, inside those stucco walls, without even realizing we hadn't been "outside." Now and then, no doubt looking like something that had crawled out from under a rock, I would go into the patio for some (usually hazy) sun, or up to the roof for some air, and I would inhale the smog of Los Angeles and look down on the dirty rooftops of one of the unloveliest sections of Southern California. And I would realize that there was nothing to go outside *for* anyway.

But none of that mattered, because I was now a part of the full-time team.

When I wrote letters home, the Richmond team passed them around and I would get letters back saying "We miss you in the fight here but we are thrilled that God has chosen you to be a part of the full-time team," and things like that. And they sent money, too, when they could.

After awhile, some of the good people on the various local teams began to notice our pallor, and felt they should get us out of the city now and then, and they would invite us to their lovely houses for swims in their pools, and barbecues. And sometimes we at the club would organize a "playday." Some of us cooks would get up extra early to pack picnic lunches and, leaving a skeleton crew behind, we'd pile into cars and take off for Griffiths Park, where we'd have strenuous games of softball and basketball and (guys only) soccer: European soccer, with Europeans who were very good at bouncing the ball off their heads. There were a lot of bloody noses and I remember the time Don Libby (American) had some teeth knocked out.

The kitchen was a dangerous place, too. Accidents ranged from minor cuts and burns to singed eyebrows: this sometimes happened if you opened the door of a pre-heated oven too fast. My own accident was the most dramatic of the winter of 1950. It was Valentine's Day, and I was testing a recipe for Mock Cheese Cake from *Better Homes and Gardens* magazine. If approved, someone would do the math—multiplying the recipe by ten or twelve—and type it up for the Dessert File.

I had often used the large grey industrial chopping/grinding machine (which could make mincemeat of bones in a few seconds) so it did not scare me. The recipe called for $2\frac{2}{3}$ cups of graham cracker crumbs, for the crust. I discovered that the machine (bolted to the floor and waist-high) was not efficient when it came to such small quantities; the crackers were not crumbing evenly, so I thought I'd help things along by pushing the crackers under the blades. And that's how I nearly lost the end of my left index finger. A whirring blade went clear through the bone, mangling things along the way. I didn't know that at the time: I just felt a bit of pain but much chagrin—how could I have been so careless? Surreptitiously, I went for a Band-Aid. But Gwen Anderson took one look and began dashing around the kitchen, pulling dish towels out of drawers and wrapping them around my finger and my hand. ("Gwennie" was a favorite of us younger ones; she was like a big sister, with a droll wit that could make a disaster seem hysterically funny. In crises she would say things like "Now don't get your tail in a knot" or "Don't get your bowels in an uproar.") But now here was this *serious* Gwennie, walking me— swaddling towels and all—to the doctor (friendly toward MRA) just a block away. I sat in his waiting room for some minutes, watching with fascination and some alarm what was happening to the dish towels: they were turning red. And the pain was beginning. When the doctor saw what must have looked like bloody rags he took me ahead of his other patients and, without injecting any local anesthesia, went to work. The nurse wafted smelling salts underneath my nose, while vocally marveling that I wasn't passing out. The pain was excruciating, but somehow the thought of what it must have been like in pre-anesthesia days when you had to have something like an appendectomy, helped: I don't know *how*, but it did, and I managed to be a wonderful Stoic.

After a lot of snipping, the doctor took twelve stitches between the tip of my finger and the first joint, and then he took X-rays. He did not tell me, then, that I might have to go through life with a partial finger. I went back—splinted and bandaged— to my room at the club and was put to bed, and someone filled a prescription for codeine pills. The codeine numbed the pain and oddly enough made me euphoric, which was nice because visitors began streaming in and they all wanted to know the details of What Had Happened, and I found myself on a non-stop talking jag. Lots of people brought bouquets of flowers, too. Never mind what foreign dignitary, or movie star, or prize-winning journalist might have been visiting the club that day, *I* was the Big News. It was rather thrilling.

Someone must have completed my recipe, for Mock Cheese Cake did go on the menu. My finger did heal, but was not restored to full normal activity for a year or so. The nail never grew back properly; the slight deformation is a constant reminder that all this really happened.

I guess MRA's Finance Team paid all the doctor bills. So far as I know, there was never anything like a legal contract with parents whose minor children joined the full-time team. If (for instance) my mother had been given accident insurance forms to sign, she would have been astonished and probably *insulted*: the implication would seem to be that she didn't trust the team to take care of her child, and this would make her feel like an outsider. That any of the faithful would sue MRA was unthinkable: we were all family. Of course my accident had been my own fault, but it did indicate something about the general lack of supervision in the kitchen, and I suspect that there were meetings about this during my recuperation.

After my accident, I didn't return to active duty in the kitchen for some months, but there were lots of other activities, such as chorus; and now and then we would climb into team cars and make excursions to schools and colleges and women's clubs and city council meetings, where we would put forth our ideology. We recast "The Drugstore Revolution" and I was in it, and my friend Barbara Bluejacket—who was in her senior year in high school at Hermosa Beach—was the lead; our first performance was in her school. After the final curtain, Barbara spoke from the stage about how she was just an ordinary girl, but she wanted to make her life count. We took the play to San Francisco and to a number of schools in Los Angeles, and after each performance we would explain, from the stage, about our ideology—in the vernacular of those teenagers who were far more tough and sophisticated than the ones I had known in *my* high school. We would look over the footlights at hundreds of pairs of eyes staring out of white faces and Mexican faces: there was always the "moment of truth" when we'd know whether we'd won or lost the audience. It seemed we always won. Students would crowd around us, wanting to know everything from Did we have dates in MRA? to How could they keep their parents from splitting up? Some of these kids were self-conscious, some were skeptical, but they all seemed hungry for what we had.

We had learned, in high school, how to be articulate about MRA in a teenage idiom—catchy phrases, all the right slang. Now that we were full time, we were learning to speak in more sophisticated terms so that we could convince visiting congressmen and senators and European diplomats who came to the club that MRA was the answer to the problems they carried around in their briefcases. Often, after spending many hours on our feet in the kitchen, we cooks would take off our aprons and wash our greasy hands and put on our good dresses; the fellows who were working in the boiler room or making holes in the walls for new piping would put on their dark suits. Then we would all sally forth into the large dining room and line up on the stairs to the mezzanine and sing with the chorus to the dignitaries we cooks had just fed. The MC of course always let it be known that most of us in the chorus had just come from the kitchen and the dishwashing room and the basement, because this demonstration of a "classless society" was always impressive.

I remember the time that U.S. Senator Harry P. Cain came to dinner. He was very impressed with the food and the service. The chorus sang various inspiring songs, and I was one of several who stepped out of the chorus line to speak to the Senator and his assemblage. I told him that I had helped cook his dinner, and that I believed that if a lot of different women from different countries could work together in peace and harmony to produce a good meal, then democracy could work anywhere. My testimony, and that of the others, must have impressed Cain; when he got up to speak he said that if young women could work out democracy in the kitchen, then "any other problem before us is of relatively minor significance."

We quoted that, extensively. It was a real feather in our caps.

Being articulate about our ideology was a kind of two-edged weapon; as we convinced others, we convinced ourselves, too. We had phases of doubting, but they were accepted as a normal part of our life. In fact, if you *didn't* go through doubting phases, you were "not being real." When you *were* "being real" and "shared" that you had doubts, you would then trace these doubts back to some kind of self will, and would have to ask yourself: Where do I need to change? And then it was simply a matter of "getting back on the ball." It all had to do with *acceptance*. It was much better to accept something as one of God's mysterious ways than to try to understand it. At times I doubted, but I never wondered.

Perhaps that is why even now I find myself ignorant about some things that most children wondered and asked about as soon as they could look at picture books. In high school I got straight A's but absorbed little knowledge because I had never wondered, on my own, about stars and planets and molecules, or how the earth came to be, or how Democrats differed from Republicans. Explanations and answers and solutions are like balls that roll into the right holes of curiosity and wonder. If there are no holes, the balls will roll right by. I knew people from all over the world, but I'd never wondered what their countries were like. I had never been curious about what economic and religious factors, what great writers and painters and thinkers, had shaped these countries; I had never learned anything about history or geography or culture. Yet I felt "identified" with the destinies of other nations; and the fulfillment of that destiny depended upon acceptance. We said: "Philosophers have explained the world; our job is to *change* the world."

THOSE OF US WHO WERE BORN into MRA grew up with all the answers before we understood the questions. We took our early responsibilities seriously. I remember, when I was eight or nine, talking to some friends about finding the answer to family squabbles, and about listening to God. "You don't hear a Voice or see writing on the wall . . . you just sit, and listen, and write down what comes, and then *do* it." Once I tried to stop a heated argument on the playground by saying: "But this is what causes wars, and you can't expect the world to have peace if you kids can't get along together." I knew the Answers. But I didn't know much about wars, or family squabbles, or any of the things that went on in my friends' homes.

During my first year at the club, I learned a lot. Not about the problems for which we had the answers (there was no time for such research) but about fatigue, for one thing—"bone fatigue" and mental exhaustion. And I learned about the discipline and sacrifice demanded in "living alongside other people." We knew that whatever we were meant to do in the world depended on our unity and our love for one another, and we knew that anyone who isolated himself in an attempt to live his own life within the framework of the team could jinx the whole works.

It was rather like a monastic concept; we had to be a community, not a crowd. We had supposedly given up our ambitions for worldly careers (some had given up careers which had already brought some measure of importance) and we had given up our right to determine how we would serve, or whom we would marry, or *if* we would marry, or where we would go, or what clothes we would buy. All these things were decided under team guidance. But there were still opportunities for self-will and ambition and lust and all the other things. Even monks have their professional hazards. That is where sacrifice came in.

What *I* had to sacrifice was my image as The Stoic. I had always kept my "feelings" inside. Now it seemed I had to let all these people walk in and out of my own private world, which I'd always kept secret even from myself. I had always hated to cry in front of anyone; dramatic scenes had always embarrassed me. (For years I thought I hated opera, because when I was young my sisters would listen to the Saturday afternoon broadcasts from the Met and sob over things like Mimi's demise.) But now I was supposed to "open my heart." I had to have "feelings." I thought I didn't have any, but one day someone sat me down and told me she felt I was dead on the outside and smouldering embers on the inside; that I had to be willing to be hurt without closing my heart (we had a word for closing one's heart: "Clank"). So I thought I'd better try to come up with some feelings, because if you didn't have them you would shrivel up, and if you did have feelings and could harness them, you would be a creative power for the new world order. "What about the *guys*?" someone would ask: "Is there anyone special?" If you said No, you'd be suspect: either you were dead inside, or not being absolutely honest, or you had a more serious problem. But if you had a crush on someone, that was wonderful: you could *use* those feelings, by giving them up. Someone wrote a song that began "Harness all the heartpower in the whole wide world" which had something to do with the channeling of one's energies being the key to freedom.

Some who had joined the full-time team found it hard to give up smoking and drinking and other various attachments—which, though they weren't specifically prohibited—in MRA there weren't any "rules"—were just not *done*. Since I had grown up in MRA I had avoided a lot of worldly complications, but I had managed to hang on to my moods, an indulgence which I felt to be a legitimate luxury of the Artistic Temperament, which was what I thought I had. But moods had to go. Moods, and preoccupation with private plans (like taking a nap or reading a book) because at any moment you might be called upon to show some important person around the place, or you might have to sit next to an important person at a special luncheon; and if you were stubborn or rebellious you might lose an opportunity (for The Work) that might never come again. If you tried to superimpose a cheerful countenance on your mood, you would not fool your teammates; they would say you were being "unreal."

PERHAPS THIS WAS ALL a normal part of growing up. Learning to admit and to use "feelings" and yet to "live above them" involves primarily an effort of the will. Growing up is not easy even under the best circumstances. And it was not an easy time for us younger ones, or even the older ones, at the club in those days. None of us knew just exactly what we were supposed to be doing. The club represented a new situation in MRA; there was no precedent to follow. Mackinac was a summer training center; everyone who went there helped with the work. British MP's did dishwashing, baronesses cooked, and so on. Caux, the headquarters in Switzerland which had opened in 1946, was not at that time open all year round, and at Caux there were at least fresh air and mountains and lakes. The situation at the club was analogous to a relatively small number of people staffing the equivalent of a large hotel as well as running an international convention day in and day out. It presented a new challenge to the practicability of our ideology. Was it humanly possible to keep going? Could we concentrate on remaking the world when, for instance, there were not enough cooks to do dinner, switchboard people had to run elevators, and all the sopranos in the chorus were in bed with colds?

That year, and the other years I spent at the club, were full of the intensity of that experiment. I was learning to think as an adult about problems outside myself; I was beginning to grasp some of the large and general practical problems you can't really grasp unless you have lived in the middle of them. They were years of hard thinking, and of hard work.

BUT ABOVE ALL, they were years filled with music. Quite possibly, music was what kept us going. Music was one expression of our philosophy about the "New Renaissance" that America and the world needed. But music was more than "a vehicle," a propaganda medium: it was something on a personal level— for me, anyway. And I think for many others as well. More than any of the other things we did, singing seemed to reveal and to integrate the two selves in each of us: through music, the secret incommunicable personality that is everyone's dignity and isolation was fused with the personality that was trained and molded for the propagation of the ideology.

It was while singing in the chorus that I felt most truly myself and at the same time most sincerely and most happily dedicated to a Cause. The songs we wrote and rehearsed and sang, in French and German and Italian and Chinese and Japanese, somehow made everything worthwhile. Singing in the chorus was speaking from my heart, conveying things for which I had no words.

No matter how tired we were (and we always were) we put our *all* into singing. I think I put into it parts of me that I didn't know existed—and that I wouldn't understand until years later. When we sang, it seemed that we were above and outside ourselves, and time; that we were communicating from soul to soul with something that transcended language. It was a superlative joy to sing about the new world. In those chorus times I could say with the Psalmist: I am delighted with my inheritance.

At "The Club" in Los Angeles (June, 1950), the International Chorus performing for the guests; Faith is just visible (fifth down from the pillar, right row; her sister Nancy is the third girl behind her).

The Defectors

How can anybody leave The Team?

WHAT WAS MY INHERITANCE? We who were born into Moral Re-Armament and grew up in its atmosphere were perhaps like "born Catholics" who wonder what it would be like to see the Church for the first time: outsiders cannot imagine what it is to inherit the way of life. Our parents were supposed to want us to make our own decision, when we'd reached some age of reason, but they couldn't know what we were up against in trying to make such a decision.

What we had inherited was more than an idea or a philosophy; it was a *spirit*. The literature of Moral Re-Armament did not talk about the spirit of the dedicated men and women in the movement, because that would have been counterproductive: the important thing was to get the message of MRA across to the millions. But there was one document, the Preamble to the Articles of Incorporation, which I always thought came close to expressing, in words, the heart and soul of MRA:

> Riches, reputation, or rest have been for none of us the motives of association.
>
> Our learning has been truth as revealed by the Holy Spirit.
>
> Our security has been the riches of God in Christ Jesus. Our unity as a world-wide family has been in the leadership of the Holy Spirit and our love for one another.
>
> Our joy comes in our common battle for a change of heart to restore God to leadership.
>
> Our aim has been the establishment of God's Kingdom here on earth, in the hearts and wills of men and women everywhere.
>
> The building of a hate-free, fear-free, greed-free world.
>
> Our reward has been in the fulfillment of God's will.

31

That was the spirit I thought of as my inheritance. Perhaps the term is *élan vital*—the creative spirit in an organism, the spontaneous rapport which exists between individuals as if they were organically of one mind and heart. It was the most precious thing we had and we knew that everything depended on the sustaining of this spirit. Therefore, to protect the source of this power, nothing was more important than keeping the air free from bitterness and jealousy and ambition and pride—all the things that could divide mind from mind, and heart from heart. That was the constant battle, and it made things pretty intense.

What is both necessary to understand, and most difficult to communicate, is the psychological effect of being brought up in the atmosphere created by this spirit. Each of us was in a sort of psychological cocoon. For each of us, of course, it was a little different because of individual temperament and the distinctive features of our own families. Some of us found it easier than others to say: "I have now made my *own* decision to live Moral Re-Armament." The fact was, none of us could really know "freedom of choice." We were inexorably bound to the life, because the choice was presented as between God and inevitable decadence. It was black and white: we would be a part of the disease, or a part of the cure. So what this atmosphere gave me, and others, was the secret conviction that I had a very special destiny. It was either MRA and the fulfillment of this destiny, or a deadly and anguished nonentity. Theoretically, we were "free" to choose for ourselves. But is it possible to exercise one's free will when the very concept of choice is unknown? We born-into's grew up thinking alike and speaking alike; we moved along parallel paths; in such a milieu, dissent was inconceivable. Our whole environment forestalled any objective look at our way of life.

So for us, to make a choice between The World and what we had been preconditioned to believe was God's plan would be to do violence to our whole psychological structure. Some who tried to "give up MRA" came back to the prodigal's welcome. They would state that they'd discovered MRA was the only way after all. Whatever "individualism" had caused them to leave was renounced; they would henceforth deny themselves for what they were now convinced was the will of God. They were back in the heart of the family, they were back in the fight, they were again Friends of God.

It didn't take the cumulative years of childhood to become a captive of this atmosphere. Even a few years in it had a potent effect. When people new to MRA would leave, we would feel sorry for them, and we would say: "Once you have seen the answer, you can never forget it." (Or, in a lighter vein, "The banana that leaves the bunch gets skinned.") These people would generally follow one of several patterns. Some, who had found God through MRA, felt that by abandoning it they were abandoning God and therefore He was justified in washing His hands of them, and they would proceed to "go down the drain." The more "revolutionary" they had been in MRA, the farther down the drain they would go. Others of the departed would rationalize, and conjure up a compatible concept of God—a consoling Deity who wanted them to lead "a normal life." They would insulate themselves and—as we said—settle down in a grey rut of mediocrity, and never find the fullness of God's plan. Of these two classifications, there was always more hope for the unmitigated rebels. They might become desperate enough to come back. The lukewarm, alas, probably could not be reached, for they were lost in layers of complacency.

Although it was impossible for me to make any kind of choice, there were times when I was not at all "delighted with my inheritance" and wished I'd never heard of MRA. Which was difficult to imagine, since without MRA I would not have come into the world anyway; and, things being what they were, there was nothing I could do about it. It would have been foreign to my nature to make a dramatic exodus, even if I made a dramatic return the next day. I was dramatic enough to imagine this, but I knew I couldn't do it. I didn't live in blacks and whites but I admired those who were "all or nothing." They, I thought, had *guts*. But I couldn't really imagine being on the Outside. No matter how difficult life could be with the team, it was nevertheless *something*: to leave would be to step off a cliff into nothingness.

There was something powerful and indefinable that bound me to the life, and that left its mark on those who broke away. It was more than the training we'd had and the conditioning of our consciences through a common idiom and a common thought-process. It was an ineffably infectious quality which, for all its elusiveness, was the heart and soul of MRA. It was this which gave impetus to the songs and plays, and charged the air and overwhelmed people as soon as they'd step inside an assembly or a team center. It was something electric. It had to do with language and commonly-accepted values, but in its essence it was wordless. Its outward expression was fixed in inflections, tones of voice, looks of understanding between people: a kind of ideological telepathy. For anyone long in this cosmos, any kind of objective analysis is both emotionally and intellectually impossible, because the mind and the emotions are fused in an organic whole. The cosmos becomes one's self; one doesn't exist as a separate entity, as an individual, outside of it. Anyone outside for very long feels just plain homesick.

That word we used a lot, "heartpower," was a bit more sophisticated—more twentieth-century—than "charity." Our spirit had the unified intensity of a front-line troop in hand-to-hand combat with the enemy, but perhaps it was heartpower that kept the passion from burning itself out. It was a passion which sustained its dynamic in the warmth and humor and compassion of a family, with each member sharing one another's joys and troubles. Together we wept and laughed, confessed and chastised (it was your duty to "challenge" someone if you felt there was a moral flaw somewhere). We were not a cozy fellowship of kindred spirits but a family of fighters who cared not only about the cause but about the fighters. Frank Buchman had said that we should "live to make the other fellow great." And Frank's idea of "teamwork" was: Train ten men to do the job better than *you* can.

And God, He too was one of the family. Perhaps it was this sense of a mystical bond with God—which we considered not at all extraordinary but the normal way to live—that gave us an unspoken but unshakable and impenetrable sense of superiority and infallibility. Our life together was in many ways utopian. Outside was darkness.

SOMETIMES, DURING THOSE MONTHS I spent at the club, it was dispiriting to see the enormousness of our task. I hadn't gone to Los Angeles expecting the lush palm-tree and orange-blossom sort of life which is the fiction of Southern California, but neither had I been prepared for so much desert. There were times when we all seemed to be stranded on some vast, arid, bewildering plane; but always we were sustained by our sense of destiny. We had accepted the challenge to bring the world under God's control. We knew that we might not see ultimate victory in our own lifetimes, but it was inevitable that we would win, because we were God's instruments: through us He would remake the world. And we needed to feel this sense of guarantee, for we couldn't have kept going if we hadn't felt the certainty that, no matter how things looked, we were predestined to be victorious.

BUT IN EARLY JUNE, 1950, something happened that shook me to the roots, and made me wonder if this sense of infallibility and inevitable victory had more to do with faith in our leadership rather than in what we called "naked trust in God." There was never any announcement, but *via* a kind of grapevine we in L.A. learned that certain ones of the "older gang" had *left*. Some of these—including ultra-popular Jackie Scott—had been among the first teenagers to go full time with "The Drugstore Revolution" and then with "The Good Road." They had been doing great things in Europe; they were our heroes. To us younger ones they represented the reality and adventure and glamour of all the things we talked about, in connection with our generation's part in remaking the world. The news was shattering. Their leaving was beyond comprehension.

I had known some of them fairly well and couldn't think of them as Traitors. And so—for perhaps the first time—I wondered, and I asked questions. I didn't expect any answers, and I didn't get any; but I asked *myself*: "Have they discovered some stumbling block that I—that we—haven't come to yet? Why hasn't it worked for them? What *happened*?" These "youths" had written many letters, for us all to share, about the complacency of America and about how all Europe—especially Germany—was "desperate for an answer." How could they know all this and still place their own interests above the crucial need of the nations? (And how could God let them do it?)

I couldn't justify their exodus but I couldn't condemn it either. I could only try to accept the hurt, and the emptiness. My friends and I at the club were like bewildered children whose heroes abandon them. What about us, we wondered. Who among *us* would pull out? And what of the others who had left, even before that summer—those who we had said would surely come back, and who had not come back?

What all of this did was to bring me face to face with a question: *What if all the leadership should crumble?* The question itself was not the point, for the eventuality of the leadership crumbling was something I could not imagine: but the issue arising from this hypothetical situation was a very real one. Just supposing the leadership should go, would I stick it out or would I get out while the getting was good? Which meant: What are you really committed to, remaking the world or "the team"? Which do you love, and which are you serving, the vision of a world rebuilt or these people and this atmosphere of Moral Re-Armament? Had my motives for being with the team been unworthy? If so, did I have any right to stick around?

It was during this turbulent time that Blanton Belk, Jr. began talking about leaving. Blanton—the son of our dynamic pastor in Richmond—had been in the Navy and had been something of a playboy before he joined the full-time team. A lot of the girls had serious crushes on Blanton, but to me he was more like a big brother, and we confided in each other. He was a great tease; one never knew when to take him seriously when he made noises about leaving: he bounced on and off the ball with amazing resiliency. But this time he said he really *was* going to pack up and leave. Janie Belk and I remonstrated with him (Barbara Belk, who had "changed" me, was among those who had left from Europe, and was engaged to her high school boyfriend) and then some of the guys and a few of the men had a session with Blanton and got him all changed again, whereupon he went to work on *me*. I wrote in my diary, on June 28, 1950:

> Blanton told me yesterday that I'd never be able to leave the gang because the Lord has too strong a hold on me . . . and he said that that was true of him, too. I think he's right. . . . The situation in Korea is very serious. We've never been so on brink of war. What can we do?

Well, obviously what I had to do was stick with the team: it was my patriotic duty and anyway, I had breathed the MRA air too long to imagine existence without it, and so I went on, with a kind of desperate, wordless hope that God would be merciful even if He knew that I was not the sort of person who would go down with the sinking ship.

But at the end of that summer, something in me seemed to collapse. I felt empty and washed out. The perpetual activity deadened me. I was in my twentieth year and my youth, I thought, was all gone. (As were the twenty pounds I had always wanted to lose.) I must have looked pretty awful. I didn't know anything about the mortifications of the saints, but I took a secret pride in the dark circles under my eyes; soon there wasn't much glamour about that, either. The grown-ups concerned with the needs of us younger ones decided I needed a change of pace and place, so I was sent to stay for awhile with a family in Van Nuys. The parents were on the local team, and had jobs: they had two children, and my chief job was to look after the very energetic four-year-old. The other thing I was supposed to do was cook and serve dinner for a family of four. Now I had proved myself extremely proficient in quantity cooking: making five gallons of coffee was easy. At the club, though we put "caring" into the cooking, we followed timetables and got food into the steam tables and the "hostesses" took it from there, and the guys did the dishwashing. It was quite beyond me to make *a* pot of coffee and to have the different foods done at the right time and put them on the table: an entirely different mental process was involved, and I wasn't up to it. Dishwashing for the small family was a relief: it meant I'd survived another meal challenge.

All of that, along with the effort demanded to play Hopalong Cassidy with young Tommy Eastman, was too much; every small problem seemed insurmountable, and I spent most of the time in tears. Just before I had some sort of nervous breakdown, I was flying home to Richmond, for a long time of doing nothing: that's what had been prescribed.

I don't think it's an exaggeration to say that I was in a state of battle fatigue. It happened to many of us, and I guess it was partly our own fault, because we were always trying to prove ourselves, and therefore we got all worn out and reached the point where we couldn't push ourselves further, so we sort of collapsed.

RICHMOND WAS BEAUTIFUL that October. I had not seen autumn for several years, and I collected colored leaves and spent hours over the ironing board, preserving them in paraffin. I loved breathing the fresh Virginia air (after all the Los Angeles smog) and I loved our small Richmond apartment—especially because I knew we wouldn't have it much longer, since by then Nancy and Margie were full time and my mother had been invited to resign her job and join the team.

In the first month of 1951 there was an MRA world assembly at the Shoreham Hotel in Washington. I spent a week there and met many of the young Europeans I'd been hearing about, and saw many of my best friends who had become secretaries and were singing in the chorus and acting in the plays; I longed to be with them again. But the team went back to California, and I went back to Richmond to do something I had vowed I would never do: I took a secretarial course.

The course not only gave me skills, it was therapeutic. There was something of "normalcy" about it. And there was even a bit of social life that spring, because some of the MRA fellows I knew had been drafted and were stationed at Camp Pickett, in Virginia. They would come into Richmond on weekends, and some of the other young Richmonders on the team were home for one reason or another, and we would often get together and have long discussions. It seemed we were all doing a lot of thinking and philosophizing during those months, which were the first ones we'd spent in a relatively normal atmosphere since we'd gone full time. (Even a draftee's life was more "normal" than life in MRA: it didn't need to be explained.)

Mario Petrilli and Dave Robb and Jimmy Moncure were at Camp Pickett—Jane Belk and Jack Hipps and I in Richmond—and we all seemed to be groping for something. Obviously we were trying to "find ourselves." Jane Belk and Jim Moncure found each other: they got married a year or so later, and I was a bridesmaid. In an attempt to "find" *myself*, I wrote a long and involved opus which I titled "Retrospect and Introspect." (I don't know what became of those long yellow sheets I typed, but I suppose they clarified my thinking.)

When summer came, I let it be known that I had regained my equilibrium, and soon I got a wire inviting me to Dellwood. So I took my new inner stability and my new secretarial skills back to the full-time team.

Cooking for Uncle Frank

Fingerprints on the glass-topped table

ALL THAT HAPPENED after that now seems like a different lifetime. It was during that year at Dellwood that I began to have an inkling about something being not quite right in the nature of the movement itself.

In April my friend Betty Wilkes, who had been one of Frank Buchman's "special cooks" in Switzerland and who was now back cooking at Dellwood, was summoned to Manhattan to cook for Frank. He had been ill and was recuperating at Han and Virginia Twitchell's Upper East Side townhouse. Peter Howard—a British journalist and a principal Leader of the Work—was there, as was Paul Campbell, who was Frank's doctor and Peter's sidekick. Wherever Frank Buchman settled, however briefly, that place became the nerve center of the movement, and after a few chaotic days at the Twitchell's, Betty knew she needed help and she phoned me at Dellwood: Could *I* possibly come?

Well, this wasn't even a matter for guidance. When you were invited to do something for Frank Buchman, your teammates could manage to get along without you. And of course I was thrilled. So I took the train to the city, and was met by Betty and my old buddy Blanton Belk, of whom I hadn't seen much since that grim time in L.A.*

At the townhouse, phones and doorbells rang constantly; people came from the MRA office on Fifth Avenue (secretaries to do letters for Frank and Peter, couriers, higher-ups involved in strategy-planning which took place at morning coffee, lunch, afternoon tea, and

---

*I *think* Betty and Blanton were "just teammates" then, but some years later they got married, and some years after *that* Blanton became president of Up With People—an MRA spin-off that became an international Musical Road Show (its most famous *alumna* is the now-famous actress Glenn Close).

dinner); Betty and I planned meals, shopped for groceries on Third Avenue, cooked meals for the household and sent Frank's special trays up to his room *via* the dumb waiter. The Twitchell's townhouse in the East Seventies had become MRA's temporary headquarters.

Sometimes Betty and I joined the others for lunch in the second-floor dining room. There were some strange and unnerving luncheons, at that glass-topped table, when John Roots was present. John was, presumably, also a Leader of the Work, but apparently Peter and Paul thought he was badly in need of drastic change. Something mysterious and secretive was going on: a few words would be exchanged, and then there would be silence, during which Peter would concentrate his brilliant, intense gaze on the hapless John—all the while drumming his fingers on the glass-topped table. Afterwards, Betty and I would polish the fingerprints off the glass, giggling (Betty was a great giggler) and wondering *what on earth* was going on in this cat-and-mouse-game. All we knew was that John Roots was being "challenged." (My diary entry from that time: "Being with Peter and Paul is terrifying but stimulating.")

There were dinner parties too, and one or another woman from the MRA office would come over to help cook and serve. Sometimes, in the evenings, Frank and his entourage would go out—once to a dinner at the Waldorf Astoria for Frank's friend Queen Juliana of Holland, once to Broadway, to see "Call Me Madam"—and on the night they went to see "The King and I" the Twitchells also went out, so Betty and I, giggling and feeling like school kids playing hooky, stole out to Radio City Music Hall to see "Singing in the Rain." It was Betty's treat: she had some money. We fairly danced back to the townhouse afterwards. I have never understood what that movie had to do with changing my life, but I felt even then that it was some kind of turning-point.

"Frank is *finally* leaving," I wrote in my diary. (The thing about Frank was that no one could know exactly when or where the spirit would move him and I guess we had got a bit worn out.) When we got word that Frank was actually on his way down from upstairs, we all gathered by the front door, to say good-bye. Someone mentioned that Betty and I had cooked his meals, and he thanked us (if you hadn't known better, you'd have thought he was just a nice, kindly, elderly gentleman). We told him how much we'd enjoyed it, and then he said, with that well-known twinkle in his eye, "Oh no, you haven't. You've had a Hell of a time." And then he was whisked off.

There wasn't time to ponder those words (Did Frank mean something Bad or Good, about having a Hell of a time? Every utterance from him was supposed to have a deep significance) because things were heating up at Dellwood. Peter had had a briefing session with us, and told us that "Dellwood is full of teeming masses."

And so it was back to Dellwood and the teeming masses and sometimes over ten hours a day in the kitchen. The air was charged with positive activity and big plans were being made, we gathered, in inner-circle meetings—but there was also something strange and *negative* going on, which reminded me of Peter Howard's fingerprints on the Twitchell's glass-topped table.

There was one specially-called "family meeting" (no guests were allowed at these) during which many of our leaders "shared"—with many tears—individual and collective sins. It was rather like a high-level self-purge. I think it had something to do with why "The Good Road" never got made into a movie, but emotions were so rampant that it was difficult to get the facts; anyway, the meeting was about forgiveness, not facts. We all of us ended up on our knees, and we must have looked very funny kneeling on the floor and praying into our chairs. Peter Howard was there to give a sort of general absolution, and a Benediction. Everyone went away supposedly feeling a renewed commitment, born from humility. Our leaders had stripped themselves of spiritual pride—they were sinners, just like us. (Frank Buchman, or someone before him, had made *Jesus* into an acrostic: *J*ust *E*xactly *S*uits *U*s *S*inners. But that was strictly for insiders.) We were all supposed to have been brought back to unity (which I hadn't known we had lost) and Renewed. But what *I* felt, and couldn't say, was insecurity, disillusion, and an obscure sense of unresolved conflict in the inner sanctum. What had happened was supposed to be something Victorious: I thought it was depressing.

But there wasn't time to wallow in depression because, in May, there came an S.O.S. from Mackinac: the winter skeleton crew there was feverishly preparing for a full summer program, which would include a World Assembly, and there was a desperate need for cooks. So we Dellwood cooks had a guidance session about who felt committed to Dellwood and who felt God wanted them at Mackinac. Two days later four of us were on the train to Michigan.

By now the Island natives knew that "the MRA" was very big and important; they must have realized this the summer before, when—during the first twelve days of June, when ordinary tourists were just beginning to come—one thousand, six hundred and eighty-three delegates from thirty-two countries (sixty-four of them from seven Far Eastern nations) had descended on Mackinac for "the World Assembly for the Moral Re-Armament of the Nations." A larger assemblage was expected for this summer of 1952, so MRA had rented space in the Grand Hotel.

MACKINAC'S GRAND HOTEL is known for its Greek Revival architecture, its panoramic view of the Straits, and for having "the longest porch in the world." Its "serpentine" swimming pool was famous for having had Esther Williams in it, during the summer of 1948. She was in the starring role of an MGM movie (I got to watch some of the "shoots"—Jimmy Durante was there, too) and the whole pool had to be drained and then repainted to match the color of Esther Williams' swimming suit. So nothing much surprised the Islanders any more. Nor could they complain: MRA had brought new life to Mackinac by expanding summer tourism. The ferry boats were loaded as never before; the horse-drawn carriages and the bicycle rental shops did a booming business.

"Mackinac is THE place to be this summer," I wrote in my diary. It was exciting, as well as exhausting. I would spend hours in the kitchen of our main residence, Bennett Hall (at sea level) and then would mount a rusty old bike and pump uphill to the Grand Hotel on "the bluffs" where I would help with telephones and room allocations. I was a member of the chorus, too, and the Mackinac Singers were always in demand, often at short notice. We all did a lot of non-recreational biking that summer.

When September came, those of us who remained on the island drew a collective breath of relief. As we wound down from fever-pitch intensity, nostalgia crept in—but not for long, because September was the month for planning ahead. One of our songs had the refrain "Red leaves are falling, and the long road is calling. . . ." The ordinary summer tourists had left, the gift shops had closed, the natives were laying in their supplies for the drab winter months ahead. The fog horn sounded lonely, and louder than ever. The little French-Indian children from Harrisonville, their settlement in the middle of the island, were coming out of the woods to go to the small schoolhouse with the few children who lived in the houses along the lake. Our meetings and assemblies were over, the local-team people had gone home, about three-fourths of the full-time team had left for Europe; it was time for the remnant to discern the next move. God would tell each one of us where to go, and the design for each individual would form into a blueprint that would reveal God's plan for the coming months in America.

Most of my contemporaries would be heading West, and I had visions of going back to California too; but some of the team mothers, including my *own* mother, had been having different thoughts about my future. So in mid-October I was on my way back to Dellwood, where I would have guidance and consultations about where I should pursue a (temporary) career in the world: it was thought that I should take a refresher course in stenography and try to get a job in publishing and take some courses in writing . . . all these things would be valuable, later.

It was clear to me that New York would be the place. My mother wasn't so sure, but her teammates' guidance checked with mine; and there was an MRA person in Manhattan with whom I could stay, at first.

I *had* once enjoyed the thrill of a paycheck—during my recuperative time in Richmond I had a job, during the Christmas season, at Thalheimer's Department Store. I sold, or tried to sell, fancy ties and such in the Men's Furnishings Department. The thrill of a paycheck was all out of proportion to the actual pay, which was the minimum wage—75 cents per hour. Still, it was *my* paycheck: proof of my existence as a person.

But in New York, my salary would have a crucial value: I was to be self-supporting. Or anyway, that was the challenge. Learning to handle money would be important, but of course there was much more involved in this "new move" and I had some guidance, which I shared with the various people involved in this decision, and they thought it was "valuable." There were many things I needed to learn and to do, I felt, and as long as I was in the framework of the full-time team I would not learn them. I wrote down:

> You have often used MRA to give you a personal feeling of special destiny, of superiority to the masses. And yet you have often felt a deep inferiority with people of the world who have struggled and risen on their own—and with people on the team who can live in the heart of the team and yet know so much about everything. The life you live with the team becomes narrow and confining and you become stale and narrow-minded and opinionated and live from cookshift to cookshift and become more and more afraid of meeting new people. You don't take time to learn things and you can't concentrate on what people are saying when you have the chance to learn from them. So you crawl further and further into your shell. The time has come to burst out, to get out into the world. . . . This is the only way you will become a whole person who can be used fully in the revolution. When you get out into the world perhaps you will find a real passion to remake it. When you face the world and human nature realistically you will find many second-hand convictions becoming a reality. Your easy, protected life is over. You have grown as much as you can in this framework. I am offering you a new field in which you will grow and grow . . .

New York, New York

High Fashion and Low Spirits

Now of course there is nothing essentially new about someone setting out to find a job in New York City. There are stories and books about the starry-eyed youths who come to the city and look up at the skyscrapers with reverent awe and set out to "find themselves" in this crazy city. It is a perennial literary theme. There is nothing new: yet it is entirely new each time it happens. If the newcomers have read some of those stories, they may find that New York is full of things they had not read about and for which they could not have prepared themselves. The young women who, so as not to be stereotypical, have shed their illusions and have come to pit themselves against hard, cold, cruel Life with all its unpredictable elements may feel they have been cheated out of the glamorous misery of an intense and unwritten drama—they may find themselves living quite normally. There is nothing to write home about. They have come in a procession, bearing their small vessels of talent or idealism or ambition, and they are allowed neither the limelight nor the sweet satisfaction of a sacrificial offering.

NEW YORK IS NOT SO MUCH a place as it is a state of mind, or a way of life. It offers opportunity and disappointment and mediocrity, so mainly it is a challenge, and newcomers must adjust to their perceived demands of the challenge. Some adjust easily, some with difficulty, and some not at all.

I had an advantage because I had not come to New York to "find myself" or to "prove myself": MRA's ideas of success and failure were different from those of the world. I had come to

New York with the full backing of the team, and therefore everything was bound to work out, for whatever might be the inscrutable design of Providence.

Providence, or the Holy Ghost, felt like the summer sun, shining down on me: surely He who clothed the lilies of the field and knew the number of hairs on my head could easily find me a job. With one of those large, folded, obvious maps I tramped the pavements and filled out applications with facts that must have looked peculiar to personnel people. I had none of the usual requirements, except for "stenographic" skills, so I had to leave lots of lines blank (colleges attended, salaries received, reason for leaving last job) but I filled out lots of other spaces with a summary of my experiences in cooking and planning meals for hundreds of people, singing in an international chorus, working with people from many nations to train youth from all over America to think and live ideologically, and so on. I left these stirring testimonials in many flashy personnel offices of magazine publishers, and I didn't hear from any of them. Then someone suggested the Hearst Publishing Company, so I tramped over to the West Side where the Hearst Corporation had a huge building and a very dingy employment office. After the application routine I was given a typing test, on which I managed only 40 words per minute and made a lot of errors, because I was nervous. But it so happened that there was an opening on one of the Hearst publications—*Harper's Bazaar* magazine—and I was sent back to the East Side, to the *Bazaar*'s offices, for an interview with its new Managing Editor, who needed a secretary.

Robert Gerdy (whose job was *features*, not *fashions*) was very polite and a bit shy; he asked if I would phone him the next afternoon at three o'clock. When that time came I was with some people from the MRA office seeing *Cinerama*, which had just opened in New York. (It was impossible to get in, but MRA people always managed to surmount all obstacles; we even had good seats.) At three I absented myself to make the phone call, and Mr. Gerdy said the job was mine if I wanted it; I said I did, and he said he was "just delighted" and could I begin the following Monday? I got back to my seat in time for the famous Roller-Coaster Ride, which had the audience screaming and gasping and excited—my mood exactly.

My salary would be $40 per week. Since I had worked for

no salary at all, this seemed like quite a lot of money. Take-home pay would of course be rather less than $40, but what difference did a few dollars make? And of course I thought about the irony. I could imagine myself working for, say, *Good Housekeeping*, but a slick *fashion* magazine? We all thought it was ironic and amusing—and therefore certainly "guided."

In the typical New York success story, the newcomer begins in some miserable cold-water walk-up flat and works his way up to a smart apartment in a building with doormen and terraces which overlook the East River. For me, the sequence was reversed: I began my New York adventure in a modern, tailored apartment on the eleventh floor of Manhattan House, Section A. Manhattan House had been built on the site of the old car barns, and takes up almost a whole square block. It was one of the first "new" buildings then, fronted by a driveway that curves down from East 66th Street, sweeping along a glass front and white pillars, and there are doormen on duty. From a distance, Manhattan House—with its projecting glass-walled balconies—looks, as a taxi-driver described it, like a huge bureau with all the drawers pulled out. I was staying with an older woman, an MRA person from Atlanta, who was also an old friend of the couple whose apartment it was: they were off on a trip, Nan was looking after their two Siamese cats, and writing a book. The apartment was also a studio, because the man was a freelance artist. The living room's whole south wall was glass, with a door to the balcony: it was like a window, framing South and East Manhattan and the bridges over the river and, at night, all the twinkling lights studding the dark silhouettes of the skyscrapers. I could stand there and survey my kingdom. I was eleven stories above whatever lay in wait below. The tenement houses across the street, on whose roofs I could look down and see kids playing ball, and the very real and noisy Third Avenue El which rattled by below the balcony, were the only reminders that the city stretching out beneath my gaze was not entirely a fairyland.

THEN BY DEGREES I moved *down* the social scale. This was partly due to circumstances, but mostly to do with a growing desire for independence: I wanted to make it on my own, like the other "peasants." I stayed with MRA friends on the East side and then—

boldly—moved into something called the Hotel Warrington on 33rd and Madison, which was being renovated and was full of plaster dust.

I didn't stay there long, because my mother packed up my belongings and put them in a locker at Grand Central Station while I was at work, after I'd told her that a man tried to get in my window in the middle of the night. (I had asked: "Who is it?" and he had said "Oh pardon me, Ma'am," so I figured it was just a mistake—maybe he was a workman who had been surreptitiously using that room to sleep in, when it was empty— and I went back to sleep.) My mother said "And then of course you locked the window." That had not occurred to me, so Mother said she thought I'd better find a room that was several stories above ground-level and that was not connected to a fire escape.

A few days later I moved into something advertised in the New York *Times* as "an apartment for young business women." It was gloomy railroad apartment on 34th and Lexington where I would have "cooking facilities" and a room at the end of the narrow hall, and "breakfast," for only $10.50 a week, and a landlady who carried about her an aura of rather unwholesome mystery and psychopathic possibilities. Mother thought it sounded "safe."

After a day at work in the editorial offices of one of America's leading fashion magazines, where my boss, who was responsible for the literary features, would confer with people like Sir Sacheverall Sitwell and W.H. Auden and Cecil Beaton, and would dictate letters to governors and diplomats and royalty, I would go "home" to a supper of crackers and cheese. Sometimes I would buy ground beef and fry a solitary hamburger on the greasy stove in the large dark kitchen where all the silverware and utensils were kept in a big cardboard carton on the floor. "Be shuah you wash youah silverware befoah you use it," my landlady would say: "You don't want ta get soahs on youah lip." And sometimes I kept a few supplies in the communal refrigerator. This however was risky, since the fridge was never very cold and usually something in someone else's paper bag was going bad.

At first I rather enjoyed the pinch of poverty. And it amused me to make luncheon reservations for my boss at fancy restaurants like The Colony and L'Aiglon and then, on *my* lunch hour, to leave the flurry of photographers and models and rush over to the Woolworth's by Bloomingdale's where coffee was still only a nickel.

Inevitably, however, things began to change. As I became more involved in this new life and more immersed in the mechanics of daily existence, I began to have unquieting thoughts. My world had been so greatly enlarged that I no longer knew where I belonged in what seemed to be a vast macrocosm of human complexity. There was this new and forlorn feeling of no longer being Somebody. Here I was, in a city of eight million. I was among the millions not as part of a task force presenting plays, nor as a part of the chorus singing on the stage in a reserved hall at the Biltmore. I was just a New York working girl, and there were plenty of me. I had never thought I wanted to be Famous, but the obscure hope of becoming noteworthy in my own right had after all been deep inside me. When I was very young I had dreams of becoming a famous artist, then later an actress, a writer, and a singer. Being a part of the full-time team had nourished my feeling that I was Potential; that I would one day have a great impact on my generation. (I had never acknowledged this feeling, but it was there.)

Now, here was New York and My Generation and the harsh reality: I would not suddenly be Discovered. There was nothing to discover. I began to think that the most I could hope for was to be an "average" human being, for I was beginning to suspect that I wasn't even quite normal.

I was a critic of a world which had lost all reference to me and a "prophet" of a world which seemed less and less likely to come into being. The more I learned about *this* world, which I had viewed from a kind of moral utopia, the more I wondered about the new world which it was MRA's mission to bring to birth. The raw material was not so much raw as soft, I analyzed: human nature was padded by layers of complacency which only the most revolutionary could penetrate—and I was not the most revolutionary. I didn't have that "fiery passion" to give people The Answer. My position seemed to be one of example rather than exhortation: if I had any position, it was faith rather than works. (I wrote this down in my diary with a vague notion of what it meant.)

The fact that I didn't wear makeup made me different from the other girls at work: I was a curiosity to them. So, I reasoned, if I was an *intriguing* curiosity, if I seemed to have a "quiet secret of peace and purpose," perhaps that—rather than the militant—was my "role." Then maybe some would ask questions, and I would take them to Dellwood, and they would be—if not "changed"—at least impressed.

I tried to "operate on this level" (another cliché) but the process of applying my so-called philosophy to this enormous and unknown world became more and more unreal. One day, Carol—the secretary of one of the executive editors—and I were talking about Richard Nixon, who had just been elected Vice President. I made some vague, laudatory remark about him, and Carol asked me a very normal question: "Why do you think he's so great?" Nixon had been to the club; I had even shaken his hand. MRA considered him an ally and a statesman "above politics." He had said, in June of 1952, "There is no question that the great struggle in which we are engaged in the world, between the forces of freedom on the one side and communism, dictatorship and totalitarianism on the other, will be decided in the hearts and souls of men. The Moral Re-Armament movement is one of the greatest factors winning that struggle."

But what did I *really* know about Richard Nixon? I had been "challenged" by Carol, I thought; and in the empty silence of my room that night I wrote all sorts of self-recriminatory things in my journal (I had begun to keep a journal for non-diary-type ruminations). "You are nothing but a chameleon," I wrote to myself. "You take on the color of whatever atmosphere you are in and you never bother to find out the facts and do your own analyzing and form your own convictions. You have always managed to get by with vague, general moral aphorisms about a person or an issue . . ."

As I sat over my journal, gazing out the window at the dingy Bickford cafeteria on the corner of Lexington and 34th Street, I remembered another conversation which suddenly took on a new and depressing significance. The production manager of *Harper's Bazaar* was a practical, blunt, single, middle-aged woman who wore flat shoes and no makeup—a solid, rather refreshing incongruity among all the lady editors with their varnish and their cigarette holders and their Paris hats which they wore all day. They were intimidated, it seemed, by this Mary Hanshon—they respected her, because she was *herself*. One afternoon when I was sitting at my desk Mary Hanshon shuffled in with an armful of proofs for "Gerdy" to go over. As she waited to see my boss, we somehow got on the subject of writing. She said: "Writing was never one of my ambitions." I told her that I had no ambition to become a "famous writer," but that I wanted to learn certain things through a writing course I planned to take. I don't remember exactly what led up to it, but suddenly she looked at me over her glasses and said: "Don't be *mediocre.*" And I began to feel that's exactly what I was: mediocre.

I had been in New York long enough to have seen the conflict between two worlds, the one I had come from, and the one I was now—at least physically—a part of. I was suspended somewhere between the two. According to the age-old pattern, this was the time when I might have broken from the past in a rebellion against inherited tradition. I could not have done that, for no matter what I lacked, I had a conscience, and I had pride: it would have been dishonest to reject, just because it was my tradition, all the things I believed; it would have been childish and irrational and damaging to my ego to do something that predictable. Had I been a true child of my century, with a fair amount of intellectual curiosity and emotional stability, without rejecting all the past I might nevertheless have set off on The Search, wandering down the lanes of new philosophies. According to the pattern, this is the time when young intellectuals might realize their social consciences and go all out to alleviate the plight of the struggling masses, affiliating themselves with suspicious organizations. It is a natural time for crusading, for championing one cause or another. Or, if the person has a mystical bent and has decided that the world is at best merely an object for contemplation, he may investigate the religions of the East; or at least talk about them, and perhaps buy books on Yoga. He is full of ideas and questions; he and his friends will discuss them late into the night over beers in a dimly-lit bar or in someone's Village apartment, in the flickering light from candles stuck in wine bottles, dripping their wax down the sides. The point is not to find the answers but to enjoy asking the questions.

The trouble with me was that I was not asking those eternal questions about Life and Society and Values. I did not know about the little groups who sat discussing existentialism in the numerous Italian coffee houses below Washington Square South. I had never enjoyed asking questions just for sport, or for intellectual stimulation; and anyway I could not play the role of the intellectual contemplating his unanswered questions because I had no unanswered questions. A question cannot go unanswered unless it has first been asked. And I had never asked questions, because I already had the answers.

And so, although to someone looking on from the outside the dilemma had all the marks of the classic conflict between the inherited way of life and the big alluring world, because I had never questioned the basic tenets of my inheritance, I was not consciously at any crossroads.

THEN CHRISTMAS CAME with all its cheerful distractions, and I sent out more than a hundred Christmas cards informing friends all over the country that I was now a New York working girl. Probably the most daring thing I did that season was: I had a martini. Alone. I had slowly walked by several cocktail bars and then found an anonymous-looking Child's Restaurant, and I went in and sat at a table and had a martini, which I thought tasted terrible.

At Dellwood where I spent the holidays, everyone wanted to know all about my adventures in the Big City, and I told them about the job, and even about the martini, which had been more silly than wicked, but which was a part of the whole adventure, too. They listened and even teased me, and the more I talked the more convinced I became that I was rather special, and that my life was pretty exciting, after all.

January is always a strange anti-climactic month. Everyone returns to the daily grind and to all the things that had been set aside for the holidays. In January of my first year in New York the glamour and novelty of the big city was beginning to wear thin. It was not easy to gloss over the unpleasant bits of local color—the drunks and the bums, the greed and the lust and the poverty that stalk the city at night and in the daytime too. No one who comes to New York is really blind to these things, but it is possible for a while to accept them in the large, sweeping embrace of the whole sensational city. You take it all in stride, the bad and the good, until the time comes when these things begin to get under your skin with a gradual, almost imperceptible contaminating effect. You think of the crowds of people rushing everywhere, and of the individuals who pass through these mobs, unnoticed; individuals whose suicide you may be reading about in tomorrow morning's newspaper. And you understand how the greatest city in the world can also be the loneliest city in the world.

One of the paradoxes of big cities is this: the same circumstances which produce loneliness also kill solitude. No one who is not a real extrovert can stand New York for very long unless he discovers the difference between true solitude which is selfless and false solitude which is the refuge of pride. The cliché of "finding one's self" leads to an isolation, a separation from everyone else, so that one cannot give anything or receive anything—least of all the clue to his own identity. There is only the cultivation of the personality, which amounts to feeding the illusory image of one's self, dressing it up in things it was never meant to wear.

Even at an early age, when I first began a diary, I was obeying some obscure urge to distinguish myself from the masses of other people. The secret of everyone's incommunicable personality is God's secret; half-sensing that there was such a secret, I tried to discover it and communicate my individuality, and I never got farther than an experimental manipulation of words which were always the wrong ones. I could never seem to hit on the startling, revealing word or image which would unlock the key to that inner sanctuary. It had always been that way with writing: always solitude was loneliness that led to more blindness, and self-consciousness, and misery.

And so, that first winter in New York, in seeking to "find myself" in experiences mulled over in my journal, in the isolation of my room, I was very much in danger of losing even what I had.

My MRA friends, and other secretaries at the *Bazaar*, would ask: "Do you like living alone?" I said that I did. Loneliness: that was too conventional. If you could live alone, it meant that you had peace. I could not admit—even to myself—that I was lonely, but when loneliness became more psychologically disturbing than merely unpleasant, I bought a little radio. Then some kind of insidious virus got into my system. I couldn't seem to shake it off, nor could I get rid of the strange atrophy that came with it, and every day I sank deeper into gloom and depression. Worst of all was that I seemed to have lost my sense of humor. When I felt the most weak and confused and desperate, I had a powerful urge to run to the people who could make me laugh at myself and would tell me everything was really all right. I knew that at any time I could go to one or another of the MRA apartments in the city, or to Dellwood, and find understanding and encouragement. I thought it would be almost comforting to hear people ask: "Why are you so conceited that you think God can't solve your problems?"

But along with this strong urge to run to "the only people who really know me," there was an equally strong signal warning me that this was the worst thing I could do. Unless I could stand on my own two feet, I was not qualified to be a part of MRA. For that matter, I was not worthy to be a part of anything; I did not have what it took to be a part of any world I knew. I felt like a worn-out mule, and thought that both God and Mammon would have been embarrassed if I had offered myself to either master. I could not offer a lump of mediocrity to the world, and before I could make a complete submission to God and throw myself on His mercy, I had to prove that I did not need Him as a crutch. Before I could renew my commitment to MRA I had to prove that I did not need the movement as some sort of mother-image. I had to earn the right to God's mercy, I thought; He had enough free-loaders.

So what was I going to do? Well, for one thing, I would educate myself. I began a Current Events notebook. I bought a Pocket Book edition of *The Story of Philosophy* by Will Durant. And I decided the time had come for the writing course. One freezing night I went down to Washington Square Park, which is bordered on three sides by the buildings of New York University, and after crisscrossing the park numerous times (in my high heels) I finally found the right building, and enrolled in a class called The Writing Laboratory, which would be held every Thursday night in the Mills Building at 66 Fifth Avenue.

Next, I enrolled in a literature course at the Midtown branch of City College. Therefore, Tuesday and Thursday nights were taken care of, and I would not be exposed so frequently to the haunting spectre of this new thing, loneliness.

My family and friends at Dellwood were glad that I was taking these courses. They would often invite me for the weekend, and I would take with me all sorts of books and things I had written for the writing course. They always wanted to hear these, and they laughed very hard at the Character Sketch I had written about my weird landlady,* and they thought my free-verse piece about *The Dragon* (the New York subway) was quite good, if a little macabre. I may have alarmed some of my friends with some of the ideas I was getting through my courses, but there was little danger of my being led "down the garden path"— I was aware of the subtle traps, and these new excursions into philosophy were not likely to lead to any annihilation of belief. Rather, they seemed to be leading to a broader understanding of the beliefs I had always had; they gave me new angles and deeper insight, and I thought they might help to bridge the two worlds. I remember getting all excited about some of Plato's ideas, which I thought I understood, and keeping my Dellwood roommate awake very late as I pointed out the similarity between Plato's philosophy and MRA. In the literature course, we were studying Orwell's *1984*: I thought it was a horrible and illuminating example of what might happen if the "wrong ideology" took over. And so my friends at Dellwood may have had a few misgivings, but they trusted my good sense and had faith that in time all these things would prove to be fuel for the right fire.

WHAT I REALLY LIVED FOR was the writing course. Here was a disparate group of individuals whose only link was the desire to write, and—through the course—to find out whether or not they had talent. Here were people who knew nothing of my background, and who didn't ask. Everyone seemed a little odd, and that was fine, for what counted was not conformism, as in high school, but individualism. We were adults.

Our instructor, Vance Bourjaily, gave assignments; when he had read our papers, he would choose some to read aloud to the class, for discussion and critique. One of our first assignments was: Write a physical description of yourself. It would be rather like a game: Mr. Bourjaily said he would read some of these aloud and the class would try to identify the authors. This put me in a dilemma. How could I describe myself without mentioning the most obvious thing—that I didn't wear lipstick? To have included some sentence about "pale lips" would have been a dead giveaway. The solution was obvious: I would wear lipstick to my writing class. This was not moral compromise; I was

---

*See Appendix, page 235 below.

entirely justified. (I don't think I mentioned this to my MRA friends.) And my paper *was* read aloud.

As the course went on, and we did different kinds of writing—biographical, critical, "mood pieces"—I began to find a freedom from old molds of thought and expression. It was a heady thing, this sense of liberation. Was I actually becoming a real person? There was a Jewish girl in the class, and we would sometimes meet outside class—I even spent Yom Kippur with her and her family in the Bronx. Her name sounded Irish, but she spelled it *Ilene*. She did ask questions about my background and I always managed to imply things without being at all specific, which was becoming difficult anyway, for I was feeling more pragmatic than dogmatic about MRA. One night over hamburgers in The Texan on Lexington Avenue, Ilene said she thought of me as an *enigma*. I liked that. And I was content to remain an enigma, at least for a while, because "enigmatic" was a legitimate category in which one was not obligated to be "black or white." An enigma could ride several horses at once, and keep people guessing. I *felt* like an enigma, but in spite of all the grey fog about myself, there were still those basic beliefs I had never thought to question; therefore I still had not come to any crossroads.

The most basic belief, of course, was God.

Every Tuesday night, after our Writing Laboratory class, some of us would go to the drugstore across the street. I found it reassuring that in all the discussions we would have over coffee, no one blatantly denied moral values. One night, somehow, "God" got into the discussion: not the fact of God, but the question of God. I was astonished at the way these people—some were my age, some were housewives and businessmen—referred to God as a vague, more or less mythical being in which you were free to believe if you found it helpful. And I was also bewildered, because in all the discussions I'd ever had with people—in my role as "enigma" or in a frank MRA context—the reality of absolute standards and spiritual values was based on the assumption that whatever one might choose to call it, the positive factor which represented God was the common denominator. With the premise that everyone really believed in God whether he admitted it or not, people could be led to a general conclusion about the need for moral standards and a purpose in life and an ideology for democracy, and so on. I had never talked with anyone for whom the whole idea of God was not a crucial issue but a matter of indifference. How could I prove to all these people that there was a God?

Like all the others born and brought up in MRA, I had been on familiar terms with the supernatural all my life. If I was not honest enough now to acknowledge my state of confusion, I could not in all honesty question God's existence. For we had always lived like the lilies of the field—not that we took no thought of the morrow; we thought and we did what we could in the practical sense—but usually there was little we could do about things like paying the next bill. Somehow the money always came. And in every other area of life, things that were way beyond mere coincidence were always happening. The finger of the supernatural was always reaching down into the natural order, moving people and things around like checkers on a board— opening pockets, melting stony hearts, providing new team centers and spaces on airplanes that had been all filled. Insuperable objects were always mysteriously removed: the miraculous was expected.

So it would have seemed not only dishonest but ungrateful to deny God. Besides, I had a haunting fear of what God might do to me if I didn't give credit where credit was due; therefore any little nagging doubts that may have been lurking around were shoved down into the nether regions of my subconscious. I thought I had kicked them out the front door, but they had gone down the cellar steps and had taken refuge among the shadows with all the other mysterious baggage lurking there.

And so I went on trying to establish the superstructure, when all the time it was the basic foundations that were shaky.

IN APRIL, EVEN THE EXTERIOR ORDER of my life got out of hand. I had realized, in February, that I couldn't stay at *Harper's Bazaar* much longer. I couldn't afford to, for one thing; for another, the superficiality and materialism of the magazine was debilitating. My boss, Robert Gerdy, sensed that I was unhappy, and he asked: Was it just the money? No, not just that, I answered, and I didn't have to say much more because (as I would soon learn) he too was fed up, and was secretly planning to leave the magazine. Nevertheless, he tried to get me a raise: Would an additional ten dollars a week help? he asked. I said it would. After some weeks of negotiating with Hearst's financial people, he informed me that I would be getting a *five* dollar raise. He said he'd thought a ten dollar raise was "a modest request," and "This company is *cheap*." By March, we were both (clandestinely) looking for new jobs—I was dashing around to magazine personnel offices during my lunch hour and he was feverishly composing letters to editors of such magazines as *Look* and *The New Yorker*. I would type those letters, and was instructed to take the carbons home with me: some to keep for a while, some to destroy. (Bob Gerdy did indeed go to *The New Yorker*, as back-of-the-book editor.)

Meanwhile, my landlady had turned into a Jekyll-Hyde character, with the evil side predominating. For no apparent reason I had been switched from her Good to her Bad List (Girls with Malicious Tongues). That she wanted me out was made frighteningly clear. I was stubbornly determined to stick it out, until my mother and sisters (who had heard her rantings on the telephone) convinced me that it was unsafe for me to be under the same roof with her. Although I felt brave and "wise as a serpent" I agreed that it was better, in this case, to be "harmless as a dove"—best to move out and let her think she had got the better of me.

So I had to find not only a new job but also a new place to live. Once again, I tramped the streets, taking the Business Opportunities and Rooms-to-Let pages of the New York *Times* into phone booths. My metabolism had evidently hit an all-time low; I was depressed, and it rained every day. With the advent of summer, my shaky foundations were very shaky indeed.

The Village Misfit

Climbing The Seven Storey Mountain

IT WAS THE SUMMER of 1953, and I had a small room in "Katherine House"—a sedate Women's Residence on West 13th Street in Greenwich Village. It was run by something called The Christian Union and was somewhat dwarfed by the huge Salvation Army women's residence right across the street, The Evangeline. (The Evangeline always had a long waiting list and the Salvation Army ladies did not hesitate to refer waitees to Katherine House.) I lived on the third floor, and my window overlooked a tree.

The Village was (and to some extent still is) one of the places in New York where most of the streets had preserved their individuality. There were trees, and small stores, and houses which did not all look alike; you could sit by your window and hear the footsteps of the people walking by, and fragments of their conversations. It was an oasis in the relentless machinery-hum of the city. On Saturdays, in the early 50s, strange bearded creatures in Bermuda shorts would stand in the line at the A&P for groceries. On Sunday afternoons old men played chess in Washington Square Park and young women in shorts or black tights, and young men in sport shirts, would cluster in the circle around the fountain, eating Good Humor bars and playing guitars and bongo drums. No one looked out of place in the Village.

And no one should have *felt* out of place, but I did. I was not really a part of the Village. I wasn't a part of *anything*. I felt isolated from everyone and everywhere. Most of the time I was a passive onlooker, watching what was taking place on the battlefield that was myself. I didn't know what forces were in combat, and I didn't know who or what would win. I would

59

administer first-aid to both sides. I can't remember the exact feeling—the memory (mercifully) has a way of protecting us by blurring these things in the course of time. But in those days I was still writing things down in a notebook, because writing things down was one way to confirm my continuing existence; and now when I read the things I wrote down I can remember a little of how it was.

There would be the panic. A twisting weight in the diaphragm and a melting in the knees. My heart would pound and my mind would soar like an escaped kite, and then I would be in a long dark tunnel. There would be flashes of light: I would reach out, and then the waves would come again like the big waves that come close to the beach, suddenly—so big you do not know whether to dive under or jump over, and then it is too late and you are sucked under and your face is in the sand and you feel the foam frothing over you.

I would wonder if this sensation was real or imagined, and then I would realize that didn't matter anyway because I no longer knew whether there was any such thing as "real." I would tell myself, in those moments, that this had happened before and I had come out of it. But the one consistent feeling each time the big wave hit me was that it would never break. Each time, I could not imagine anything going on from that moment. Everything would be blank space and I could not even remember what I had been thinking about.

I would be able to cry, a little, and then the waves would subside and I would lie exhausted. Then the next phase would come—one of numbness, almost a delicious feeling. Things were real, yet I was not real among them. And strange things would happen: I would smell the summer air and feel a breeze and be filled with an overwhelming sense that all these things were created for me alone. The tree outside my window: its greenness was for me. The furniture in my small room was there to comfort me; the table, the chair, they existed at that moment purely for me.

It didn't matter whether I was sane or not: I was among friends. It was like waking up after a nightmare in which you were dead, and being relieved that you weren't dead after all—you have been given the gift of life and you want to savor each morsel of it.

But I knew that tomorrow I would be in foreign lands. The

language would be different. There would be no identity. I wrote down streams-of-consciousness like this:

> What is reality: Water is wet—stones are hard—but maybe only to me. But I must cling to the thread. And know that it is there whether I can feel it between my fingers or not. . . . To cling to your faith, your beliefs, fanatically, desperately, knowing that to loosen your grip a tiny bit is fatal. Let it slip even the slightest bit and you'll never have it again. Loosen the cement around the foundation stone of a bridge—one tiniest budge and everything will fall down all around you.

And I would wonder: Just how does one go about having a nervous breakdown? Do you throw yourself on the floor and scream, bang your head against the wall, or what? How does one actually go over the line that it is so agonizing to stay on the edge of? I didn't know how to let go—how to flood myself out of consciousness. (Obviously I also didn't know about alcohol.)

> The most vital thing: to know reality. To believe with fanaticism. Stick your neck out in every area of life. Make a fool of yourself. No set of values is stable unless there are absolutes. *Believe* in absolutes . . .

And while I wrote this down, I was really wondering the same things Tolstoy had wondered: What is bad? What is good? What does one live for? What am I?

I had no control over the rhythm of war and peace. I wrote: "Things I used to think important I no longer think important. Peace can be in the middle of an atomic blast. War can rage in the middle of a symphonic Sunday afternoon. Both can come at any time. It is good to have war because then you love peace." I wanted tranquility, at whatever cost. And I couldn't have it because of this Thing inside me, which in more rational moments I called my Will. I began to fear it like a demon, the "roaring lion who is seeking to devour you."

My *will* was to be dreaded above all. I had often been "challenged" about my self-will. I knew that *everyone* had self-will, but the difference between me and the others in MRA lay in the degree to which we could consciously recognize and surrender our wills. The dictionary says that to be self-willed is to be overtly "obstinately or perversely insistent on one's own will." I had lived too long in the milieu created by continual renunciation of one's own will to be *overtly* obstinately or perversely insistent on *mine*.

The will is a conscious faculty: my self-will was buried under many layers of conscious motives and controlled actions; it seemed to lie almost in the unconscious, in that dark place which I did not understand and therefore feared. What *was* my will, and what would it do to me now? Was it really so intent on evil that it would destroy me rather than lose its prize? And what *was* its prize? And what if it *should* destroy me? I had no desire to go on living, but if I was powerless against my will, I was also powerless against something stronger than my will: the instinct, common to man and beast, for survival.

The worst times of all, that summer, would come after weekends spent at Dellwood. Actually they would begin there, and their effects would intensify. At Dellwood I'd see my friends, work hard, and hope that people felt sorry for me because I looked so awful. Then the depression would begin and I would try to hide it. Everything would suddenly seem unreal; things went on in a kind of two-dimensional dream.

My mother would come downstairs to prepare Sunday afternoon tea for the team family and guests, as I would be cleaning up the kitchen in frantic, inarticulate desperation. Mother would say: "What's wrong, anyway?" And I would tell her I didn't know. She would work in charged silence for awhile, as I tried to prove that I was fighting this black cloud, and then—with her eyes throwing unhappy sparks—she would say: "What I sometimes think you need is a good kick in the pants." And then she would say something about the curse of self-will that I'd inherited from her.

Now there was nothing I wanted to do more than kick myself in the pants and everywhere else. I hated myself; I wanted to destroy myself. Then someone else would come into the room and I would swallow and smilingly plunge my hands into the dishwater. If the person said something nice to me (and people always *did*: they were fond of me and knew I was working hard) I would almost burst into tears. I found that I could gain momentary control by hitting my knuckles or my wrists with the handle of a heavy knife.

Finally it would be time to get the train, and as much as I wanted to get away there was always that peculiar feeling, such as I used to have when I was very small, leaving mother and going to school, with a lump in my throat.

On the train back to the city there would be rosy-faced infants and puffing mamas with arms full of flowers from "the country." I would look at them and wonder what it was like to be "normal." The train pulling into Grand Central felt like a foreign planet coming to earth: everything was unreal and peculiar.

Back in my room, I would try to read but I could not concentrate. My mind would race off in all directions between each line; I'd read the same paragraph over and over. I had heard that a person who is having a nervous breakdown can't concentrate or read, and I hoped that something would happen soon. Perhaps it would be discovered that I had some strange metabolic disease (I took comfort from this thought) and soon I would be lying in a hospital bed and people would be saying: Forgive us, we just didn't understand.

During those tortuous days, I felt as though I had lost all sense of harmony with the universe. I myself and all the people and objects around me were formless presences in a moving stream that was rushing somewhere without direction. We hurtled through tunnels to work in the morning, fighting the mobs in the subways; merely arriving at work in one piece seemed to involve enough effort for one day, and there was still the whole day to get through.

Sometimes on my lunch hour I would go to a nearby square that had trees and benches, and the sun would warm me like a comforting sort of blanket and the fog would clear, for awhile. It was not as though the sun burst through the fog to reveal sharp peaks of reality: when the fog cleared, I felt suspended in a sort of space, where things were floating, where nothing much mattered and nothing touched me.

One night I sat typing names and addresses on envelopes in a dingy letter shop on West 19th Street, where I sometimes worked to make extra money, and where I could do a certain amount of thinking while my fingers worked automatically. Suddenly I made what I thought was a great discovery: that living *in* the world while not being *of* the world had to do with realizing that there were different *realities* and one could simply choose in which reality he wanted to live. That, I thought, should end the conflict and confusion: it was simply a matter of being consistent with whatever reality you settled on.

New York was a mirror of a disintegrated society—a world

of shifting values and relative standards. Who was to say that there were Absolutes? One had to realize that people lived in different dimensions, according to their own standards; once you were aware of this you could select your particular reality and exist in that reality: it was a matter of existence, of *being*, rather than of pursuing some goal.

There was something healthy in this reasoning, for I had at least become free from the familiar thought-pattern. I was thinking independently, if not very intelligently (I had not heard of existentialism) and my thinking was not directed at reaching any conclusion. There was, I thought, nothing *I* could do to lift myself out of this vacuum.

During those days there were times when I felt a sense of destiny—as though there were a pattern, the forming of which was above me and had nothing to do with my efforts. There were days which seemed to be filled with a meaning beyond and above the commonplace appearance of things; and there came a new sense of the value of aiming for perfection in each task, however small. My tasks were, in fact, *very* small: I was working in the enormous building of the American Book-Stratford Press, one of the largest book manufacturers in the country; but I was working for a kind of subsidiary project which had been the bright idea of one of the vice presidents. The job had to do with producing a new line of 25-cent children's books called "Jolly Books," but there was little for me to do besides rejecting silly manuscripts and spraying plastic fixative on freshly-pulled galley proofs. I watered the plants and kept the office dusted, and chatted with Dorothy McKittrick, who was a Catholic and lived in Brooklyn, and who was the associate editor of Jolly Books—a position which did not keep her very busy either. I admired her sense of humor and her stability. Of course I couldn't let her know the real me, since *I* didn't know the real me; but later on we became very close friends.

Something strange was happening to my motives, it seemed: I no longer felt guilty if I couldn't see how I was affecting the world through each thing I did. I was taking a day at a time, and trying to please God by doing small things well, and this idea of serving was somehow satisfying, and seemed to need no other reason to justify itself. At night I would repeat some lines I had memorized (memorizing was one thing I discovered to be helpful in preventing the mind from going round in circles) from *The Village Blacksmith*:

> Toiling, rejoicing, sorrowing,
> Onward through life he goes,
> Each morning sees some task begun,
> Each evening sees it close;
> Something accomplished, something done
> Has earned a night's repose.

It was not a very inspiring Night Prayer, but it consoled me in some mysterious way.

I do not think that I have overdramatized all this: in that summer of 1953 I was in a real crisis. I had certainty about two things only: that (as I put it) "everything has crumbled"; and that I could do nothing about it. I also memorized *Invictus* by W.E. Henley, and walking from the subway to the office I would say the lines: "I am the master of my fate: I am the captain of my soul." I think I must have enjoyed the irony (if I enjoyed *anything* in those days) because I had never felt less the captain of my soul.

I was helpless because the old formula didn't work. The familiar diagnosis of conflict being a tug-of-war between the ego and God no longer helped, because I no longer knew who I was or what my will was or who God was. I was no longer the same person who had written:

> The important thing is to feel the Lord close—real—guiding you. Whether you can prove that he is God or not—what does it matter whether it's your imagination or not—that doesn't matter either because you know how you feel when it's there and when it isn't . . .

I COULDN'T REMEMBER what it was like to feel even *emotional* "certainty." God, as a voice dictating to me in my Quiet Times, was gone. I wondered vaguely how long He had been gone before I'd realized it . . . how long had I been listening to my own voices?

Those who have studied the psychology of conversion say that in a true crisis, which is moral and spiritual and physical, along with a total sense of helplessness there must be a hidden knowledge that only God can do anything: if there is only one-half of the necessary condition for conversion, a sense of crisis and helplessness, there will be ultimate despair, and possibly suicide.

But the other half of the necessary condition for conversion is a "creative despair." Kierkegaard and others wrote that despair would be impossible to man if man had no intuition of the eternal; and in my despair there *was* the feeling that I was in the grip of some intelligent presence.

So far as God was concerned, all I could think about Him was that if there was such a being, He was different from anything I had ever imagined. And all I could do was wait.

Along with helplessness and "creative despair," another condition was necessary: before I could arrive at the beginning, I had to be brought to an awareness of what I was looking for: the ground had to be prepared to receive the seeds. But to some extent the seeds had to be identified before they could bring forth life. And then two strong lights broke into my darkness: first, that there was such a thing as Absolute Truth; second, that the salvation of my sanity lay in finding that Truth.

IT MAY SEEM ODD that these two convictions were so "new." Many people know that 2,000 years ago a Roman governor named Pontius Pilate had asked: "What is truth?" I must have read that sentence, but it had never occurred to me that men had been losing their heads ever since that time precisely because of the question mark after that short sentence. We in MRA had spoken of "the truth" but not of capital-T Truth. Absolute standards were our foundation, but I had never wondered about *the* Absolute, the cornerstone on which all other standards depended. We had of course been trained in "right and wrong" but I had never thought about their basis. I didn't know that sociologists had written about "morals without religion" or that there were humanistic and altruistic "ethical systems." And so I began to understand my disintegration. Everything in my past had been built on the sands of subjectivity. There had never been anything outside myself that I knew was *there* no matter where *I* happened to be at the moment; I knew of nothing which existed apart from, and independent of, this thing I called myself. I had always been guided in my response to reality by my own *feelings*. Truth was tested by one's reaction to it; faith was something you had to accept "blindly"—which meant emotionally. We had concentrated on sensible feelings, experiences, and instincts, in ourselves and in others, to substantiate the conviction that there was a God and that He had chosen us to help Him change the world. God, in fact, was the most subjective concept of all.

WHAT HAD I UNDERSTOOD about God? In those first twenty-two years of my life, the question had never come up. If some bold person in MRA had said "I'm not sure I understand God" he would be swiftly put in his place by someone saying: "Ah, but He understands *you*." Knowing God was simple: you took time every morning to listen, and to write down what came. If we would obey our guidance, God in His inscrutable way would take it from there and work the necessary miracles. ("When man listens, God speaks; when man obeys, God acts; when men change, nations change.") As individuals, and as a world force, we depended on the guidance of God.

But who *was* God? It had never occurred to me that God was a Who or a What. We talked about the guidance of God, the direction of the Holy Spirit, the Cross of Christ: to me they were pretty much the same. My knowledge of the Trinity was limited to that line in the hymn: "God in three persons, Blessed Trinity."

I am not saying that everyone was as theologically ignorant as I was. And with all the doctors of divinity (mostly English) in our midst, there *had* to be theological knowledge—but it just wasn't considered important. Our individual and collective spirituality was a kind of natural mysticism based on "contact with the Holy Spirit." When outsiders raised theological questions, they were brushed off by references to the scholastic philosophers' arguments about how many angels could stand on the head of a pin. Theology as such was irrelevant—as was, for instance, the science of politics. I had never learned about Democrats or Republicans or liberalism and conservatism because the important thing was to create real statesmen who would put the good of the country and of nations above partisan belief: it was "not *who* is right, but *what* is right."

We read the newspapers and discussed the issues behind the headlines; we read the New Testament and analyzed the strategies of those "first lifechangers," Peter and Paul and their—*our*—other friends. Pentecost was celebrated, in our "family meetings," not as the birthday of the Church so much as the forerunner of Moral Re-Armament—which had been originally known as "A First Century Christian Fellowship." ("It is," explained Frank Buchman in a note to a supporter [1922] "a voice of protest against the organized, committeeised and lifeless Christian work" and "an attempt to get back to the beliefs and methods of the Apostles."

If I had any concept of God, it was of a nebulous Something whose reality existed in terms of my own experience and on the authority of those who had been "living under guidance" longer than I had, those who were "more changed" than I was . . . God was the silent voice inside me. God was "conscience" or whatever you chose to call it, and you had to choose very carefully when you were trying to change someone. (You personally, or the team as a whole.) I *did* understand the reasoning behind the strategy: it was *ideological.* If you got specific about Jesus Christ or the Holy Spirit, you'd risk alienating Jews or agnostics or Moslems or Buddhists—especially the Buddhist *monks*, in their saffron robes; they rarely left their monasteries but they were now beginning to flock in droves to world conferences in Caux. Basically, you could refer to God as a universally-perceived Presence and you'd get your point across. So I guess as far as *language* was concerned, the end justified the means.

We listened to God, we got His guidance, and we checked our guidance by the four absolute moral standards of honesty, purity, love and unselfishness. But by what Absolute did we check those "absolutes"? One's guidance could be "challenged" and in fact that was the value of "sharing" it—a kind of checks-and-balances system. But guidance was challenged on moral, not theological, grounds. If a decision based on guidance turned out to be disastrous, which sometimes happened in the case of the higher-ups, no one would have said "But God couldn't possibly have said thus-and-so, He doesn't act that way." No, it would be clearly a matter of self-will. And we would *all* pay the price of someone's self-will.

It was assumed that even the least among us could receive direct, clear messages from God, and that therefore our guidance should be heard. Now and then my own guidance included some "gems" as we called them—but these gems were not inspired passages that would be quoted in other meetings or in letters to people in other team centers—they would hardly provide the "keynote" for the next world assembly. More often my guidance was a kind of mental exercise—an evaluation of our way of life— an attempt to understand it better, through reasoning. We were all encouraged to do this sort of "reasoning"—it would make us more committed. The problem was, if your mind had nothing new or unusual to feed it, you could only go around and around within the same narrow frame of reference. It was a deductive process that went back to the already-accepted premises and then would build up again along the same familiar lines. With nothing to change the mathematics you were bound to arrive back at what you'd set out to prove—two and two always made four. The same premise, the same syllogisms, always led to the same conclusion.

I would write down sweeping generalizations such as "Ours is the most materialistic, immoral generation the world has ever known," and no one would "challenge" *that.* They would nod their heads wisely: no one would say: "Prove it!" It would have been of value in our "training" if, when someone made such generalizations, he would be asked whether he was justified in this sort of speculation about historical forces and issues—had he studied world history, did he know about the other materialistic and immoral generations throughout the ages? But no one challenged my basic assumptions, because they were *our* basic assumptions.

Now and then I would have a dialogue with myself about my own basic beliefs, presumably to intensify my commitment to MRA and to integrate the "real me" with the revolution: but I suspect I was also trying to justify my belief in God. I wrote down dumb things such as:

> What are you really sure of? I know that there is a God and that it is possible to get guidance from Him. I know this because all my life I have seen God at work in little and big ways. I know he can speak to humans because I've experienced it and I've seen others have it. I'm convinced that the happiest, free-est people on earth are those who live close to the Lord. . . . I'm sure MRA has the answer to the world's mess.

But it was the same old formula. I was just moving the old familiar furniture around and putting it back where it had been before and ending up with the house in the same order.

There were times when I would write down an observation that turned out to be a *fact* about the nature of God and His operations—something I'd arrived at all by myself, and when people would look thoughtful and say Yes, that's true, I would be filled with a strange sort of exhilaration. It seemed to be a part of a different order, and it gave me a security that transcended whatever dilemma I happened to be in the throes of. Perhaps I realized, in some obscure way, that an actual *fact* about God was the one thing I could be sure of—one thing that would always be the same, because God did not change. And sometimes I felt this strong desire to get at the root of it all, and find certainty. But then I would become suspicious of this desire, and would bring my theological speculations back down to the moral and practical level, and would continue operating (and "developing") on the surface. The layers underneath had not been strengthened: the surface had only been polished up a bit.

God was true because He guided me. But my belief did not altogether depend on bringing God into my daily orbit: I also knew God as children know the reality and wisdom of fairy tales, and through incommunicable elements in art and music and nature. It was obvious that there was something beyond man: a power he could neither explain nor contain.

I knew that God held the fate of nations in His hands, but it was also God Who whispered in our ears how many gallons of potatoes to cook for dinner so that there would not be any waste. God loved everybody, of course, but he loved *us* in a special way. The Holy Spirit was always hovering over our centers; we had a special and mysterious telephone line to God. He knew the secret places of our hearts—and how much money we had in our pockets. He held the secret of our individual destinies: now and then He would give us a hint or two, sometimes even about whom we might marry. (But about this, He always told Frank Buchman first.)

Whether or not any of us had private ideas about the nature of God, we all knew that He was our only security. He had gotten us into this business of changing the world and only He could carry us through this superhuman task. I suppose it was a privilege few have had, this growing up in a milieu in which the subordination of everything to the guidance of the Holy Spirit is never questioned. Nevertheless, when I look back, I am astonished by how we took for granted our sense of the *reality* of the supernatural. The way we spoke about what God had said to us, and what He had done through us, must have startled many people. No doubt some thought that in our "communing with God" we were assuming a relationship which even the saints dared not speak about—that our intimacy with the Holy Spirit would scandalize the mystics of old. And yet this wasn't really presumption, or lack of humility, on our part: it was confidence, and innocence.

And in my own innocence God understood and guided me step by step. But all the time that He was guiding and I was trying to be obedient, there was a deep and obscure hunger in the shadowy places of my soul. Something was missing, there was a gap; and I half-sensed that it was the one vital thing on which all else depended—not only my effectiveness in changing the world, but also my sanity.

It had to do with motive. God had a plan for my life: I was chosen to help remake the world. That's what I had always said, and believed—but why *was* I, at all? There had been growing in me a gnawing hunger to identify the one factor that would tie everything together. We had absolute standards, but did we have an Absolute? Wasn't there somewhere a solid, unchanging factor that would be its own reason for being? Something infinite that would absorb all of me into its depth and height and limitless reality, something that was the reason for my existence? Something that had to do with my Being, not my Doing: Something that, simply, *was*?

Before I could find this Absolute I had to be brought to a place of nothingness, where I had abandoned all previous claim to knowledge of God. For when the voice inside me turned into a hazy and terrifying jumble of contradictory voices and shadowy suggestions, when the warm feeling of assurance was gone, then God was nowhere, for He had never existed outside of me.

Prayer had always been as natural and as unconscious as breathing. When I prayed, I didn't need any mental image of God sitting like a Buddha, inclining His ear, because the atmosphere seemed charged with divine receptivity. But in the summer of 1953, when the line had gone dead, and there seemed no dimension in the darkness, perhaps that was when I learned about prayer for the first time. I have read that love and prayer are learned in the coldest and driest hour when the heart has turned to stone; and in that summer, when I had no love and no words, I prayed the prayer that is a mute gaze at something—a half-instinctive, unfeeling, lifting of the mind and soul to whatever is there. This would not be possible for anyone to do if there were *not* something there. And perhaps salvation begins in that moment, for one cannot even half-consciously desire to find God unless God has already found *him*: if He did not first love us, it would be impossible for us to want to love Him.

Somewhere in all this blackness I had begun, partly as a result of that course in writing, to *read*; and now I found myself turning to books with the desperation of someone hanging on to a cliff. There was no particular order in my reading: I had an odd collection of paperbacks that seemed strangely consoling, such as D. H. Lawrence criticizing certain American classics I had vaguely heard of, and a small Bartlett's Familiar Quotations, and a haphazard collection of *avant garde* magazines I had picked up at the little musty bookstore across from the New School for Social Research on Twelfth Street.

The first perceptible result of the reading was that I discovered I was not alone. As I read and half understood some of the lines Whitman addressed to his soul, I felt a sense of identity. There was the *Song of the Open Road*:

> Now I examine philosophies and religions.
> They may prove well in lecture rooms, yet not
> prove at all under the spacious clouds and
> along the landscape and flowing currents . . .

The fact that other humans in ages past had wrestled with moral values and metaphysical abstractions was a profound relief: the mere fact of their struggling to communicate what they only intuitively grasped gave me a sense of identification with something outside my own isolation. One of our MRA dictums was: "We're all the same underneath." Human nature, I knew, was everyone's common bond. But the individual complexities of the human intellect was something else. Now I knew that other people had asked questions, even the questions which neither I nor they quite understood ("My voice goes after what my eyes cannot reach") and their anguish at being incapable of expressing the questions made me feel a part of humanity restlessly and wordlessly united in a common search.

AND THEN, ONE DAY, I found the book that was destined—in the divine scheme of things—to be the beginning of everything.

I was browsing in the paperback section of the 8th Street Bookshop, and I saw a fifty-cent New American Library edition of *The Seven Storey Mountain* by Thomas Merton. I remembered the name, Thomas Merton, because he had been a friend of Robert Gerdy, my boss at *Harper's Bazaar*. I knew that Merton was "a famous Trappist monk and author," but I did not know what a Trappist was, and I didn't know much about monks. I wondered if the book would have anything about Bob Gerdy, so I looked at the index—sure enough, *Gerdy, Robert* was there—as were other interesting names and things and places: communism, Columbia University, Duke Ellington, Greenwich Village, Harlem, France, and *Freud, Sigmund.* I bought the book and began to read it.

After the first few pages I seemed to be not so much reading a book as entering into an experience; I began to feel the book had been written for *me*: here was this Thomas Merton talking about all those things I had been wondering about—like Truth, and the Absolute.

I suppose there were many reasons, aside from the working of grace, why the book captured me. For one thing, here was the sort of writing I had always been looking for: a style utterly honest and simple—the way *I* had always wanted to write. Of course I wasn't the only person mesmerized by the book: there was already a Merton cult flourishing in America and England and France—but I didn't know that. I didn't know that when the book was published in 1948 it became phenomenally popular, that it was a selection of numerous book clubs, and was on the bestseller list for many months; that almost overnight the author who had left the world to disappear in the Order of Cistercians of the Strict Observance had become a sensation; that all sorts of people who had never before known about Cistercians or monasteries were devouring books on the contemplative life.

What I *did* know was that Merton spoke like a voice inside me: everything he said brought a response from some deep place I had not known existed. I had a strange sense of identification with this monk: he spoke in words I knew; he was himself someone I knew. He was a mirror for the obscure but nonetheless corporeal image I had of myself, the person I hoped would emerge through my "New York phase"—someone sophisticated, urbane, clever, respectably "bohemian," and popular—not in the mundane sense, but appreciated and understood and accepted by a certain enlightened minority. And Merton was also a mirror that reflected the generation with which I identified, and for which I was supposed to have "the answer"—the generation between and after two world wars; the anguish of the intellectuals on the campuses, the moral confusion, the paradox of their idealism and their cynicism; their disillusion and passion; their obscure hungering for an *absolute*, a universally comprehensive *something*.

My "answer" had been based on an oversimplified and superficial evaluation of this generation, and of human nature. I knew nothing of the undercurrents that would soon surface and find a name— The Beat Generation, and Britain's Angry Young Men. I had always been so busy "seeing through" things that I hadn't seen the things themselves. That's the way it was, in MRA. Had I taken seriously "surface appearances" I might have learned that basic problems could not be solved categorically—that all young, angst-filled college "intellectuals" were *not* just kids "with moral problems"—according to MRA, most Intellectuals had Moral Problems. We always said that rebels (with or without a Cause) simply needed "a big idea to live for." Which was, of course, remaking the world; that was the biggest challenge, and Moral Re-Armament was the way. It was all very pat. But I had no conception of the complexities in the natures of these "intellectual savages" or of their sincerity and I had a totally inadequate idea of the logic and solidity demanded by an answer that would satisfy their minds and hearts.

Thomas Merton had been one of them. He spoke in their idiom and laid bare the roots of the disease, with all its peculiar manifestations. I had read many "change stories," but this one was different. It was not a before-and-after testimonial, highlighted by a dazzling "central religious experience," ending with a moral discourse through which the author would cleverly superimpose his convictions on the reader. This was, instead, the straightforward story, in retrospect, of a twentieth-century man's long and gradual and painful ascent to Truth: long, gradual and painful because it was the transformation of the whole man: mind, body, and will—all drawn together through love into the heart of the Truth.

Merton did not write as though he were hovering over his audience, and he did not pander to the baser appetites of that large mass known as the "general reader." Nor did he write in the pedestrian manner of one having a Message. It was more as if his story were a long contemplation. Many people have written books about God; the subject did not automatically make the books good. This man was a poet, and he didn't shed his talents when he put on his cowl and scapular: he didn't throw his five senses overboard when, at the age of thirty-three, he set out to write about his conversion and monastic vocation. He used them all—yet he was spontaneous and artless. With no false selves to unlearn, he achieved a realism that surpassed the efforts of many writers of the School of Realism. He didn't *try* to write with candor and humility and humor; he simply *was* honest, and simple; and his humor, which some critic called "Augustinian wit," was a part of all those things.

Thomas Merton wrote about his parents, his childhood in France and England, his years at Cambridge and Columbia, his friends— all the small and idle details, reminiscences, fragments of memories and conversations that were a part of the pattern. And thus he let his story unfold against the tremendous canvas of twentieth century post-Christian society.

There were parts that nearly choked me: passages with a naked beauty, stripped of all sentimentality; passages expressing the childlike simplicity that is found in the professional artist who has penetrated to the one reason for everything and has left himself outside. With great ease Merton would move from detailing some homely incident to almost Biblical prose, and prayer, and expressions of fierce joy, and back again to the halls of Columbia University. With ease he moved from the mysticism of William Blake to Jazz at Nick's in Sheridan Square, in the Village. Psychological observations of modern man in search of a soul were interlaced with paragraphs of apocalyptic vision, and with memories of his apartment on Perry Street and the mailbox on the corner into which he fed poems and book reviews, which would be rejected. All these transitions in his prose were part of a sublime whole—somehow they all fit together.

I was surprised to discover that some people in MRA knew about *The Seven Storey Mountain*. One friend's mother said that it was only "a poor man's St. Augustine's Confessions." By which she meant, I gathered, that Merton wasn't such a terrible sinner and therefore his "conversion" wasn't all that important. Some people like their sinners really wicked. (And of course we didn't know, then, that the first draft of the book had been rejected by the Trappist censors: all the specific incidents described would, they thought, scandalize the young girls in convent schools who would be reading the book). What I thought, when my friend's mother said this, was: Merton could not have written someone else's story . . . and perhaps he was, for our age, what St. Augustine was for his. In Augustine's day, sin was sin. In the Middle Ages, sin was understood in seven deadly categories and called by name. In our age sin doesn't often take on such dramatic and pagan and violent appearances: it is more subtle, and its very violence often masquerades as mediocrity, and all the forms of sin can make themselves look almost respectable. Thomas Merton, with (even in the "cleaned-up" version that was published) all his carnality, his passions, his scrapes with the law, his intellectual pride, was of the generation that tries hard to be startling but that cannot be unique even in concupiscence.

Apparently some critics were annoyed by this young man who presumed—with such authority—to interpret the monastic life. But Merton did not write for those who read the eminent French theologians and liturgists: he wrote for people who wouldn't be reading treatises on monasticism, or even classic conversion stories like Newman's *Apologia.* He wrote for "ordinary" people— he spoke to *me.* Yet he didn't speak so much as he illuminated what had always been in me: it was as though he had beamed a light on an embryo, making it free to begin life, and to grow.

I emerged from the book a different person. I did not have the answers, but I knew more about the questions and I knew that there *were* answers. And I knew that I was on my way to finding them, and that I was being propelled by something outside myself.

The Seven Storey Mountain was a book about God. About the relentless pursuit of the Hound of Heaven for the lost sheep. All my life I had said many words about the way God works in peoples' lives: but now I was overwhelmed by the power and the persistence and the mercy of God—His omnipotence. All alone on a page before the text of the book were the words of St. John the Baptist:

> For I tell you that God is able of these stones
> to raise up children to Abraham.

And so, in the autobiography of this Trappist monk, I had begun to find the Europe that is the heritage of every American; and I had begun to find America. I had begun to find an interior life, and I had found hope.

I found much more, too: in that book I discovered the Church, but I didn't know that until later. What I did know was that I had begun to discover Who and What God was; and that was enough to keep me pondering for a long time.

During this pondering-time, the movie *Martin Luther* was being showcased in Manhattan. I went alone to see it, and came out feeling that the movie had been the affirmation of something: I didn't know what. Presumably, the movie was anti-Catholic . . . but it had a *positive* Catholic effect on me, which may have had to do with my new interest in things monastic. All those austere (looking back, I think they were more cadaverous than austere) monks with their Gregorian chant were my first audible and visible contact with *liturgy*.

I had been telling many of my friends in MRA about *The Seven Storey Mountain* and I was disseminating the books all over. At work I had an electric typewriter—no doubt one of the first—and on it I would write long letters about the interior life to my friend Barbara Bluejacket, who had temporarily left the team and was working in Los Angeles: she wrote back long letters about what Thomas Merton was saying to her, too.

In January, when I had a bout with the flu, I read the Pocket Book edition of *The Imitation of Christ*, with those red and black stylized illustrations by Valenti Angelo: and I felt I was reading Thomas á Kempis for the first time.

My reading, in fact, was becoming more and more specifically Catholic. There were books by authors with dissimilar backgrounds— authors of different styles, purpose, and approach—but there was a common element in all of them. Whether hagiography, apologetics, or essays on Democracy and the Church in America, they communicated a sense of freedom and of joy. There was a unity of perspective and a clear, logical and vital application of basic Christian principles to what MRA called "the burning issues of our age." There was a humility, too, because of an underlying assumption that God was the Absolute and that everything else, in the temporal, political, or spiritual order, was real and important only in relation to that Absolute. (Perhaps this was when I first began to wonder about MRA having the total answer to all those burning issues of our age.) I read articles that burned with passion for a cause but which were also full of peace and calm practicality and wisdom about patience and God's timing.

These authors—this galaxy of men, alive or dead, famous or obscure, didn't hammer away at truths: they created an atmosphere in which truth could be apprehended. It was simply *there* and there was no reason why anyone who had an eye should not perceive it.

In some of the novels I read, especially those of Graham Greene, the characters—adulterers, "whisky priests" and so on—were not two-dimensional exponents of an idea: they were real flesh and blood people with unpredictable responses to the reality of sin and to the presence of grace in their lives; and they said a lot to me about how nothing needs to be profane—that ordinary human love and all it involves can lead from the concupiscence of the flesh to sanctity.

This is what all those books were saying to me: Man's destiny is to love and serve God in this world and to enjoy Him eternally in the world to come. Every action and every thought and every possession is a part of this, and this is the way you will find your identity as a child of God.

And then, as fall came, all the fragmentary details of my daily life seemed to coalesce, as if there were a hidden connection in all the things happening around me. Conversations I had with people about irrelevant matters—casual remarks people just happened to make—everything seemed to be part of a design.

FROM KATHERINE HOUSE I moved uptown into a large, airy apartment on East 87th Street: this was yet another MRA apartment, but it was not "charity"—I, and the others there who had jobs, paid for our rooms and our estimated share of food. I had begun a night course at New York University, called "Great Epochs and Great Figures in English Literature." The books we read seemed to have a far deeper significance than could have been intended by whoever had planned the course, which was designed to relate literature to the general atmosphere (religious, political, economic, cultural) in which it was created. For me, this course was an introduction to Western Civilization—about which I knew nothing. It was a revelation, and I was fascinated. I began to feel a nostalgia for the thirteenth century when, although unsanitary and "superstitious and ignorant" the world was "Catholic and universal." There was the solid faith of the men and women who lived by the labor of their hands; the clear-eyed poetry of the first Franciscans: and all the literature, whether pious or cynical or ribald, was part of this universality. Our instructor, Professor Ralph Bates, was an Englishman who had a brilliant and original turn of mind—he had written books about the Spanish Civil War (about which I also knew nothing) and he frequently stated that "So far as I have been able to detect, I have no particular religious beliefs." Yet he managed in almost every lecture to work in what seemed to me some startlingly Catholic affirmations. He knew a lot about the saints: their dates, and their contributions to the culture of their times, made history came alive for me—it was about real people.

And then I began to fall into one book after another in an effortless way. I read *The Apostle* by Scholem Asch, and I saw *The Robe*—a movie which, in spite of its Hollywood trappings, taught me a lot about early Christianity. That movie, in fact, had the same effect the course was having—it showed me the connection between history and Christianity, which is perfectly obvious to most people but which for me had always been abstract.

The more I read, and learned, the more surprised I became that so many people knew about God. People had been discovering and rediscovering Him for a long time. They had gone at Him from all angles—personal, professional, scientific, mystical. They had sung to Him and written for Him and painted for Him: God had been the focus of their lives.

Before I read *The Seven Storey Mountain*, no one outside our own orbit had impressed me with any facts about God. Somehow I had the notion that we in MRA were the only ones really qualified to understand Him: we were on the inside track. We all read *The Imitation of Christ*, for example (and for spiritual purposes), but no one had ever said to me the things that Thomas Merton was saying, and saying with such authority. Merton wasn't on any of our MRA reading lists (we didn't have *lists*, of course, but books would be recommended). One of his books, though, *The Waters of Siloe*, was quietly waiting on a shelf at Dellwood to be discovered: I discovered it, and always wondered how it got there.

We in Moral Re-Armament followed in the tradition of the Apostles' practice of common ownership. I don't remember anyone ever quoting from the Holy Rule of St. Benedict, but we followed his admonition: "Let all things be common to all [Acts 4:32] . . . but let no one call anything his own or claim it as such." (Holy Rule, chapter 33.) And in a way God too was common property. How astonished they must have been, those people new to our "family meetings," when one after another we would rise to our feet to share our thoughts, our failures, our ideas, and would preface our sharing by the calm statement "God said to me . . ."

And because God, and the spiritual life, had been more common than personal—and because we felt we had no right to privacy and secrecy in these matters—God was personal only in the sense that any experience He gave us was meant to be passed on and used with other people. Therefore I was introduced to an entirely new idea when I read, in Merton's *Seeds of Contemplation*:

> If we find God in our souls and want to stay there with Him, it is disastrous to think of trying to communicate Him to others as we find Him there. We can preach Him later on with the grace He gives us in silence. We need not upset the silence with language. . . . The inviolability of your spiritual sanctuary, the center of your soul, depends on secrecy. . . . Keep all good things secret even from yourself. If we would find God in the depths of our souls, we have to leave everybody else outside, including ourselves.

Although I would never have dared to say anything like that, when I read those words I felt I knew what Merton meant; that this was the way it was supposed to be, with God.

God—"I am Who am." It is impossible to recapture the feeling I had when I read those words—the answer to Moses' question— and suddenly say them, logically and clearly, as the answer to the whole riddle. The implications ripple out in a circle that gets wider than time, and language is left drowning in the overwhelming simplicity of it all.

From the Belly of the Whale

The Pamphlet Rack at St. Patrick's

O N PALM SUNDAY, 1954, at eight o'clock in the morning, I went to Mass for the first time. A Catholic friend at Dellwood took me with her to the church of St. Francis of Assisi, in Mount Kisco: I would not have braved it alone.

The church was very crowded, and that was my first surprise, for I still had the Protestant notion that eleven o'clock was Church Time, and especially so on Palm Sunday. We had to sit near the back, which was fine with me, since I was all shaky with that self-consciousness that afflicts most non-Catholics, the First Time.

I had the feeling that this would be a kind of "test." Would I be disillusioned, or would all I had been reading about Catholicism "prove itself" in the way these Catholics acted at their Mass—which was, I knew, for them their "central act of worship"?

At first I had no idea what was going on up there at the altar. At intervals, between getting tangled up in all those colored ribbon placemarkers in the *Cardinal Spellman Prayer Book & Missal,* which someone had lent me, and trying to kneel and stand and sit at the right times, I could see the priest, dressed in purple, walking back and forth in front of the altar. All the activity was, I thought, "preparatory" and I wondered when the Mass would begin.

But when I heard the volley of little bells ringing, I knew that the Mass had indeed begun, had been going on for some time, and now the important part was coming. And by that time, I knew that there *was* something here: *something* came into the lives of all these people, while they knelt. They were here to worship. Whether or not they knew the Mass backward and forward

81

in Latin, whether they were still struggling to wake up, simply
and obviously didn't matter; what *was* obvious was that they
were in that church to offer God their praise, their gratitude,
their sorrow for sins—whatever they had on their minds was
directed to Him. He was God the Omnipotent and He cared
about their collective personal woes and petitions and thanks.
He, God, was real to them.

And the fact that no one had noticed me, an outsider, was
perhaps the most impressive affirmation of all.

After the priest turned and faced us and intoned the "Ite, Missa
est" (and I knew what that meant) I came out of the church
not just feeling but knowing that I had worshipped God for the
first time. I seemed to have lost all my Protestant horror of "ritual":
all the kneeling and standing and crossing had been perfectly
normal. Intellectually, I knew that since we are not pure spirits
but are spirits in bodies, the body has to worship too; but now
I *felt* the truth of this. I felt strangely peaceful and exhilarated
at the same time.

This sensation had something familiar about it and then I
remembered how, after singing with the MRA Chorus, I would
feel as though everything in me had been used; every part of
me had been involved in a single and intense and consuming
action. After pouring everything into a song, I would feel exhausted,
and empty, and yet somehow expanded; cleansed and purified,
and at peace.

After that Palm Sunday Mass, I was very pleased to go back
into Manhattan with palms that had been blessed.

The rest of Holy Week that year was somehow a continuation
of that first Mass. And now that I had actually been inside
a Catholic church, I felt brave enough to do what I'd been
wanting to do every time the Fifth Avenue bus slid me by
St. Patrick's Cathedral: I went inside. This was on Holy Thursday
evening, and I stood in the back for about five minutes and
wondered why all the people were filing so quietly and intensely
down the right aisle and around the back and then back up
the left aisle. (I had not yet read anything about the Blessed
Sacrament and the Repository.) And on Good Friday I surprised
myself and everyone at the office by going to the Three Hour
Service. My boss said of course I could take the time off, and
then said: "I've always been scared to go inside a Catholic church."

I said that so had I, but I was inching my way in little by little.

I stayed for the whole three hours; it was pouring rain outside but of course the Cathedral was packed and everyone seemed to be exhausted with that peculiar emotional tension which comes with the last days of Lent. I was astonished at the energy with which everyone knelt and stood and sat, and with the continuity of the discourses. And I knelt and stood and sang with all the others, and I joined in the litany—"This is my first litany," I thought—which went very fast.

On Easter Sunday I was at the Cathedral again, along with five thousand others, for the Pontifical Mass celebrated by Cardinal Spellman and assisted by one hundred seminarians and clergy and two choirs—or so all the newspapers reported. I didn't have a ticket, but somehow I managed to get in and I found standing room in one of the aisles. It suddenly became very quiet, because it was time for the Consecration, and then there was the little volley of bells; and then all I could hear was the subdued shuffling of feet as what seemed like multitudes made their way to the altar for Holy Communion and then back to where they had been sitting or standing; and those who had been standing knelt right down on the cold floor, good Easter clothes and all. When the Mass was over with a final triumphant blast from the organ, I went out the center aisle and I'll never forget the feeling I had when I got to the wide-open doors: what had been Fifth Avenue had become masses of hats, banked everywhere; and people with or without hats were still filling the bordering side streets and Rockefeller Plaza. The most startling thing was the silence. Even the movie cameras periscoping above the heads in the human sea appeared to be holding their collective breath. The hundreds of policemen were quiet, too: they had all been hearing the Mass through the loudspeakers.

DURING THE WINTER of that year I had read *The Sign of Jonas*, Thomas Merton's journal: his thoughts and prayers and experiences set down, day by day, during his first five years as a monk. It was when the prophet Jonas was traveling as fast as he could away from Nineveh, where God had ordered him to go, that the whale swallowed him up and took him to where God wanted him to be.

It seemed that *I* had been traveling in something like the belly of a whale, too. I had been responding to the secret workings of grace; I knew I was headed for somewhere, but I didn't know where; and it had not seemed necessary to find out, because the whale knew.

But one day came when, apparently, God decided it was time for *me* to find out where I was and where I was going. Ever since I'd read *The Seven Storey Mountain*, a solid interior life had been developing itself inside me, without any fanfare or reflection on my part. I was a child happily bathing in a new atmosphere. Now I became aware of the nature of this mental and spiritual climate which had brought me back into a unified existence: the space I had been breathing in was the clean air of Catholic philosophy and tradition and culture. Realizing this, I began to be curious about the *specifics* of it all: atmosphere was one thing, but just what was Catholic *doctrine*? What, in black and white, did Catholics profess? What did their catechism teach?

I didn't know how to find out; but the whale was still swimming. One day after work I went into the Cathedral again. My old self-consciousness came flooding back, for it is one thing to be in a Catholic church when something is going on and you're part of a mob, and quite another to—as Catholics say—"make a visit." This is something born-Catholics can never quite appreciate. So I hovered at the back, by the holy water font, trying to be invisible, looking wistfully at all the people who knew exactly how to genuflect and light candles. And then I spotted a refuge: the little pamphlet room. I ducked inside, thinking: How original, how quaint, this idea of having a small store right *in* a church. I still felt ill-at-ease, though, and hoped the little nun behind the counter would not ask if she could help me, and I wondered what I'd answer, if she did. I could say: "Just browsing, thank you" but then she might ask if there was anything particular I was interested in and I imagined myself replying: "Oh no, just the whole Catholic Church, that's all." This amusing thought helped me to relax a bit, and gave me a bit of courage; so I wasn't too embarrassed when I placed on the counter my hastily-selected handful of edifying tracts: *How to Pray the Rosary, The Way of the Cross, Sacraments*, a pamphlet (heavily documented) on Martin Luther, and a twenty-five-cent *Catechism for Inquirers*. I paid for my purchases and left the little store and the Cathedral feeling very pleased and as though I'd overcome a major hurdle; I could hardly wait till I was alone and could discover what was in all those booklets.

The *Catechism for Inquirers* was the important one. For as I read in the back, in small print, the "convert's Profession of Faith," I came upon a certain phrase which had a footnote that, in the words of Pius IX, said:

> It is to be held of faith that none can be saved outside the Apostolic Roman Church . . . but, nevertheless, it is equally certain that those who are ignorant of the true religion, if that ignorance is invincible, will not be held guilty in the eyes of the Lord.

I felt I'd just arrived at Nineveh. That footnote-statement seemed more like a solid *place* than a sentence of words. It startled me into the realization that I had a responsibility: that something, now, was up to *me*. That it was my move, now, whale or no whale.

It was not that I was terrified of losing my immortal soul— I was not even aware of having that kind of soul, nor had I ever thought about "salvation"—but it was inescapably obvious that an *interior* acceptance of Catholic ideas was not enough: I had lost my qualification; I could no longer plead that "invincible ignorance." It was so completely logical: the next step had to be taken. I had to find out the whole of this Catholic faith, and if it turned out to be true, what I would do next would *not* be a matter of choice.

To become a Catholic! I could hardly say the words to myself. The sentence sounded unreal, and I could not *feel* that such a thing was possible for me. And yet while the whole tremendous idea scared me, it had that air of indisputable common sense. God had given me the gift of reason, and this was not subject to what somebody else might say the Holy Spirit was telling him or her about me (the way it had always been, in MRA); nor was it subject to some kind of interior illumination that was supposed or presumed to be the guidance of the Holy Spirit.

There was a passage in *The Seven Storey Mountain* that I had underlined:

> . . . They stand in the stacks of libraries and turn over the pages of St. Thomas's *Summa* with a kind of curious reverence. They talk in their seminars about "Thomas" and "Scotus" and "Augustine" and "Bonaventure" and they are familiar with Maritain and Gilson,

and they have read all the poems of Hopkins—and indeed they know more about what is best in the Catholic literary and philosophical tradition than most Catholics ever do on earth. They sometimes go to Mass, and wonder at the dignity and restraint of the old liturgy. They are impressed by the organization of a Church in which everywhere the priests, even the most un-gifted, are able to preach at least something of a tremendous, profound, unified doctrine, and to dispense mysteriously efficacious help to all who come to them with troubles and needs.

In a certain sense, these people have a better appreciation of the Church and of Catholicism than many Catholics have; an appreciation which is detached and intellectual and objective. But they never come into the Church. They stand and starve in the doors of the banquet—the banquet to which they surely realize that they are invited—while those more poor, more stupid, less gifted, less educated, sometimes even less virtuous than they, enter in and are filled at those tremendous tables.

And now I knew that for me, the time of "gazing on hungrily with a curious reverence" had come to an abrupt end. Although I could not *imagine* myself doing such a thing as becoming a Catholic, and I guess I'd never done anything I hadn't been able to *imagine* doing, "imagination" suddenly seemed irrelevant. Furthermore, I could *feel* the reality of the fact that this could happen: this was an entirely new feeling, and a new concept of reality. And so I found myself entering into a dazzling new strata of freedom: I knew, with a calm and absolute certainty, that all my trepidation and temperamental cowardice could not possibly stand in the way of what my reason told me I had to do. There was no reason why I could not transcend my natural limitations and there was every reason why I should simply proceed to take the next step.

And I found out that the next step was something called "taking instructions." But I didn't know any priests. I couldn't imagine even talking to a priest: but by this time imagination really *had* lost credibility. Whether or not I could imagine going to a rectory, any rectory, and knocking on the door and asking to see a priest, I knew I could do it if I had to. But this was made easy for me, too, as everything else seemed to have been: my Palm Sunday friend, Nancy Hawthorne, with whom I was in touch now and then, said she knew a priest, a Father Eugene V. Clark. He had been stationed at St. Francis in Mount Kisco, but now he was teaching in a Catholic boys' school somewhere in Manhattan. Nancy said she would be happy to put him in touch with me.

A week or so later I got a letter from this Father Clark. He said he'd heard from our mutual friend that I was interested in having some further information about Catholic teaching and the Church, and that he was happy to be at my service . . . that he'd be most happy to talk to me no matter what my "questions, hopes, or plans might be."

I was touched and rather charmed by this gracious invitation— for that's what it seemed to be; so I wrote back to Father Clark that Yes, I would be most happy to meet with him at his convenience, and he took it from there: if it was all right with me, we would meet at 7 in the evening of May 14th, in the rectory of St. Ignatius Loyola Church, on Park Avenue between 83rd and 84th Streets.

As he would later explain, he was then stationed in what he called Greater Harlem, teaching English and history at Bishop DuBois High School. He didn't think it would be wise for me to go into *that* neighborhood, so he came to mine: he knew that I was then living in St. Ignatius Loyola's parish (which was more than *I* knew) and he had managed to "borrow" a rectory room from the Jesuit Fathers.

I was then living in that MRA apartment, on 87th Street between Madison and Park: our building was right next to the Park Avenue Synagogue. *That* I knew, but I didn't know that the Jesuits were in the neighborhood, too. My knowledge of the neighborhood was pretty much limited to transportation facilities: Fifth Avenue (for the bus); Lexington and 86th (for the subway.) I'd never had occasion to take a stroll down Park Avenue, so I'd never passed by St. Ignatius Loyola Church and rectory until that evening.

And then I passed by it, *several* times: I was a bit early for our appointment, so I walked around the block two or three times, concentrating on my umbrella—there was a slight drizzle— trying to look nonchalant. But I was ridiculously nervous. When the time came for me to present myself at the rectory, though, I was beginning to feel (along with nervous) rather heroic, or courageous. This was, I thought, probably the most heroic/ courageous thing I'd ever done. (I think only converts can appreciate this.) And indeed, this did take a lot of courage: it was a big step, because of what it represented. Until then, my whole gravitation toward the Church had been *interior*; now I was taking the first *outward* step. As long as a thought is in the mind, it is safe. Once it is spoken, it's in the public domain. This step meant that there was now something "on the record" and therefore there could be repercussions. It was in every way a departure from the behavior-pattern of the past: I had not "checked" this step with anyone in MRA and I hadn't even told more than two or three people about it. Nor was there any dynamic personality to whom I had transferred my security. It was entirely impersonal, and it was the first time I had ever acted solely on intellectual conviction. (And the first time I'd had a *concept* of "intellectual conviction.") I had never taken an Important Step without first telling a lot of people about it, in order to register their reactions, by which I would test my "motives." This time, even if people had been horrified or even mildly disapproving, it would not have pitched me into conflict about whether I was doing the right thing.

My decision to take instructions did not represent a decision to become a Catholic: it represented a decision of the mind and will to submit myself unconditionally and everlastingly to the truth, whatever it should turn out to be. The thing was to find out if the idea I had gotten of the Church was the refined concept of the literary elite whose books and articles I had read, or if it was really and actually and universally the Catholic Church. If it *was* the truth, the final decision—I knew—would not be a matter of choice: I had acknowledged such a thing as truth and I had to be consistent with that truth. Beyond all feelings and fears and loyalties, finding reality was my ultimate responsibility.

But it was not because of what all this represented that I was trembling, when I approached the rectory. The fact was: I had never spoken to a priest. I had never even pictured myself face to face with a black-suited official representative of the Catholic Church; and there is always something a little terrifying about doing something you can't picture yourself doing.

As I went up the steps to the rectory, I felt conspicuous, though no one was watching me. I opened the door and went inside, and told the plump lady at the switchboard that I had an appointment with a Father Eugene V. Clark. Was he here? I asked. "Yes, he is," said a male voice which turned out to be Father Clark's. He had appeared from somewhere down a hall, and we shook hands and then I followed him to a tiny room which had a desk and a chair, a few musty books, and a crucifix on the wall.

I couldn't have been more surprised by this Father Clark: somehow I'd pictured him as a white-haired, benevolent, fatherly sort of priest who would call me "my child" and settle down in a stuffed armchair and fold his arms and nod understandingly while I talked. Instead, here was this young, handsome cleric—maybe English, I thought. Actually, he was mainly Irish, and from the Bronx . . . but there *was* something in his manner which reminded me of the English people I'd known—a certain unmistakable charm which, though I did not know it then because I didn't know about the Irish, was unmistakably Irish. *English*-sounding Irish. He was obviously polished and urbane: very much a priest of the world, in a quiet sort of way. He seemed a little shy, too. He sat down on the edge of the desk, and I sat on the edge of the chair, and looked up at the crucifix. *I* was shy, and got all tangled up and tongue-tied as I tried to summarize all that had led to this moment at the rectory of St. Ignatius Loyola. But somehow I knew that Father Clark understood all I was struggling to explain, and that he knew more, too: he seemed to know *me*.

When I had finished talking, or had come to what seemed like a stopping place, Father Clark began to speak with respect and generosity about the spirit of Protestantism. Though he probably suspected that I was very close to accepting Catholicism, he apparently felt obliged to speak to me as though I were a good and educated Presbyterian; and I felt almost ashamed that I *didn't* have any strong Protestant loyalties. He made Protestantism, and the faith of *my* father, sound very attractive. Anyway, it was clear that this was not one of those priests many Protestants warn about: it was almost disconcerting that he didn't seem at all eager to lure me into the Catholic Church.

The priest's job, he said, was to help people find the grace that has always been available to them: that the main thing is the person's touch with God. Then he gave a breathless kind of survey of what we would be studying if I wanted to take "a regular course of instructions," and he said that if I *did*, I should have no preclusions about the outcome. I was simply to study, and either things would quite naturally fall into place, or at least I would have learned a lot. And, he said, so would *he*. We talked a little about Thomas Merton, and Gerard Manley

Hopkins, and Cardinal Newman and the Church in England, which was Father Clark's particular enthusiasm; and Msgr. Ronald Knox and G. K. Chesterton.

Nothing could have been more obvious than that Father Clark was "a priest forever according to the order of Melchisedech" and was delighted with his job. He was a friend of God, and the simple, undramatic—respectful, not "familiar"—way in which he talked about God made me feel that I was a friend of God, too. There was a grace and a delicacy in the way he used his hands and a sensitivity in his expression when he spoke and listened; something poetic in his whole manner, but there were also flashes of something tough and almost roguish, and it occurred to me that if he had not been in black he might almost look like an Irish cop. Especially when, as we were walking down the street afterwards, he pushed his black hat back at a jaunty angle and told me about the young demons he taught at Bishop DuBois High School. I found out later that he hadn't been out of the seminary for very long—he might have almost been a contemporary—but he had the authority and maturity that comes with the grace of Orders; and I knew then why every priest had a right to be called Father.

We had talked about many things in that hour and a half, and I had a strange feeling that I had been a Catholic all along, only I just hadn't known it. Did I want to take instructions, he asked? I did. And so we decided to continue once a week, and he gave me various books to look through, including the bright yellow, paperback, very English *This Is the Faith*, by Francis Ripley. It was not, strictly speaking, a "catechism." It had been published by the Birchley Hall Press, which had been secretly set up and supported in Lancashire in the early 1600's. The Hall had a chapel used by Catholics in penal times, and adjacent hiding places for priests. Birchley Hall Press had printed "many Popish pamphlets" in those dark days of the seventeenth century, and it had published its first book, *This Is the Faith*, in 1951. The jacket blurb said: "This may be excellently described as a book for enquirers into the teachings and practices of the Catholic Church; as a commentary on the Catholic Catechism; as a handbook for all who teach Catholic doctrine or as a textbook for students."

I left the rectory with *This Is the Faith* and with my head spinning, with a glorious sense of adventure and with a dizzy exhilaration that comes with disciplined thinking and reasoning. In fact I felt as though I had *thought* for the first time. I had seen a glimpse of the territory we were going to make our way through, and I knew already that this inquiry into the nature of Catholicism was not merely a formal routine, but that it was going to be a broad study of life itself.

Where had I got the notion that theology was something dead— at best, irrelevant and in any case unreliable? Theology—it was historical fact, and scientific fact, too, for the facts of theology were true in the same sense as scientific facts about the fall of a stone to earth. How had I got to be twenty-three, I wondered, without having really found out about *life*? If you wanted to find out about life, and if you proved to your satisfaction that behind all evolution there was a Creator, then you had to find out about this Creator: and that was theology. You do not know what anything is until you know what it is *for*. Man was made; therefore he must have been made by an intelligent being who knew the purpose of his own action, and who must have given us some clues about what he had made man *for*. He had given us intellects so that we could grasp his revelation about us. And to grasp all that was the highest act of the intellect.

The newly-ordained Father Clark. When Faith met him (in 1954) at St. Ignatius Loyola, the Jesuit church on New York's Park Avenue, she had expected "a white-haired, benevolent, fatherly sort of priest who would call me 'my child' and settle down in a stuffed armchair."

Instructions

Father Clark and *This Is the Faith*

THE EVENING FOR THE FIRST INSTRUCTION came, and it—the "instruction"—was more like a discussion than a lesson. We started at the very beginning, taking no premise for granted. We established the fact of the basic need for religion, going back to primitive man and his practice of "natural religion," his instinct to worship, to offer sacrifice to something above and outside him, his impulse to cooperate with this power in the rhythm of nature. We observed that there must be an intelligence behind the universe; that the universe either had a beginning and thus a Beginner, or that it was infinite, which implied an Infinite Being. We studied the argument from design and motion and other proofs for the existence of God—somehow even Einstein's theory got into the discussion—and then we proceeded step by step down the avenues of reason and logic.

The phenomenon of things "falling into place" began immediately. I had had the feeling of synchronization through my reading, but this was different: spiritual truths and metaphysical notions had already settled and locked themselves in my depths, but now pieces of fact and logic began to mesh like pieces of machinery.

After another session or two, I got some astonishing news from my friend Judy McGill. She and her sister Caryll had been in MRA for some years—not full time, they lived in the Bronx and had jobs in the city—but they often went to Dellwood on weekends to help in the kitchen or dining room or in the office, where there was always a need for good stenographers and typists. Judy (who didn't know I was taking instructions) called me at work to say Guess what, Caryll was going to a priest for instructions! As calmly as possible I said Guess what, so am I. Judy said: "Call Caryll." I did. "We have something in common," I said, and then it was *her* turn to be astonished. She told me she'd been dating a Catholic, but that her interest in Catholicism had actually begun five years ago when she was working as a page in the Children's Room of a New York Public Library branch, where—when time permitted—she read children's books about saints.

She said she'd been seeing a Dominican priest. I asked how she was progressing, and she said she *wasn't*: the Dominican had a very set method of instruction which allowed for no deviation. "I don't think we're on the same wave length," she said. He was spending much time on *sin*, and she wanted to go on from there, and tried to explain that she had been brought up in a movement that concentrated a lot on sin and guilt, but he didn't seem to understand. His "approach," she said, was "elementary."

I told her that Father Clark knew a lot about MRA and understood what we didn't need to spend time on. I asked if she would like to join us if he agreed. She said fine, and Father Clark said fine, bring her along. So now there were three of us in that little room at St. Ignatius.

SPRING TURNED INTO SUMMER, the un-air conditioned rectory got stuffy, but we went on. We studied matter and spirit, the creature man, what this thing called the soul really was, how we knew there was such a thing peculiar to man, why the soul was immortal, the existence of evil and even evolution. I found a new respect for—or perhaps my first awareness of—the power of human reason. We went over the theology of the Church, from the apologists and the schools of Alexandria and Antioch, the early Fathers and Doctors of the Church (some were also stylists of Greek literature). Then the Scholastics, who had confidence in human reason being able by itself to recognize the existence of God, and confidence that reason and intelligence can alone establish the credibility of revelation on historical and philosophical grounds.

The theologians through the ages had done their job of explaining doctrine in a systematic manner, using natural knowledge and its laws to make the divinely revealed truth more intelligible.

(What a wonderful gift from God was this thing human intelligence, I thought.) And so, using our intelligence, we proceeded from the fact of God and the historical fact of His having spoken to man, to the New Testament—to finding out about Christ who, according to St. John, was God's Word.

All of this was leading up to the Divinity of Christ, which I'd never doubted because I'd never thought about it. I believed it, but I did not *know* it, and there is a vast difference between believing and knowing. We looked at it now, examining it from all sides, analyzing evidence from ancient poets and philosophers through the Old Testament prophets to the ways Christ Himself presented His credentials.

The reality of it all began to burst with terrific impact on my consciousness, and I could see why this was *the* fact upon which all else depended. They say that the acceptance of the divinity of Christ is the pivotal point in most conversions, and it is not hard to understand why. If you say that Christ was indeed the Son of God, then you've just about lost your case for your private concept of Christianity: if Christ was God, then all He said would have to be accepted—at least by the intelligence, and then, if you were a self-respecting Christian, you would have to follow with your will and decide to live accordingly. If Christ was God, then all He said was true, and all He did was for all time. If He founded a Church, then that Church was a very specific body of truths for all Christians.

So, therefore, it was very important to find out if Christ was God. We studied all the evidence. Did this man do all the things He said He would do? He healed people, He raised the dead, He fed thousands from a few loaves and fishes—certainly He was at least some kind of wonder-worker, but there were all those things that He predicted about the future. The most crucial test of all was whether or not He really did rise from the dead after three days.

There were the charges of those who said of course this man rose because He wasn't really dead in the first place. But the testimony was very specific about that—in fact the event seemed to have been arranged in every way to obviate all future doubts. The Roman soldiers were trained, they knew what they were doing—they knew how to make sure people were dead. None of the arguments held water. And there were all the disciples after the Resurrection, saying: "See for yourself." If this had been a trick on the part of the disciples the Jews would have exposed it, because they knew it was the heart of the Christians' faith. Yet there was St. Paul thirty years later talking about it, and no one challenged him on the fact of Christ's Resurrection.

I felt a little like a detective: St. Paul said that there were still eye-witnesses alive, and we observed that no one called these eye-witnesses up for cross-examination. The Jewish leaders and the Roman governors could have made the early Christians a laughing stock by producing the dead body of their "living" Lord. There is no evidence that they even tried that. Instead, there were many witnesses and five literary summaries of the Resurrection; Matthew and John give eye-witness testimony, Mark gives to Rome the witness of Peter, Luke gives the witness of a doctor, who tells his hearers that he has "set down in order" what he had "diligently searched out." Paul was himself converted on the evidence of the Resurrection.

I saw that all the details of the Crucifixion and Resurrection had been recorded not for pious meditation but for very definite purposes of *proof*. And for the first time I began to understand Easter. St. Paul said: "If Christ has not risen, then our preaching is vain, and your faith, too, is vain." It seemed to me that no one could know the joy of Easter unless he knew in the depths of his being how everything depended on Christ's keeping His promise. How much more it was than a mere sentiment, a pageant of the followers happy because their Master was back with them, back again after all the crushing bewilderment of Good Friday. Christ was indeed risen, even as He said.

WHEN I WAS IN SCHOOL, history was not my favorite subject. History had to do with dates and battles and laws and other impersonal things that always slipped off the surface of my mind after I had passed the exams, which I usually did pass with A's. MRA had trained me in the knowledge that God had figured largely in American history; Divine Providence was the keynote of our American Heritage (William Penn had said: "Men will be governed by God or they will be ruled by tyrants"; Benjamin Franklin had said that if a sparrow could not fall to the ground without God's notice, an empire could not rise without His aid). But

I had never thought of history in connection with *belief* in God.

We had learned now that "faith" was not a *feeling*: it was an intellectual act; its object was truth, its result was knowledge. It was a matter of the mind, and then of the will. Faith was based on reason and on the authority of God. Supernatural certitude was a gift of God, but reason alone could lead to a solid knowledge about the origin of Christianity.

When I told a friend that I was taking instructions, she asked: "Does the Church really expect people to believe what it teaches even if it goes against their own reason?" I had not yet learned that the Vatican Council, which had defined the dogma of Papal Infallibility in 1870, had also condemned "blind faith," saying that it was a sin against faith if the obedience of faith was not in accordance with reason. But I knew enough to tell my friend that Catholics did not have to grit their teeth and say "*I believe*"— they could *know*.

I had always tried hard to "have faith" (and people were always half-teasing me about living up to my name) but God had already given me what He had given all humans: an intellect and the power of reasoning so that even without *supernatural* help one could come to knowledge of the existence of God and to many things His existence implied.

Christ was the Son of God. He had been born at a particular point in time. Of course I knew the Christmas Story but I'd never thought of it as *fact*. So now history was becoming interesting, and I suspected that a "retrospective" of what happened after Christ's death was going to have personal importance for my life. Christ, the Son of God, was also God; therefore everything He taught was truth and all who called themselves Christians had an obligation to live in accordance with that truth—with *all* of it, not just the parts we would choose.

We were approaching the chapters on "Why Organized Religion?" which would include a lot about the authority of the Church, but first we spent some time on Pentecost, and what it had to do with history. Here were these men, Peter and the others, still faint-hearted, sitting in that upper room, waiting for something to happen.

Perhaps they were mulling over the instructions they'd received from Christ—very specific instructions. They were to define His teachings: "It is granted to you to understand the secret of God's

kingdom; for those others, who stand without, all is parable."
(Already, among those who stood without, there were individuals
who preferred their own private interpretations.) They were to
teach—to go out and make disciples of all the nations, to preach
the Gospel to the whole of creation. They were to govern: "All
that you bind on earth shall be bound in heaven, and all that
you loose on earth shall be loosed in heaven." And they were
to sanctify, baptizing all in the name of the Father, and of the
Son, and of the Holy Ghost.

It was a staggering commission Jesus had given them. He Himself
would not be with them very long: He had laid the groundwork,
but the rest would be up to them—though not entirely, because
He had made a curious promise that when He was gone, He
would send another—a "comforter," the Paraclete—to guide them
and to make clear all the ponderous things He had spoken about
in parables. And He had said this truth-giving Spirit would be
with them forever.

So when they were all together in that upper room, quite suddenly
"there came a sound from Heaven, as of a violent wind blowing."
Jesus had kept His promise. Not that they had doubted His word—
but people are always a bit startled when what they expect really
happens. And what happened transformed those twelve simple,
largely-uneducated men. A blazing fire came and forged their
fragile faith into a certainty stronger than Jewish persecution
and Roman tyranny. They understood now; they were ready now
to die for the faith, and they went out to "re-make the world,"
as we in MRA said we were doing. Pentecost was the hour of
birth of the Church: the new faith had entered upon the stage
of history.

DRUNK WITH THE NEW WINE of Confirmation, these provincial
men began to speak in many languages, for their faith embraced
all mankind, so the strangers and natives and pilgrims in Jerusalem
that day heard the message in their own tongue. And then the
disciples set out to preach the Good News "in Jerusalem and
Judea and Samaria and even unto the ends of the earth."

In Moral Re-Armament we used to say that what the world
needed was a New Pentecost. Frank Buchman had said in a speech:
"At that first Whitsun God spoke to a group of ordinary men.

They changed the course of history. May He not today have a plan which can solve the problems of a troubled world?" We all knew we were not *literally* expecting a new Pentecost, complete with tongues of fire and a babel of languages. (We had the languages, but we also had interpreters.) Still, I accepted it in a vague, symbolic sort of way. But now that I was seeing Pentecost as an historical incident, the birthday of the Church, I began to think that what we had really been saying in MRA was that what we needed was a new Church. And perhaps that is what we *did* mean, for we said we were to be a community guided by the Holy Spirit—as if the original one were no longer in existence. (It had never occurred to me that it *might* be still in existence, because I didn't know much about what had happened *after* Pentecost.)

The two chief characters in the drama of the early Church were of course Peter and Paul. Peter was only a fisherman, and not even a terribly successful one. His enthusiasm often outran his human capability. When the tests came he failed: when he realized he was walking on water he began to sink, and when he was asked about Christ, he said he didn't know Him. Yet Peter was the first to know who Christ really was: "Thou art Christ, the son of the living God." And then Jesus told Peter who *he* was: that he, Simon bar Jona, was the rock upon which he would build His Church.

That, too, I had accepted in a symbolic sense. What I did not know was that after the experience of Pentecost, everyone accepted the pre-eminence of Peter among the other Apostles. They talked about "the disciples and Peter," so they must have known that Christ had given him a special place. Even Paul, who didn't always agree with Peter, knew it was vitally important for them to be in agreement, and he always checked with Peter in matters of policy. The whole Christian body recognized that Christ's play on words (in Aramaic *Kephas* is a man's name; with a small k it means rock) was the expression of Peter's special function, that this rested upon the original intention and deliberate decision of Christ Himself. Later on there were theories advanced in a different explanation of Peter's special place, but many scholars—including semitic ones—have disproved that the passage in Matthew 16, 13-15 could be a later Roman forgery. Historians of all kinds have accepted the validity and the authenticity of the passage, and the literal meaning of the Aramaic idiomatic images of binding and loosing, the Gates of Hell, and so on.

Paul was a very different personality, with a different role. While Peter was still busy with forms of organization in the first Christian community in Jerusalem, Paul was plunging into interpreting, defining, instructing, for what Jesus taught was not confined to simple moral precepts. Frank Buchman had said in a speech, and it was our general belief, that God had shown Himself in a special way through the Person of Jesus Christ so that a new "plane of living" was made possible for mankind: through Christ people could find a new way of life based on absolute moral standards and the guidance of God. In the Sermon on the Mount, Christ had interpreted the Ten Commandments; we in MRA had summed them up in the Four Absolute Standards.

But Christ had said other things: He had made statements that threw the intellectual Jews and the Greeks of the day into turmoil. They wondered by what authority this man could claim power over the ancient laws, and predict things about coming catastrophe, judgment, eternal life. (Who did He think He was, God?) It would have been fine if this man had been content to make lame people leap about, and blind people see, and evil spirits depart with the swine, if He had not implied, and even said outright, that He was doing these things to prove that He was God. When He made Lazarus come forth—Lazarus who had been in the tomb three days—the Jews had had all they could take, and decided to put Him to death. And then there was the Resurrection.

Those were the things Paul had to explain to the scholars, the skeptics, the barbarians, and the new converts who soon had their own ideas about it all. He ranged over Asia Minor, Greece, and the Mediterranean islands, speaking and writing. Trained by a Jewish scholar, he used all his intellectual gifts, rationalizing, relating, setting down in logical argument proofs that Jesus Christ was indeed the Son of God, one *with* God, and that His Truth was "the whole of God's plan." Speaking at Ephesus, before he went to Jerusalem, Paul said:

> I have never shrunk from revealing to you the whole of God's plan. Keep watch, then, over yourselves, and over God's Church, in which the Holy Spirit has made you bishops; you are to be the shepherds of that flock which he won for himself at the price of his own blood.

So now our instructions brought us to the point of investigating the Catholic Church as an institution, a visible society on earth. Our book had a forthright way of putting things: boldly it stated that Christ had founded the Church just as directly and immediately as General Booth had founded the Salvation Army, and that Christ would have done "an extraordinarily foolish thing" in founding a Church with the definite task of converting the world if he had given it no organization with which to accomplish the task: "He would have founded a rabble, and surely He who was Infinite Wisdom did not expect a rabble to do what He commanded—nothing less than to preach the Gospel to the whole of creation!"

It said "reason" demands that Christ would leave some central authority to interpret His teaching according to the different circumstances of each succeeding age.

There had to be a way for people two hundred—or two thousand—years later to be sure they were getting the full message. "Stand firm, then, brethren," said St. Paul, "and hold by the traditions you have learned in word or in writing, from us." He warned about the future: "I know well that ravenous wolves will come among you when I am gone . . . there will be men among your own number who come forward with a false message, and find disciples to follow them . . ." He wrote that those coming forward with a false message would often seem to be very saintly people, directly illuminated by the Holy Ghost: "Friends, though it were we ourselves, though it were an angel from heaven that should preach a gospel other than the gospel we preached to you . . . if anyone preaches what is contrary to the tradition you received, a curse upon him!"

As the centuries unrolled there were many of these "saintly" men who yielded to the temptation to take one aspect of the truth and make it the *all* of truth: they preached a fine-sounding message that was however not the full and complete Gospel of Christ. Their disciples were those who found it easier to magnify a part than to embrace the whole.

In the *early* centuries it was quite clear cut: either you were, or you weren't. Heretics were condemned so that others would not be led astray. Certain vagaries of Christian thought were defined as heretical so that the great body of Christians could be sure what the Church was; there was excommunication so that all the trees and all the dead branches could not obscure the forest and everyone could be quite sure of "the Church of the living God, the pillar and foundation upon which the truth rests." (1 Tim. 3,5,15)

But with the Reformation, it was not so black and white. The theory of an "invisible church" had become popular. Men of stature and good will, and an idealism incompatible with the *human* element in the Church began to speak about an "invisible society," the One True Church independent of human institutions. But even these men did not succeed in obscuring the visible Church, for in every age just when it has seemed to vanish it emerges again, whole and complete, the visible institution containing and preserving "the whole of God's plan" which St. Paul had spoken about. Our instruction book quoted St. John Chrysostom: "It is easier for the sun to be quenched than for the Church to be made invisible."

There is a famous passage from Lord Macaulay, the great nineteenth-century historian, who was by no means Catholic:

> ... The Catholic Church is still sending forth to the farthest ends of the world missionaries as zealous as those who landed in Kent with Augustine, and still confronting hostile kings with the same spirit with which she confronted Attila ... Nor do we see any sign which indicates that the term of her long dominion is approaching. She saw the commencement of all the governments and of all the ecclesiastical establishments that now exist in the world; and we feel no assurance that she is not destined to see the end of them all. She was great and respected before the Saxon had set foot on Britain, before the Frank had passed the Rhine, when Grecian eloquence still flourished at Antioch, when idols were still worshipped in the temple of Mecca. And she may still exist in undiminished vigour when some traveller from New Zealand shall, in the midst of a vast solitude, take his stand on a broken arch of London Bridge to sketch the ruins of St. Paul's.
>
> —Macaulay, *Essay on
> L. von Ranke's
> History of the Popes,* 1840

I had an outline history book which said that one of the reasons for Christianity's success is that it possessed a book. The Bible, however, could not have been the secret to the mystery of how the Church had gone on all this time, because almost every sect throughout history and every Christian denomination in modern times claim the Bible as basis and proof for their own theories. Our instruction book had said that the sources of faith were Scripture and Tradition.

With Pentecost, the church had entered history. That the Apostles went eveywhere preaching and writing about Jesus is an historical fact. But St. Paul had written: "Hold by the traditions you have learned in word or in writing from us." What of the *word*? What of the things that were not written down?

IT WOULD HAVE BEEN HELPFUL, of course, if more *had* been written down. But no one told the Evangelists that they were writing a Bible, and that if they did not make everything very specific there would be a lot of controversy in ages to come. Today, as soon as someone begins to look important, a dozen biographers set out to produce The Definitive Biography of that person, who may or may not be dead yet, including all the details of his life, an evaluation of his significance in our times, and his message for future generations. But the Apostles did not busy themselves with their memoirs. Some left no writings at all, and some who had thoughts of writing it all down gave up in the face of such a tremendous job. St. John said, a little wistfully, "There is much else besides that Jesus did; if all of it were put in writing, I do not think the world itself would contain the books which would have to be written." Anyway, it seems not to have been God's plan for everything to be made clear in writing, for there was another way by which the truth would be passed on: word of mouth. St. Paul said to Timothy: "These things which thou hast heard of me before many witnesses, the same commend to faithful men who shall be fit to teach others also."

What had happened after the death of St. John, the last living Apostle? I had never thought about how difficult it must have been to stand firm and hold by the traditions taught by the Apostles. I had never thought about how one subtle diversion from what the Apostles had taught could lead whole nations astray. In my understanding of theology as something abstract, I did not know how the fight to testify to the one true interpretation of the doctrines of the Divinity of Christ, the Trinity, the authority of St. Peter, the Eucharist, caused many heads to roll in those first centuries. The seeds of these fussy theological distinctions were truths for which many of the early Christians were devoured by lions; but the Church survived, then to be laid almost to ruins by the Arians, the barbarians—the bloody struggle in the arena and on the battlefields, the bloodless but equally fatal cold wars in diplomatic societies and in empires all through the ages, a life and death struggle against those "deceiving influences," the continuing struggle to carry out St. Paul's charge to St. Timothy: "Guard that which has been commissioned to thee."

I HAD KNOWN NOTHING of the acts of the Martyrs, or the books and homilies of the early Doctors and Fathers of the Church, the early councils, the inscriptions in the catacombs. I had no awareness that there was anything important between the conclusion of the New Testament and the fifteenth century: I had been content to pick the story up then, accepting the interpretation of Christianity from preachers who had lost touch with that living tradition which had been passed on by the Apostles. I had accepted the word from those who had broken the link in that chain of commissioned preachers, a chain that had come down to our own day, with a unity maintained by the oral tradition of the Church.

I understood, now, that the whole of the Gospel—"the complete Christ"—was learned not only from historical records of the life of Jesus and the writings of the Evangelists, but also from the primitive Church, whose life was based on the preaching of the Apostles, centered around the one Peter, guided by the one spirit of the whole Christian Community, and animated by the Holy Ghost.

That was how the new faith had come through the world to me. That was how Christianity had come down to *now*—in a direct line, without distortion or interruption, in spite of treachery from within and violence from without. Cardinal Newman had spent many years trying to locate the One, Holy, Catholic, and Apostolic Church which Christ had promised would last forever; in an effort to prove to himself that the one true Church had always been in the Church of England and that the Roman communion was in schism, he started to write an Essay on Doctrinal Development. But in the middle of the writing he decided to become a Catholic. He could no longer write about "Roman Catholicism," because he had become convinced that there was only *one*; that modern Rome was in truth ancient Antioch, Alexandria, and Constantinople.

It was orthodoxy that had kept the whole truth intact and had prevented any one of the great and devouring ideas of the Church from swallowing any other truth. The ancients knew that in the time to come, if the faithful were to keep their balance among all the fashionable ideas of the day, from slavery and divorce to birth-control and Marxism, they would have to be sure just what Christ had taught about the principles involved in all these things: that was the purpose of dogma.

I was reading a biography of G.K. Chesterton while we were studying dogma, and learned that he had written a whole book about orthodoxy; there was a quotation from that book which I copied out in my notebook:

The Church could not afford to swerve a hair's breadth on some things if she was to continue her great and daring experiment of the irregular equilibrium. Once let one idea become less powerful and some other idea would become too powerful. It was no flock of sheep the Christian shepherd was leading, but a herd of bulls and tigers, of terrible ideas and devouring doctrines, each of them strong enough to turn to a false religion and lay waste the world. . . . This is the thrilling romance of Orthodoxy. People have fallen into the foolish habit of speaking of orthodoxy as something heavy, humdrum, and safe. There never was anything so perilous or so exciting as orthodoxy. It was sanity: and to be sane is more dramatic than to be mad. It was the equilibrium of a man behind madly rushing horses, seeming to sweep this way and to sway that, yet in every attitude having the grace of statuary and the accuracy of arithmetic. . . . She swerved to left and right, so exactly as to avoid enormous obstacles. She left on one hand the huge bulk of Arianism, buttressed by all the worldly powers to make Christianity too worldly. The next instant she was swerving to avoid an orientalism, which would have made it too unworldly. The orthodox Church never took the tame course or accepted the conventions; the orthodox Church was never respectable. It would have been easier to have accepted the earthly power of the Arians. It would have been easy, in the Calvinistic seventeenth century, to fall into the bottomless pit of predestination. It is easy to be a madman: it is easy to be a heretic. . . . To have fallen into any of those open traps of error and exaggeration which fashion after fashion and sect after sect set along the historic path of Christendom—that would indeed have been obvious and tame. But to have avoided them all has been one whirling adventure; and in my vision the heavenly chariot flies thundering through the ages, the dull heresies sprawling and prostrate, the wild truth reeling but erect.

The word "dogma" had long ago become a part of my vocabulary in the form "dogmatic," which I thought meant the tone of voice of people who spoke emphatically about things I did not agree with. If I had been aware of such a thing as religious dogma I might have thought that dogmas could be useful if what you chose to pick as a dogma was a kind of symbol that helped stir up a few embers in your spiritual life. A dogma might be a kind of motto—a Golden Rule. If an intelligent Catholic had told me that dogma meant true intellectual freedom, I would not have understood. But I would not have been too surprised, for none of the Catholics I knew seemed to be cringing in perpetual terror under the fearsome Infallibility of the Pope.

THERE WAS ONE TIME, THOUGH, that I did become aware of dogma as a reality, and I thought a rather frightening one. It was also the first time that I thought about the Catholic Church with anything more than a vague awareness of its existence. It was in November of 1950, when the Assumption of the Blessed Virgin was defined as a dogma. I was slightly scandalized, like a lot of other Americans. I can still see the newspaper headlines— maybe the whole thing has become magnified in my mind, but I *think* there were headlines—and I felt sorry for the poor Catholics who might wake up any morning and find a new doctrine in their newspapers.

One hundred years before this, the doctrine of the Immaculate Conception had been defined, and had upset a lot of people in Cardinal Newman's day. In his *Apologia* he explained that there was no such thing as a "new dogma"—that new "definitions" of dogma were the clothing and illustration of dogmas that had always been a part of Catholic belief. It was not that Catholics came to believe a dogma because it was defined: it was defined because they believed it. The definition in 1854 had come in consequence of a unanimous petition. And Newman explained that Catholics were not likely to be oppressed by new definitions if it took eighteen centuries to promulgate even one of them, as it had in the case of the Immaculate Conception. The doctrine of the Assumption had been a part of Catholic belief for fourteen centuries before it had been defined in November 1950. Furthermore,

Newman said that the normal seat of infallibility is the Pope in Ecumenical Council, and there had been only eighteen such councils since Christianity had begun.

As a matter of fact, when we were studying Infallibility, I learned that there were so many conditions upon which an infallible pronouncement depended that I began to feel a little sorry for the Pope. Later on I read something that George Bernard Shaw once said:

> The famous dogma of Papal Infallibility is by far the most modest profession of its kind in existence. Compared to our infallible democracies, our infallible medical councils, our infallible astronomers, our infallible parliaments, the Pope is on his knees in the dust confessing his ignorance before God.

During this time I was going to Mass on Sundays, and finding out about Catholic sermons. There was little of the oratorical eloquence that Protestants expect, and often get, but I was grateful for the simplest homilies, and even for the vehemence of some of the fist-pounding Dominicans, at St. Vincent Ferrer's, who were being literally true to their vocation: the Order of Preachers. My response to sermons was different from what it had been in Protestant churches, because I knew that however the preacher's own private views might enter into the sermon according to its subject, whatever he said about God was the truth. To borrow a phrase of Monsignor Knox, the preacher has, in preaching sound Christian doctrine, "the rather negative assurance of not teaching error."

The preachers in those pulpits may not have spoken with the tongues of angels, nor with the brilliance of a Monsignor Knox or a Cardinal Newman; but however badly they might express it, the truth was there, backed up by centuries of authority.

ONE DAY THE BUSINESS OF PREACHING and the idea of history and tradition combined to reveal something to me on a deeper level. It was Sunday. I had gone to Mass at St. Patrick's Cathedral, which was where I felt the safest, for I was still shy, and too clumsy with Father Stedman's *My Sunday Missal* to venture into small, intimate churches where people could look over my shoulder.

The priest climbed the stone steps to the pulpit, read the announcements, then began the sermon. I do not remember what the sermon was about, but as he spoke I had an almost tangible sense of a long smooth channel stretching behind this priest all through the centuries, like a shaft of light, beginning with the faithful in that upper room when the Holy Spirit came down, and preceding in a steady beam throughout the Roman Empire, the Dark Ages, the Middle Ages, the Reformation, the Age of Reason, right up to June 6, 1954, with this priest standing and preaching his sermon in the center of this shaft of light. Here was I, somehow privileged to be a part of this clear solid light that had been steady throughout the centuries. Off this main beam had shot little beams which wanted to illumine certain corners and to dwell in that light alone, and therefore they cut themselves off from the source. All these little lights became portable lamps with no sure, steady connection with this power station.

I HAD LEARNED A LOT in the weekly instructions, but that day in St. Patrick's I became conscious, with more than my mind, of being newly possessed of the intellectual heritage of the past. The society I had been brought up in had been uprooted from the past: now I was a part of this living tradition of sound thinking. I was an heir of all its wealth. Somewhere I had read that an individual cannot think without a memory, a society cannot think without a tradition. The past was not there to visit as an antiquarian might: it was meant to be brought in line with the present, and this conjunction was a stepping-stone toward the right kind of future.

It was a very good thing that I began going to Mass regularly. The best colleges educate the whole man: mind, and body, and spirit. To be fully instructed in Catholicism meant an orientation not only of mind and intelligence but of my sensibilities. If one is not to be top heavy, mental expansion has to be synchronized with the formation of the spiritual consciousness.

I remember the first time I went to Vespers at the Cathedral on a Sunday afternoon. I had no idea what it was all about— the solemn bowing and rising and sitting down, the removing of caps, the changing of position. But what was clear to me was this: all the business at the altar was not for the entertainment or edification of us, the congregation. The choir, the officiants, all the "performers" faced the altar. All the intensity of their vocal expression was directed there, to the altar, to whatever mysterious presence was there. And as I faced the backs of the clergy in the sanctuary that Sunday afternoon, I got the point. This was worship. We were all doing it together. Everything was unified and directed in a steady gaze toward the object of our worship.

I realized that all the material objects in the Cathedral had a purpose; that because we are not pure spirits, we grasp spiritual things through things visible: the statues, the vestments, all the furnishings—and through things sensible, the incense and the music— the Gregorian chant echoing round the sanctuary and the nave and the antiphonal rhythm back and forth from the balcony to the altar. All these things focused the attention on the essentials. All the actions, the words, the sequence of the liturgy drawing everyone into a unity, a wholeness; the joyous, articulate expression of the relation of creature to Creator. It was the complete worship, by the whole man, of the Absolute—God.

WE HAD STUDIED THE CHURCH as a visible organization: now we arrived at the chapter on The Mystical Body of Christ. "We have spent several instructions," said our book, "in dealing with the Church as the visible ORGANIZATION established by Christ to continue His work upon earth. Now we go further. We maintain that the Church is not only an ORGANIZATION but an ORGANIC SOCIETY, A LIVING BODY, AN ORGANISM with its own life-secret and its own life-stream."

Christ had hinted at the union that was to exist between him and the members of His Church when He spoke about the vine and the branches . . . "I am the vine, you are its branches; if a man lives on in me, and I in him, then he will yield abundant fruit . . ." (John 15; 1-5).

We learned that the term "Mystical Body" was not a poetic phrase but was a literal concept developed by St. Paul who was always stressing the relation between the Vine and the branches in terms of a man's body and that body's members. "A man's body is all one, though it has a number of different organs; all this multitude of organs goes to make up one body; so it is with Christ. . . . And you are Christ's body, organs of it depending upon each other . . ." (1 Cor. 12; 12-30). And to the Romans St. Paul had said: "Each of us has one body, with many different parts . . . just so we, though many in number, form one body in Christ." (Romans 12:4).

So the Church is a living body, a body with Christ the head and Christians the members of the body. I thought that perhaps that was the secret of the mysterious bond I had felt between all the different authors of all those books I had read. It was not a mechanical unity, imposed from without: branches are not stuck on to a vine. St. Paul shows through the simile of the body that in the same kind of organic union as vine and branches, Christians are united to Christ and share with Him one life, which is His life. Through baptism all Christians become cells in this organism, and as cells they are absorbed into something supernatural; they are given a share in the divine life.

We learned that "mystical" in the "Mystical Body" did not mean something *mysterious* but that for about eight centuries, Christian writers—unable to think of a suitable word for an organism that had no exact parallel in the natural order—had just spoken about the "Body of Christ" until someone in the ninth century used the phrase "mystical body" to show that it was not a physical or moral body, and the phrase had stuck.

This was the secret. It was a unity of a higher order that drew, like moths to the flame, people who had no innate interest in smoothly-running moral or social organizations. This organism was one Church, which St. Augustine had called "the whole Christ." God, said St. Paul to the Ephesians, had made Christ the head to which the whole Church is joined, so that the Church is His body. (Eph. 1:22). The Church through the centuries was the continuation of the work of Christ; that explained why the Church was and would always be "One, Holy, Catholic and Apostolic" in spite of the abuses that made Luther nail his ninety-five theses to the door in Wittenberg.

One of my friends, who was getting nervous about my interest in Catholicism, had written a letter in which she said: "History shows the Church is susceptible to corruption and decay." That would be true, if the Church were merely a human organization, a moral or social body. Our book, after explaining the metaphors of the vine and the branches, the head and the body, illustrated how this body was distinct from a mere social or moral unity through an analogy of a Mr. Smith and the Joint Stock Company. Briefly we followed the career of this Mr. Smith who managed to pass from a mere physical Mr. Smith to a moral and social person—the Smith Manufacturing Company. Obviously, if something happened to the morals of Mr. Smith or if something went wrong with the social principles of the Smith Manufacturing Company, it would crumble from within. I had already, by this time, realized that Catholic historians knew far more than did my friend about the Church's battle against corruption and decay, and they also knew that the Church could not crumble from within. Christ gave no intimation that the flock would not have some very bad shepherds, but He said the Church would go on forever; that against it even the Gates of Hell could not prevail. This could only be a Church which was something far more than a human organization.

IF THE TERM "MYSTICAL BODY" was strange at first, the word "organism" was not. There was something very familiar in this idea of *organism*. Moral Re-Armament was often explained as "not an organization but an organism." And we had often read St. Paul's words to the Romans in which he emphasized both the social function and the different responsibilities of each member of the body in the unity of the same spirit: "Each of us has one body with many different parts, and not all these parts have the same function. . . . Just so we, though many in number, form one body in Christ, and each acts as the counterpart of another . . ." Some were to teach, some to administer, some to preach—but all were united, as cells in an organism. All the different parts of the body were to make each other's welfare their common concern. If one member suffered, the rest would suffer: if one rejoiced, we would all share in the joy: the intellectual and spiritual shortcomings of individuals would be made up for by the penance and extra graces and talents of the others.

All of us who had grown up in Moral Re-Armament, and those who had been with it for a fairly long time, were used to thinking *corporately*. Even if as individuals we lacked "world vision" we knew there was for us no such thing as a "personal plan." Nor was there any such thing as a "private sin." Everything affected everyone else and The Work. So we did in a real and practical sense think of ourselves as vital cells united in an organic body.

Some of the descriptions of this organism, in Moral Re-Armament literature, sounded almost like the description of the Mystical Body in our instruction book. The effect of the world force of Moral Re-Armament, explained the English historian R.C. Mowat in his booklet "The Message of Frank Buchman," would be like that of a leaven, which gradually changes the nature of the entire lump of dough; or it would be like an organism—a plant or tree, which grows while maintaining its own essential nature until it overshadows the entire area around. The growth of MRA could not be measured by statistics and membership cards but would have, as an organism, its own inner principles of growth composed of cells. Cells were represented by homes where inspired democracy was lived, by groups of workers in factories and mines, by students in universities, by all those in different areas who were committed to the MRA revolution, and such cells were formed spontaneously as soon as a person found the experience of change and began to pass it on. The cells of MRA were linked together in a world organism, not by human organization, but by the fact that their members would seek guidance from God whereby each would maintain touch with the whole. Thus there would be a supernatural network of live-wires all over the world.

NOW, IF ALL THIS WERE TRUE, and Moral Re-Armament was indeed an organism, how was it related to this other organism which I had learned was the Mystical Body of Christ? MRA was "for everyone, everywhere"—but if its membership was established by cells absorbed into an organism, what about Catholics who were already absorbed into an organism? Surely there couldn't be *two* Mystical Bodies? The one must be a part of the other. But the Church was both an invisible and a visible society— an organism *and* an organization. MRA, it was often said, was "a production of the Holy Spirit." Therefore it must be a part of the Protestant tradition which does not recognize a visible Church. But MRA denied having any religious character.

There was not, however, time to ponder this paradox for very long. We were covering a lot of territory, though we never went too fast: Father Clark always seemed to know when we were ready to move up to the next rung on the ladder. Sometimes we veered off on tangents which turned out not to be tangents so much as windows through which were illumined modern aspects of ancient problems. We talked about politics and the press and psychology; the muddle of modern life, viewed from the perspective of Catholic social doctrine, took on order and meaning.

Father Clark talked about the "family squabbles" among the clergy in America and all over the world: healthy controversy on matters not connected to faith or morals, and I saw that there was a tremendous space of freedom with the church—freedom that is possible because of the conformity with the mind of God, that makes for unity and not uniformity. I was astonished at the tremendous space created by the Church for rational debate about controversial issues. I read articles by Catholic editors and journalists, and speeches by Jesuits in their magazine *America*: they were all based on solid moral principle but they also took into consideration the special pragmatic needs of American society. It seemed that these writers and speakers presented their cases honestly, without dependence on slogans or cliches: they respected the intelligence and the integrity of their readers. And I could see that American Catholics were beginning to restore something valuable to American life: the American tradition of free debate underlined by the Catholic tradition of *reasoned* argument: two traditions which are essential to a free society.

BETWEEN INSTRUCTIONS I did some browsing in that field of literature in which biographies and autobiographies are lumped together in the general category of "convert stories." There were pamphlets with excerpts from the *apologias* of eminent writers and scientists, ex-communists and actors, whole biographies with helpful indexes, and anthologies like *The Road to Damascus* and *The Road to Rome* which were beginning to appear in handy paperback editions.

It was probably fortunate that I had not read these stories before I did, because I might have wondered, now, if I wasn't patterning my own "road to Rome" along the paths of these others. Well-known and articulate converts, such as Clare Boothe Luce and Evelyn Waugh, Douglas Hyde and Avery Dulles, might have conditioned my responses. I could have fallen into the deplorable habit of taking my spiritual temperature as I approached each new step, comparing my reactions with theirs. As it was, I had gone into the whole thing cold, without knowing in advance what reactions to *expect*. This was new for me. In MRA, I'd sometimes impressed people by seeming "original." But actually, any "spontaneity" on my part was half-consciously based on what reactions I knew were expected, in any given situation.

But now, as I read, I could look back and see how my own unpremeditated steps and my impromptu reactions paralleled those of these converts, in many ways. Of course converts are not carbon copies of each other: each is different, for there are a thousand different approaches to the Church and no one enters at exactly the same angle. It was fascinating to see how grace had worked in all these lives along the lines of each one's own natural interests and inclinations. But all these converts had two things in common: the recognition of such a thing as absolute truth, and the compelling, relentless drive to find that truth.

Many of these converts had had the same feeling, as they got closer to the Church, that it was not after all so *new*—that perhaps they had been Catholic all along and were just now finding out. Ever since my first instruction I had felt as though someone had turned the light on, so that I could identify all these pieces of furniture I'd been bumping into from as far back as I could remember. I loved what Chesterton had said: "Dogma after dogma answered instinct after instinct." I felt these instincts had always been in me somewhere—rather like "secret writing" in lemon juice which must be exposed to the heat before it shows up.

There was, for instance, the instinct that was answered by the dogma of Original Sin.

IN MORAL RE-ARMAMENT, Original Sin wasn't mentioned much: Human Nature *was*. It was human nature that was at the bottom of all the trouble in the world. All the philosophies and ideologies had failed to give an answer because they did not have, as their starting point, the changing of human nature. Marxism had at least reckoned with human nature, we said, though Marx's approach to it was unrealistic: just change the *system*; then the natural goodness of man would be allowed to operate and we would have the new socially-minded man. We said it was the other way around: human nature had to change, and then the system could change. And to the gloomy skeptics who said "You can't change human nature" (because, we said, they were "quite comfortable with theirs") we would reply: "No, but *God* can," adding "I know because it has happened to *me*." And so ultimately the proving ground for the practical value of our way of life was the human nature in each of us. If we were willing to be changed completely and radically and irrevocably, we had the answer, and it could be multiplied on a world scale.

Although I had never spent any time pondering Original Sin, which was a very vague concept in my mind (something to do with Adam and Eve), I had often felt that there was some kind of obstacle—beyond our control—to the implementation of our ideas about human nature being changeable. There was the time when someone at Caux wrote down, and shared with everyone in a large meeting, that he had made the decision "never to think of myself again." The cry was taken up in every team center— not, I think, because this was original—more likely because someone very important had said it. So one person after another would get on his feet and "go on record" as having made the decision never to think of himself again. It was the New Thing we were all supposed to do. I couldn't do it, possibly because I was stubborn and rebelled against "following the crowd" or self-willed (unwilling to "pay the price of radical change"). In any case, it would have been dishonest for me to say that I too had made the decision, for it seemed like presumption: How could I be sure I would never think of myself again?

I think I had always felt hopeless about pleasing God. I had always been told about my self-will, and I had a great inferiority complex so far as God's Elect was concerned. I never did anything really bad, but my motives were presumably all—in the last if not the first analysis—hopelessly disordered. Even the *motive* of pleasing God had to be scrutinized because it could so easily be selfish: one had to be sure it was not for what one could get out of it. *Humility* was suspect, too, because there were so many forms of *false* humility, all having to do with "spiritual pride." If I didn't try hard enough to do the right thing, it was because of laziness or apathy; if I tried too hard, it was ambition or conceit (or fear). So there was this constant oscillation between despair and presumption.

WE WERE NOT SUPPOSED TO be like the penitents of old: the hair-shirt complex was not allowed, because we were supposed to-be Joyous. But it was also wrong to coast along unconcerned about sin, because our sins and our mutual failings were our common bond, the basis of our unity. Yet it was also wrong to count on failure.

We had to make a moral decision, fully intending to stick to it, and when we would fail it would be a painful and humbling experience. All this was fine if you could maintain a healthy balance between sin and forgiveness. There were some extroverts who could manage to go on day after day in this kind of rhythm, willing to make mistakes, eager to change and start again with much optimism. But for most of us it led to introspection and self-consciousness. It was as if we could never do anything without seeing ourselves doing it, out of the corner of our eye, pricking and prying with the moral needle. We were conditioned to feel responsible for our motives; this made us more self-centered than ever. And then we had to feel guilty about *that*.

So THERe WAS ALWAYS THIS CLOUD of guilt hovering above me. I always felt sinful. And when I could locate a specific sin to feel guilty about, I felt guilty because I could not *feel* sorry: my sins were always too abstract, and hadn't seemed to affect anyone. It was thought that in order to deal radically with human nature, one had to be positively smitten with the full significance of what one's sin had done to other people (and the world) and then to feel like a worm and weep many tears and apologize before an assemblage. After you had done that, you would know that God, and your teammates, had forgiven you: thus restored to unity, you could get on with the business of changing the world.

I guess I'd always thought that The Guilt Complex was the exclusive property of Moral Re-Armament. I'd had no idea that guilt had been scrutinized by worldly philosophers, and psychologists such as Carl Jung. If I had known that the guilt I lived with was what Jung calls "the Shadow," the dark side in every human being as the primitiveness, violence and cruelty in the whole human race as the result of original sin, and not personal guilt, I would have perhaps understood something about the mercy and love of God, and of Christ the Redeemer.

Our instruction book was unhesitatingly precise. It said that Original Sin was the condition in which we were all born because of Adam's disobedience; that it was different from Actual Sin, i.e., sin which we commit in our own lives; that Original Sin does not deprive man of anything which is natural to him, but is really a deprivation of the supernatural relation God meant us to have with Him, with an accompanying slowing up of some of man's natural gifts.

These, the book said, were the effects of Original Sin:

(a) IN THE SOUL	loss of divine grace, privation of heaven, ignorance in the intellect, weakness and malice in the will, concupiscence in the heart:
(b) IN THE BODY	loss of extraordinary natural gifts; the necessity for work; sickness, death, corruption;
(c) ON EARTH	unfruitful soil which must be tilled, animals ferocious and beyond control . . .

Therefore, we could not expect perfection in this life on earth. The ultimate Perfectibility of Man was a myth. All we could expect was a continual struggle against the powers of darkness.

This sounds very depressing, but—oddly enough—I was the opposite of depressed. In fact, I felt an overwhelming sense of hope and joy, because now I *knew* what was expected. It was objective. These were the *facts* about human nature. You couldn't change it in desire but you could change it in effect. And that had to do with the *will*, which has a specific part to play in freeing us from slavery to the animal nature, which we cannot change. Once you know what to expect as a result of Original Sin, you don't have to be obsessed by sin and guilt.

The book then went on to Actual Sin: what it was, what we could do to avoid it, and how to avoid "occasions of sin" (which, I thought, were pretty remote for me at that time of my Spartan existence). Anyway, a great burden of confusion and anguish rolled off me and melted away in the awakening sense of God's love for us and His mercy (after all, He understood our nature) and His justice—in telling us specifically how we could be pleasing to Him. The First Commandment has to do with worshipping God, and I thought: How wonderful that there are simple and specific ways to fulfil our first obligation ("filial devotion") and to know that God accepts our offerings, never mind the state of *our* minds, or souls, or bodies. Worship and adoration are

not things you *feel*: they are things you *do*. I began to realize
that the Church has a very sound grasp of psychology; that theology
is, in a sense, Christian psychology. I suspect that if I'd ever
been psychoanalyzed, I'd have been diagnosed as a neurotic with
chronic anxiety and obsessive guilt. I now know that moral
theologians have a word for this syndrome: scrupulosity.

Scrupulosity indicates a lack of trust in the mercy and power
of God. It means you think God has put you in charge of your
subconscious—that you are responsible for all the results of your
actions—that if an action or a decision turned out to be wrong,
it was because you had known "deep down in your heart" that
your motives were not pure. If you are afflicted with scrupulosity,
you've got to pay full attention to the *facts* about God, and the
facts about what He wants from His children. If you concentrate
on absolute truth, and *the* absolute, God, then you will not be
blown about by the seductive winds of your own subjectivity.
Your self-centered muddle will give way to the peace and tranquility
of order; the sense will become subject to reason, the reason
to faith, and the whole personality to the will of God.

You will not feel you have to probe your subconscious.

The guilt that we all share because we are descendents of Adam
is different from the "guilty conscience" we don't exactly "share"
but which many of us *have*, in varying degrees of intensity. I
had always had an active conscience, but it was not an instructed
one (it had never occurred to me that a conscience could be
"instructed") because I thought conscience was a feeling, and
that the feeling was the infallible test. But conscience is, first,
a judgment of the intellect concerning right and wrong, and this
has to do with sin, which is also not defined by a guilty conscience.
I learned about sin and penance in instructions (and I would
learn through experience) that one does not plunge into the
confessional to rid oneself of guilt. If you say to the profile of
the priest through the grille that maybe, perhaps, your motive
in something or other was not wholly pure, the priest will say:
Did you know or didn't you? He will (if he is a good and patient
Confessor—and if he knows you're a convert) remind you that
sin is an evil thought, word, or deed committed with full consent
of the will. He will give you short shrift—literally—if you are
monopolizing the Box while all those people are waiting in line
to confess *real* sins.

This can be humiliating, but also educational. Next time, examine your conscience—what have you done or thought or said that you *knew* was wrong? Or what hadn't you done that you should have done? It is all right to be very objective about sins of omission and commission. If you *felt* really sorry, that was a help; but feelings are not essential for absolution. Go into the Box, express your sorrow for having hurt God (you *are* sorry, whether you *feel* it or not) and say the Act of Contrition (which includes your Firm Purpose of Amendment) and the priest will assure you that God has indeed forgiven you. Then whether you *feel* forgiven or not, you *know* that you have been restored to friendship with God, and you go on your way confident that He will guide you.

It is not because we are so good at recognizing God's voice that we can be confident, but precisely the reverse: we are so dense that to think God would not make things very clear would be to accuse Him of overestimating His own creatures.

After that chapter about sin—Original and Actual—I realized that all my life I had been preoccupied with sin and guilt and conscience but had never understood Christ as Redeemer. That He had died for our sins was always somehow abstract. Now it occurred to me that if one doesn't know about Original Sin and the old Adam, one can't comprehend the dimensions of Christ, the New Adam.

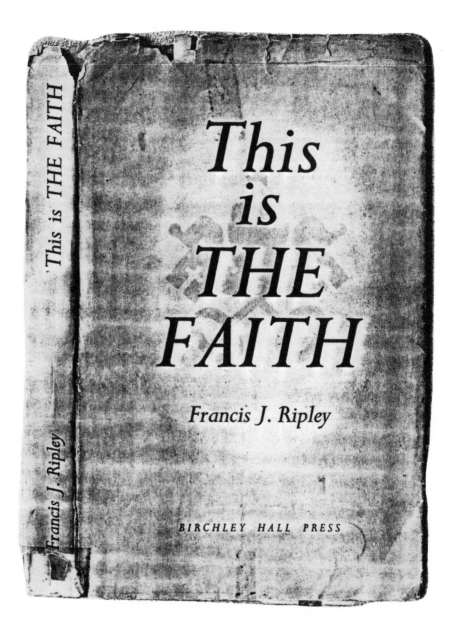

This
is
THE
FAITH

Francis J. Ripley

BIRCHLEY HALL PRESS

In pre-Vatican II days, there were many manuals intended for "non-Catholic enquirers" as they were described in the Foreward to this 1951 book of lectures given by Father Ripley, a priest of the Liverpool diocese in England. Faith still has her (now crumbling) copy.

The Boom Is Lowered

Mackinac or Rome?

WE PANTED ON THROUGH the sticky summer of 1954, and every day I took *This Is the Faith* with me, to read on the Fifth Avenue bus (if I had a seat) and to Bryant Park, behind the New York Public Library, on my lunch hour. All of New York that summer seemed to be—in the words of Gerard Manley Hopkins—"charged with the grandeur of God." The whole world seemed full of poetry. I was living on a sustained pitch of excitement, conscious all the time of an overwhelming feeling that was like being in love. And in a sense perhaps that is what it was, for real love is a reverence and an awe for the mystery that is every person, and a desire for oneness with that person. And loving the Church is not a mere romanticization of the aesthetic externals but a deep and compelling desire to worship her essential being, which is not a thing but a Person. And a longing to lose one's self, to be totally absorbed into this great and powerful love.

And then, somewhere along the line, *conviction* came. The knowledge that one has *certainty* is the first essential; the *feeling* of certitude is a great help, but *conviction* is something else: it does not come automatically with being *convinced.*

"Conviction" was a familiar word. I had always felt a personal lack of it, in Moral Re-Armament. I *believed*, but I did not have that fiery passion so many others had—the conviction that made them "burn" to see other people find what *they* had found. Conviction meant being "on the offensive" which meant, to me, strain and effort: even the thought of such conviction had made me feel tired ever since I had tried, with all my youthful fervor, to "spearhead the revolution" in my high school.

This new conviction was different. (It is, I have learned, something which makes most converts rather tiresome to most "born Catholics.") It was the overwhelming desire to *share*. Not to justify my position, not even to justify poor old Holy Mother Church in the jaundiced eyes of the prejudiced and misinformed, but a longing for everyone to know all that was their natural heritage. Monsignor Knox had said, in his book *Off the Record*, that "The truth has a claim on us; it deserves to be told, and in proportion as it makes itself known to us we daren't let it go untold; we are false to our own natures if we try to bottle it up. And, apart from that, the people we are fondest of are precisely the people to whom we have the duty of making known the truth as we see it."

Whether it was a matter of duty or not, I *had* to share it. The more I understood, the less I could contain it. For the first time, I thought I could be really articulate about something. I *knew* what I had learned, and I could talk about it to anyone without fear of my mind suddenly going blank, and without being circumspect about the small cloudy areas in my own understanding. Our instruction book was full of very precise definitions: each word was used because it had a certain meaning, and because the definitions were true to themselves. They did not try to orient themselves to the reader; they were not worded in a way that would catch his attention and win his approval. He could take the words or leave them; at least he knew exactly what they meant. For all their semantic accuracy, the sentences were simple and beyond no one's grasp. Simple, yet with enough meat in them for a hundred sermons.

I couldn't see why every Catholic shouldn't be articulate about his faith; there seemed no reason why all Catholics, regardless of their education, couldn't speak with something of a theologian's accuracy. Even the most elementary catechisms (which were ubiquitous in the pamphlet racks) have the same precision: with or without literary flourishes, the substance is there. One might, if one were clever, explain things differently to different people, making analogies suited to each person's own personality and capacity, but one always knew what the one, definite, objective point *was*.

All this was so exciting that I thought surely everyone would rejoice with me, and would want to hear all about it. It soon became apparent that this was not the case. Some of my MRA friends seemed wistful, and said they were glad I was "finding a faith." And there were some whose attitude was: "Fine, if this makes you happy, go right ahead." It seemed to be no matter of concern to them that the Church's interpretation of Christianity was the only one that logically held water. There was one person— an MRA borderline case—who told me that he would be a Catholic too, if he believed in God. It was the only system, he said, that made sense. He had the Monsignor Knox translation of the Old and New Testaments at home: he liked Knox's style.

The reaction that most took me by surprise, though, came from people whose idea of the Church was based on misconception and ignorance. They actually thought that the Church taught that Catholics consider non-Catholics not Christian and therefore outside salvation; that Catholics aren't allowed to read the Bible; that Catholics "worship" the Virgin Mary and other saints, and must "do everything" the Pope says. And so on.

Then there were those who were better informed about the Church, but who were prejudiced. They thought "Roman Christianity" added up to "lust of power, saint-worship and Jesuitry." At least one knew where they stood: prejudice was, at least, a response, and almost anything is better than *no* response.

For a while I had tried to compress my weekly instructions into letters to certain people I thought would be interested— or at least relieved to know that accepting Catholicism did not require abandonment of one's rational powers. They were not interested. And these letters were to the people I cared most about—those with whom, as Monsignor Knox had said, we had the obligation to share the truth as we saw it. I really wanted them to know the whole story behind all this commotion; I suppose I should have been prepared for this complete lack of comprehension of all I was (I thought) putting so lucidly, for I had lived a long time in the same atmosphere. We were, in a sense, victims of a singular point of view, and only a very considerable jolt could free us from the confines of our own outlook. It was psychologically incomprehensible that there could be something we had not seen. I *thought* differently now, and then I realized that I also *felt* differently. Something irrevocable had happened—something that was bound to cut like a sword; a basic point of departure that was the cleavage in the line of communication, as if a telephone line had been cut. I puzzled this around for a while, with the feeling that I was on the brink of an important discovery. And then I knew what had happened: I'd had a startling experience which had come at such a chronologically natural time that I hadn't realized it was the crux of the whole matter. It was the experience of revealed truth.

And this is where language is no good at all. I will never be able to describe what happened, or even when it happened. I had become convinced that the Church was God's revelation of Himself—that it was the fullest possible way of life. And then, all of a sudden, I understood.

I knew people who pitied Catholics because, they said, they had lost two things, which were the two things that I had *found* in the Church right from the beginning: reason, and freedom. I had read in some book: "Only when you see Catholicism as a great opening of doors, a widening of all your liberty, will you begin to see the Church clearly, as she is."

The implications of this had suddenly become clear. In one rather dizzy moment, the indefinable but profound sense of the *infallibility of MRA* faded, as a kind of veil lifted and revealed something that was everything. It was not a matter of having been wrong: it was that there was something so profoundly right, and so tremendously big. It was like taking a first breath with two lungs when you had breathed with only one all your life. No one could have told you what having two lungs was like: that would have been like trying to explain color to someone who could see only shadows. In that dizzy moment, everything was different. And in that same moment I realized the limitations of communication. Anything I might say would be like a Tower of Babel to anyone who had not had, from within, the experience of knowing this total claim, on the mind and the will and the heart, of revealed truth.

I began to feel that I was in possession of a very dangerous secret. I thought of my friends who were so convinced about their way of life, and I almost felt I should *protect* them. Because nothing can ever be the same for someone who has caught even a glimpse of revealed truth.

THOSE WERE DAYS OF an exhilarating and almost exhausting widening of all my senses. I was taking in so much that I felt the giddiness you feel when you are breathing very fast and very deeply, blowing up a balloon. Everything that had ever been fed into the reserves of my mind was shaking itself out, crawling out from under damp leaves, out from the dark musty corners of the subconscious—coming out, coming up for review in the clear cold light of reality, and then being assigned—one by one—to its proper place in this eternal perspective. Everything was making sense with the kind of exactitude of the printed message when the hands are in the right relation to the typewriter keyboard. Get your little finger in the right place and the rest is automatic; the words spell themselves out properly.

Meanwhile, my thoughts about Moral Re-Armament were suspended somewhere. I didn't know how all of this would affect my inherited way of life, and I didn't try to imagine the outcome of anything. There were moments when I felt I was understanding MRA for the first time—catching the first view of it from the outside, like a child who is familiar with all the inside details of his home suddenly seeing it from far away, as part of the landscape. The experience of finding that Catholicism was indisputably *reasonable* had put MRA in a new light; but not in sharp blacks and whites. The cumulative effect of all the experiences and graces of my years in the movement made complete objectivity impossible; and there seemed to be more paradoxes than ever.

In my first flush of Catholic reading, I got the idea that if I became a Catholic I would receive the grace through which I could become totally committed to God's will, which meant that I could be totally committed to Moral Re-Armament. It was a matter of self-sacrifice. But now I had come to realize that I had things a little backward. The Church was not an aid—it was the totality. All the truths which had formed me, all the truths everywhere, were a part of that totality—that consummate truth.

Anyway, by now the significant thing was that I had found certainty. There was no more strain to adjust to each new climate. The certainty was there like a very solid cushion: whether I was at a New York MRA meeting, or at work, or at my night class at NYU, or on the subway, or alone in my room, I was the *same person*: there was no longer the conscious transition from one reality to another. All the threads were being drawn together and I was becoming whole; all of me was going in one direction.

As for my family and friends, they *had* to be grateful for my new emotional health, because they had often worried about my "instability." So they did not ask any questions. I think they knew that whatever was happening to me was beyond them too, and so they were silent and continued to back me up in a helpless, trusting sort of way. I had written my sister Nancy (who was not then in New York) about my decision to take instructions, and she wrote me a letter which made me very happy: she said "What you said about being brought to the real starting point for the first time in your life rings bells. I believe God has led you in a marvelous way. Ever since you got a job and went to live in New York, it has filled me with wonder the way He has shown you the next step. And now you seem convinced that this is the next step. All I can say is: Praise God and more power to you!"

So FOR A WHILE all was peaceful. However, when people love you, they don't sit back forever with their hands folded if they think you are on the wrong track. When they suspect that you are being spirited away from what they believe is your God-given mission in life, they too feel a duty to *say* something. I had an ominous feeling that some kind of showdown was imminent. Toward the end of the summer, when I had a week's vacation coming up, I was presented with an idea, or actually a *challenge*, that put all my new convictions to the test.

The issue was: Are you willing to go to Mackinac on your vacation and sit down with some of your friends and have guidance about becoming a Catholic?

When I realized that this was precisely where all the preliminary conversation of the evening had been leading to, the old panic began. There it was again, the icy lump in the pit of my stomach— that ancient psychic fear rising vaporously and paralyzingly from all sorts of hiding places in my subconscious; the tidal wave that had always washed over me when my will was confronted by what was presumably ordained as God's plan for me, as revealed to certain people of spiritual authority.

I had indeed become physically independent in New York, and all I had learned about the existence of truth and the ways to be sure of it had given me the impression that I was intellectually independent, too. But my intellect was still dominated by this shadow: my inner security in knowing I was doing God's will was still tainted by my emotions, and my confidence in God's guidance was still affected by the approval or disapproval of those people whose insights had always seemed infallible. Especially those of my own family. My mother and sisters and I had always been basically of one mind and heart: any "disunity" was a result of self-will, which was usually mine. Whenever there were conflicts, I assumed that the others were right, and God was on their side. It wasn't that they acted righteous: it was just that they were, inevitably, right. That's the way it had always been.

So now, in this summer of 1954, as my mother and one sister and I sat on a concrete bench in Rockefeller Plaza, amidst all the lovely blooming flowers, the conflict was of a different sort. This time, what had come between us was not a "moral relapse"— it was something that involved an irrevocable decision which they, as well as I, knew would affect all our lives.

When in the past my motives or my convictions had been challenged, I would put up a bit of a struggle at first, but eventually I would give in, because when that indescribable panic began to suffocate me it was simply a matter of peace at any cost. I had always associated that panic with an obscure sense of sin. Now, here was this same panicky feeling suddenly threatening to trash my new and treasured balance, my security.

But somehow, during this confrontation, I realized that this was indeed the test. I knew that this panicky feeling, no matter to what extent it seemed to eclipse everything else, was *just* a feeling, and I had learned that truth was *not* a matter of feeling. I would have to fight it out. It would have been easier if I had been able to pretend that I was calm and as firm as "the tree planted by the water" in the Psalm. But they knew me too well; they knew that I was "on the defensive"—that I was vulnerable.

They said: "This is the Cross for you." I knew what they meant perhaps more clearly than they did themselves. It was not the issue of Catholicism: it was the crucial issue of loyalty to, and unity with, the team. If I went to Mackinac, that would show where my first loyalty was; that I was still numbered among the elect. If I did not go, it would imply a kind of apostasy.

I took a deep breath and plunged in. I knew I couldn't hope

to come out with my self-respect unscathed, so I abandoned all tactical measures and laid myself open to justify all their worst expectations. I said that if I sat down to "have guidance about becoming a Catholic," it would be like asking God if He wanted me to believe all He had said. Of course they didn't understand— how *could* people for whom "guidance" was a private illumination understand guidance as God's word revealed through history and tradition? I said a lot of other bold things, too, about how I could no longer be a part of something out of duty, or loyalty, or fear of atomic catastrophe.

I was clutching at what I *knew* like a drowning man hanging on to a raft. It was the first time I had dared to risk everything for what I knew objectively and intellectually to be truth, in spite of the feelings and fears of the moment. It was like hitting my head against a wall, but I had to go on doing it. For the issue that evening was not my going to Mackinac, or even my loyalties: something much more crucial was at stake. My reason was in a final tussle with my emotions. Without any consolation of *feeling* that I was right—in fact, with the familiar feeling from childhood that God was on *their* side—I told my mother and sister that no matter what state the world was in, I could not let myself be frightened or pressured into one-hundred-percent commitment to this thing that all my life I had accepted as the only means of salvation for civilization. I had a different obligation now; and if this was treason, it would just have to *be* treason—I would accept whatever punishment God should decide to inflict.

In a way, I felt I was talking to God, saying OK, God, I have learned certain things about You and Your Truth, and one thing I've learned is that I've got to live according to what my reason tells me. If I have been misled, I'll just have to take the consequences. I am acting according to what I have learned with my conscious mind; if something has gone wrong in my *sub*conscious, it's not my responsibility and I cannot worry about it. I leave myself to Your judgement.

I said all these things to God without feeling God anywhere at all, but I meant what I said, and I knew that if this whole thing which was more real than myself turned out to be a hoax, then there was nothing else. I suppose it was really "an act of hope"—in the theological sense—that I made, for I had almost a physical feeling of exiling myself from all that had been security, and abandoning myself to God's mercy.

And so, completely drained and exhausted by the physical effort of fighting an intangible interior battle without assurance of either victory or defeat, I got on the Fifth Avenue bus and went back to my room in the MRA apartment on East 87th Street. And it was then that I realized I had a secret ally in Marjorie Evans, whose apartment it was: I told her a bit of what had happened; and she gave me a phenobarbital tablet to help me sleep. Marjorie, by the way, had a strong attraction to the Church—she kept a vigil light candle in her room, and sometimes talked with a Jesuit from St. Ignatius.

There was one obscure consolation which broke into all the blackness after I got home that night: that at least, in Newman's words, I had not "sinned against the light." The very next day I got a wire inviting me to Mackinac. I wired back that I did not feel I could come at this time.

WHAT HAPPENED on my week's vacation was that I found a room-with-cooking-facilities on West Eleventh Street in the Village, and I moved in and pasted colored postcards of medieval statues from the Metropolitan Museum on the faded cream-colored walls, bought a blue broom and other essentials for practical housekeeping at the dimestore and in Macy's basement, and got organized and settled down to wait for whatever would happen next.

West Eleventh was a peaceful, tree-lined street; I loved my room, and felt it was a part of me. It seemed to have an atmosphere all its own, a built-in cheerful presence which I felt the minute I walked into it behind the landlady. In all the time I lived in that little room (which was like the tropics in the summer and like a drafty elevator shaft in the winter) I never felt lonely.

Indeed, God must have surrounded me with His protecting angels, for I realize now what terrible things might have happened to me while I lived in that room behind a door which had an ineffectual lock. The room was on the ground floor, and the door to the corridor of single rooms also had an ineffectual lock. I kept all my money in my pillow. On Easter day there was a murder in the building two doors away. But nothing ever happened to me. There were really no "cooking facilities" here but I had an electric hot pot which I discarded after it nearly electrocuted me—but that was the only scare.

When the excitement of moving was over, and I had time to reflect on all that had happened, and realized that God had not wiped me out of existence after all, I had no backwash of remorse and guilt. Instead, there was a new freedom. It was as though a nerve had been cut, making it physically impossible to test the rightness of my actions or of my decisions by watching other people's reactions to them. I was free from that immature conscience what bases its judgments partly or even entirely on the way other people seem disposed toward its decisions. I knew that I would never again search other people's expressions for the clue to my own reality. I did not have to fit myself into a category; I did not have to conform to anyone's idea, or even my *own* idea, of someone undergoing a conversion. My identity was *God's* secret.

"You shall know the truth and the truth will set you free," Our Lord had said to the Jews. The experience I had been through had been the affirmation of that sentence. I was free from my moods, my depressions, my anxieties. These things would probably continue to assault me, but I had found that objective truth that was there no matter where *I* was, and therefore if I found myself in a strange neighborhood, I could always find my way back to Square One and start out again.

Before all this had happened, I had written down some quotations in my notebook under the heading of Objective Truth. Most were from a book by Rosalind Murray, the daughter of the famous British classical scholar Gilbert Murray. She had been married to Arnold Toynbee, and had become a Catholic. She said:

> Brought down to its simplest level, we may restate the acceptance of objective truth as recognition, on whatever plane, of "what is," without regard to what we like or want. . . . Reality cannot depend on our state of mind or that of others; if it is there, that truth is independent of our own acceptance or rejection of it . . .

And indeed, there have been times since I have been a Catholic when all light and purpose were blotted out, and all the things which had brought me joy and satisfaction were empty; there was only incommunicable and bewildering pain, and I moved about under a dark cloud in a strange land. I could not feel God's presence, but I knew that He was there, in all the darkness, and that unseen and unheard friends were there too—for as the Psalmist wrote: He has given His angels charge over you, to guard you in all your ways.

Rosalind Murray went on:

> Bereft of any sense of consolation, there may be merely blind and cold adherence to what we somehow know through all aridity and darkness to be our only good, the source and end of all our being. . . . It is the interior compulsion, the overpowering, over-ruling force which sweeps all lower instincts aside and supercedes our natural inclinations.
>
> . . . It is not what we feel that matters, but what *is*; and holding on to God by a dark faith may lead us further than any responses to the stirrings of sweet consolations.
>
> (*The Life of Faith*:
> "Will and Feeling")

Our instruction book said that the Act of Faith was to say, with conviction: "I DO believe that God has given me the Church to be my teacher. I do believe it ON THE WORD OF THE GOOD GOD himself, Who can neither deceive nor be deceived."

I had made that act of faith. I had made it when I knew it but could not feel it; and now God had taken me at my word, and had given me the final prerequisite for becoming a Catholic: the conviction that is more than an intellectual acceptance of truth: the gift of faith. He had given me the grace to *believe*.

And so now something *new* flew out of Pandora's box: Impatience. It seemed to be time for something to happen. I had learned the "ground rules" and many other things too; I had been going to Mass and observing the fasts and abstinences and behaving in a manner ever mindful of the book's polite advice:

> In order to dispose himself for the reception of the gift of Faith, the convert should strive especially after the following: (a) prayerfulness, (b) humility, (c) earnestness and conscientiousness, (d) cleanliness of heart, (e) sorrow for sin.

All during instructions there had never been any question of "Have you decided yet?" In the prevailing atmosphere of detachment there had been no intimation of a conclusion to be reached . . . there was plenty of time. But I was beginning to think this detachment could be carried too far. I do not know at what precise moment I made the decision to enter the Church. Nor do I know when

I became aware that the decision had been made. I had known for a long time. And now I began to wonder when somebody would *ask*. Somebody meaning Father Clark . . . but he was on vacation.

Looking back over the road we had traveled, I wondered where all those big hills were supposed to have been. In the beginning, I thought I could see at least a few big hurdles ahead—as when you are driving in a car and see all those huge hills in your path: as you approach them, they seem to flatten out; then you look out the rear window and discover you've already gone over them.

I had read somewhere that the Church was a house with a thousand windows and that no one approaches from quite the same angle. There might have been many obstacles along the road if I had approached from a different angle, with a few prejudices, or if we had had a different sort of instructor. As it was, all the closet doors had been opened. Nothing had been glossed over: I had been given a wide-screen picture of the Church with all her human elements. I knew about the damage done throughout history by popes who competed with emperors, by priests and bishops who had got too rich or too lazy, and (more recently) by influential laymen who had what Father Clark called "a few kinks." I knew there were a number of practices and devotions dear to the hearts of various ethnic groups; devotions (and statues and art) which the Church universal could do without. So there was little danger of "getting inside" and saying: "But Father never told me about *that*."

I knew it was a Church of saints and sinners. The mystery was that it was not the sum of its parts: the Church was *more* than the individuals who belonged to her. And I believed that— no matter what her outward appearance at any given time— the Church was the realization on earth of the kingdom of God, and the natural home of the human spirit.

The Sacraments, I had learned, were the essentials; I knew that they did not depend on the personality or even the character of the priest who administered them. (I had underlined this, in my instruction book: "The Sacraments give grace independently of anything human.")

I was beginning to feel hungry for these Sacraments. I would go to Mass and watch the faithful file up to the altar rail for Communion, and I would think of the Psalm that begins "How long, O Lord. . . ?" How long would I have to stand at the gate, watching? For a while I had been grateful that there was no pressure—that I had plenty of time to observe all these practice, and to become familiar with them. I still had scary apprehensions about things like going to Confession, surviving Fast days, and getting up and out for Mass and Communion without that bracing cup of coffee. But these were as nothing compared to the overwhelming desire to *get in*: I had enough sense, I think, to expect that once *in* I would have all the extra graces to help me with these trepidations.

But where *was* Father Eugene Clark? He had said he would get back in touch with us when he'd returned from vacation. Surely his vacation was over by now? Or was this some kind of "testing" period? Was he waiting to hear from *us*? I was timid, but Caryll was intrepid: she tracked him down, and we resumed instructions—now in the rectory of Our Lady of Mercy in the Bronx, because Caryll had had her appendix out and this church was near her home. On the afternoon of Sunday, October 10th, as we were finishing the chapter on Penance, Father Clark said: "I think we've covered enough territory by now for you to begin to think about whether you'd like to be baptized."

There was a second of stunned silence. He had finally popped the question! Caryll and I looked at each other and then said, in one voice: "*We don't need to do any more thinking.*"

Father Clark was obviously pleased, and we were euphoric. The next thing was to set the date, and Father Clark suggested the Feast of Christ the King—the last Sunday of October, which this year would be the 31st—Halloween, the Vigil of All Saints.

c/o Manor House Mells

From

Nov. 9.   Somerset

Dear Miss Abbott,

Thank you very much for your kind letter. I'm glad that *Off the Record* should have been of any use to you. God bless you and make you worthy of the graces you have had.

Yours v. sincerely
R A Knox

Faith had discovered the difference between "hesitation" and serious doubt in Off the Record, *a book by Monsignor Ronald Knox, and wrote to thank him. Much to her surprise, the then-famous author replied: "Thank you very much for your kind letter. I'm glad that* Off the Record *should have been of any use to you. God bless you and make you worthy of the graces you have had. Yours sincerely."*

The Baptism

The Holy Ghost on Halloween

OCTOBER HAD BEEN THE MONTH of my beginning in New York; now I would disappear through the door of the last day in October and come out on the other side, in November—lost in the Baptismal garment of newness and smallness and whiteness which was also the wedding garment for that banquet. I had been called from the highways and byways, and invited to the feast; I had the garment, and I was chosen. I was here for good. I would never again be in that outer darkness where there is wailing and gnashing of teeth. My identity was my own nothingness. With that sense of the proprietorship of the children of God, I felt I owned nothing and yet the whole world was mine.

It seemed appropriate that October would be the month of our rebirth. Thomas Merton had said this, in *The Seven Storey Mountain*: "October is a fine and dangerous season in America. It is dry and cool and the land is wild with red and gold and crimson, and all the lassitudes of August have seeped out of your blood, and you are full of ambition. It is a wonderful time to begin anything at all." In October, you know that cold winds are coming, but they are God's plan, and it seems quite possible that your destiny is being painted into this plan by the unseen hand that creates the patterns and dappled designs on the dirty sidewalks of New York when the sun shines through the trees.

Once the date for our baptism was set, the next decision was where it would take place. There were any number of possibilities. Father Clark suggested St. Nicholas of Tolentine, on Fordham Road in the Bronx. It wasn't far from Caryll's home, and the

135

Bronx was an easy drive from Mount Kisco: we knew people would be coming from Dellwood.

I had been staying at Manhattan House again, Siamese cat-sitting; Caryll decided to join me for our last night as Protestants. Early Sunday morning we went to Mass at St. Vincent Ferrer, just a block away. When the little bells rang for Communion, we didn't feel wistful because we knew it was the last time we wouldn't be able to receive the Host. As we left for the baptism that afternoon, we were hounded by small costumed figures yelling "Trick or Treat!" Somehow we thought this was fitting.

We took the subway to the Bronx and arrived at St. Nicholas of Tolentine at exactly 2:20. Father Clark met us at the door, saying something about "a mob of people are here" and that he'd thought one of my sisters was me. We walked into a great silence. I had been in this church once before—Caryll and I had gone there to a high Mass—and I had been impressed with its almost Cistercian-like austerity: no bad art, no gory statues—not even any vigil candles. Perfect, I thought now, for Protestants at a baptism. And, sure enough, there were the Protestants, *and* the Catholics, seated near the back—looking a bit like a funeral party. On closer inspection, the Catholics (Caryll's relatives, and Addie Johnson and Nancy Hawthorne, from Dellwood) looked happy—some were fingering rosary beads.

The Protestants (Caryll's mother, and mine, and my sisters) sat with folded hands and fixed smiles and stoic expressions. I was sorry that Naomi Noyes, my good friend (and future apartment-mate on West 13th Street in the Village) couldn't have been with us, for moral support: she was my godmother, but had got the flu, so Nancy Hawthorne was to be the proxy; one of Caryll's cousins was to be *her* godmother.

IT WAS A SHOCK, at first, seeing Father Clark in surplice and stole, looking so *official*: all these months he had been our black-suited, Roman-collared Instructor. We had never seen him in his vested element, which is what he surely was now *in*, and handsomely so.

It was a large church, and the silence was creepy, but it didn't last long because Father Clark took over as Master of Ceremonies, telling the little group to follow him (and Caryll and me) down the aisle to the front of the Church—to make themselves comfortable in the front pews. They did. And then he explained to them (as though we were all in a friendly living room together) just exactly what was going to happen up there on the High Altar, during the first part of the Rite of Baptism.

Then Caryll and I and our sponsors were led up to the altar: Caryll and I knelt on the top step, put our hands on the Gospel, and made our Profession of Faith. We hadn't needed to memorize anything: it's rather like the marriage ceremony, where you repeat what the priest says. (And I was amazed, all over again—we *had* studied it—by how the Profession of Faith covers everything in dogma and doctrine in very precise language, so that there can be no doubt in your mind about what it is you are accepting and condemning. It is a marvel of brevity.)

Our Faith having been professed, we proceeded to the baptistry; and Father Clark, with a dignified but informal "Come on, Gang" gesture, led all the others into the baptistry, too. As we all stood around the font, he explained what would happen *here*: the significance (and origins and symbolism) of the water, the oil, the salt, the candle. And then the baptism began. We had little booklets to help us.

Priest: What do you ask of the Church of God?

Us: Faith.

Priest: And what does faith bestow upon you?

And we answered with the two words that roll the past and the present and the future into one: "Life everlasting." *Vitam aeternam.*

Priest: If then you wish to enter into life, keep the commandments. Love the Lord God with your whole heart, and with your whole mind; and love your neighbor as yourself."

The unclean spirit was told to depart, to give place to the Holy Spirit, the Paraclete. We received the salt, symbol of wisdom. We renounced Satan, and all his works, and all his pomps.

Then we were asked:

Do you believe in God the Father almighty, Creator of Heaven and Earth?

We believed. I believe: *credo.*

Do you believe in Jesus Christ, His only Son, our Lord, who was born and who suffered?

We believed.

Do you wish to be baptized?

We did.

And so we were baptized, in the name of the Father, and of the Son, and of the Holy Ghost.

And then suddenly Father Clark was saying "That's all. Congratulations!" As if *we* had done something.

But of course it wasn't *quite* "all"—there was still Confession to be got through. We all stood around, in the back of the church, waiting for the priest who would hear our confessions; by now everyone was feeling quite social—our friends and relations who had not been introduced to each other were introducing themselves, and chatting, and they were *all* congratulating Caryll and me. It was now more of a wedding, rather than a funeral, gathering.

Father Clark had not got just *any* priest to hear our first confessions: he had got a good friend, a classmate from the seminary, and when he arrived he too congratulated us. Father Clark had a few private words with him, and then this red-haired young priest went up and disappeared into the confessional box, and Father Clark escorted me down the aisle—there was the matrimonial theme again, a father giving away his daughter, I thought. As he walked me down the aisle (Caryll and I had flipped coins to decide Who would go First) he kept whispering reassurances like "Remember, you'll never see him again and he'll never see you again . . . and there's always The Seal." (Actually, having glimpsed the young priest, I was rather hoping I *would* see him again.)

I don't remember what went on inside that little box with its velvet curtain; I think the priest did most of the talking. I must have had a few specific sins to confess, but mostly I expressed sorrow for all the ways I had offended God all my life. It was not a matter of "How many times?" and the priest knew about my background. He said that perhaps the biggest cross I would have would be "disedifying Catholics" and he told me I should never become apathetic; he said something about what this day must have meant to me, and then I began to get emotional and stammered an inadequate sentence of gratitude, and I knew that he understood. Then he gave me my penance (I'd forgotten about this) and that's when the glorious reality hit me: I am a Catholic! I have something specific to do! I have a real penance to say! (Whereupon I totally forgot what the penance *was*.) Then the priest pronounced the words of absolution as I said my Act of

Contrition (I actually remembered all the words) and then he said "Go in peace, and remember to pray for me." (I had also forgotten that this is routine; I was again overcome by emotion and almost broke down.) So I said I surely would pray for him, stumbled out of the confessional, and went to kneel in a side pew, as Caryll went into the box. I prayed for her, and I think I said a Hail Mary and an Our Father, in case that had been my penance. And as I knelt there, I knew that something had happened which I would never be able to comprehend or communicate: I knew that baptism was not just an official seal on all the study and preparation that had gone before—that nothing could give any preview of what it was like to be *in*.

Back in my early days in New York when I was bereft of the feeling that I was Special and Potential (because that feeling was rooted in the prestige of being part of a movement which would surely one day be manifest to the whole world) there were nevertheless moments when I felt especially close to God. And in those moments, I knew that this was the only kind of "prestige" I wanted. Now, as I knelt there, a very new Catholic, I knew that I was a nobody. And that made me very happy, because I knew that I was a *somebody* with the only Person who counted. I no longer had to count on those fleeting moments of spiritual consciousness to convince myself of that dignity. It was a *fact* now, and for good.

And as I knelt there I had the feeling that I had just been received with great rejoicing where I could not hear it. Somewhere in that sphere where there are no limitations of space or time or language, I was being welcomed into the family. The Communion of Saints, and the family on earth, too. My destiny was now bound up with the destinies of all the people who came to that church of St. Nicholas of Tolentine in the Bronx and all the churches in New York, and of St. Peter's in Rome, the monks in the monasteries all over the world, and all those writers whose books I had read—people I would never meet in life, people whose language I could not speak—we were a part of each other, in a common life. Together we were caught up in the immensity of God's life.

> You are no longer exiles, then, or aliens; the saints are your fellow-citizens, you belong to God's household. Apostles and prophets are the foundation on which you were built, and the chief corner-

stone of it is Jesus Christ himself. In him the whole fabric is bound together, as it grows into a temple, dedicated to the Lord; in him you too are being built in with the rest, so that God may find in you a dwelling-place for his spirit.

—Ephesians 2, 19-22

It had been arranged that we would receive our First Holy Communion from Father Clark the next morning—the Feast of All Saints—at another Bronx church, where he was scheduled to say the nine o'clock Mass. He said he would take us for coffee afterwards. (Our bosses had given us the morning off.) This would be our first "Holy Day of Obligation" as Catholics, and we were pleased that we would just blend in with all the other Catholics (how nice that sounded, "all the *other* Catholics"); no one but Father Clark and we would know that we were Receiving for the first time.

After a long and cold ride on the Third Avenue El, we found the Church of Saints Peter and Paul, on East 158th Street. It was close to nine: where *was* everyone? As we stood there, bewildered, a very large and elderly priest suddenly appeared— it turned out he was the Pastor—and in a booming Irish bass he asked: "ARE YOU FATHER CLARK'S FRIENDS?" We said we were. He told us that Father Clark would be celebrating the *children's* Mass, that we should sit in the first pew and make ourselves comfortable, and, he boomed, "WHEN THE TIME COMES, YOU GO UP FIRST."

Naomi had got out of her sick bed to join us; she explained that he meant we should beat the school kids to the altar rail when it came time for Communion, so that Father Clark could come to us first.

At about five to nine, the kids began pouring in. There seemed to be hundreds of them—a moving sea of all colors, dotted with the black bonnets of the Sisters of Charity. One formidable-looking Sister spied us and loudly stated that we should be in the *lower* church, with the adults. As scores of wide-eyed children stared at us, we explained that we had just been baptized yesterday and were supposed to receive our First Communion from the celebrant of this Mass. Sister did not smile: she just said "Oh." Then a man in a *business suit* appeared on the altar, came down to us and asked Were we Father Clark's friends? We said we were, and he said we should Go Up before the children.

So much for anonymity.

The Time to Go Up, he explained, was "when the altar boy goes over for the plate." But there were *four* altar boys, and not one of them moved an inch, after the Consecration. And then there appeared two extra priests, to help distribute Communion. Even born-Catholic Naomi was a bit confused, but she suddenly nudged us and said "NOW!" So we made a dash for the altar rail, beating the thundering herd by seconds, and knelt down and tried to compose ourselves. Somehow Father Clark knew where we were, and came straight over to us with the Body of Christ.

The "cup of coffee" he had promised turned out to be an elaborate breakfast at Rockefeller Center's Promenade Cafe. Over bacon and eggs and much coffee, we talked and watched the ice skaters until our waiter asked sarcastically if we were staying for lunch, too. As we came out on Fifth Avenue, we saw hordes of people streaming into St. Patrick's Cathedral across the street. Father Clark asked: "What's going on, a wedding or something?" "*Father!*" we exclaimed. And he said: "Oh yes, it all comes back to me now . . ."

A contemporary photo of the new "Happy Catholic." Faith had always felt "some inner compulsion to write things down" and decided to write the story of her conversion, for her family and MRA friends. But after completing it, she decided that it might hurt her intended readers, and for many years it remained locked in a metal box, seen only by a few close friends. One of them gave it to a friend in publishing who, although impressed by the writing, said it was "one more convert story" (which were then "a dime a dozen") that would not sell.

A Happy Catholic

But what about the Revolution?

Signatum est super nos lumen vultus tui, Domine;
Dedisti Laetitiam in corde meo.

The light of thy countenance, O Lord, is marked upon us.
Thou has given gladness to my heart . . .

IN THE DAYS FOLLOWING my baptism, I didn't think I could
walk down the street without everyone seeing that indelible
but invisible sign on my forehead. As a matter of fact, everything
else was invisible too: I didn't *feel* as though I were properly
embracing The Catholic Life. I got a miserable cold, and I couldn't
seem to get my interior life organized, and I did not feel at all
efficient, or capable, or mature. But all this became (objectively,
at least) a source of joy when I realized that this was precisely
the way I was supposed to feel. The actual fact of baptism had
erased all sense of "preparation" for the Catholic Life. I was
all new now, and helpless; I had to let God grow me up into
the kind of child He wanted me to be.

So I abandoned myself to this new atmosphere—this new world
in the old world. Truth had been the object of my thoughts for
a long time; now I was realizing that truth does not materialize
like an arrow pointing the way—it's more like an overhead light
that illuminates all the possibilities. Well, Msgr. Romano Guardini
said all this better, in one of his books: "Much too long Christianity
has been beset with practical purposes. . . . The truth of revelation
is not given us, primarily, that we may do something with it,
but that we may adore it and live by it." And he said that real
adoration is action more difficult than *ordinary* action—that

143

it is the action of inner transformation of thought, action of contemplative prayer—the action necessary to carry the truths of revelation into the mind and interior disposition. That only thus can Christian existence be re-established, because in this century faith is no longer the all-pervading atmosphere, the generally accepted point of view. The Christian can endure only if his mind is securely rooted in divine truth.

In this new atmosphere, it seemed that all the grinding machinery in the old struggle to balance, to focus, to make my life count in the ideological battle, had been replaced by a new center of gravity. It was a dimension in which the right kind of Being would take care of the Doing. There is a Psalm that has this in it: "He sent from on high and took me, and received me out of many waters . . . And He led me to a large place." I was learning to breathe in a very large space in those post-baptismal months, and there was this sense of *eternity*, which I couldn't explain. I was alone a lot, in my small room on Eleventh Street in the Village, and it was a kind of nursery; I had to learn to walk and talk. I was on my own now: no more instructions, no charted course to follow. No one (thank God) was asking me: Now that you're a Catholic, what are you going to do with your life? How are you going to *contribute*? I felt no compulsion to plunge into the Catholic Lay Apostolate. But I was doing a lot of reading, in this "nursery" period—especially books about the monastic life and about the Benedictine approach to life and society. The more I read, the more clear it became that the contemplative life was the key to the layman's effectiveness in the world. At least I thought it might be the key to *my* understanding of the real issues in the world, and to "living the answer" in all the contingencies of each day—all of which I had tried to do in MRA.

I felt a little guilty, though, about enjoying my solitude and thinking about eternity, because I thought it probable that my MRA friends would now see their secret suspicious justified: I had escaped from the ideological struggle, I was conforming to the stereotype: Catholics do not take responsibility for the state the world is in because they are merely enduring life in "this vale of tears" with eyes gazing heavenward like the pious plaster saints in some of their churches. Catholics are concerned only with the hereafter, while Christ is being crucified again in His members in prisons and torture chambers in Russia and China and Poland and Hungary.

On New Year's Eve, just before 1955 arrived, I was with a friend from MRA and I was in a sort of metaphysical mood. I made some remark about how time no longer seemed so important—eternity seemed more real. I should have known better. The reaction was what I should have expected; and I began to wonder if I was, after all, an escapist, deluded by the concept of timelessness when the twentieth century was a very concrete slice of time and everyone had to do his bit to save a crumbling civilization. Feeling a bit alarmed and rather unstrung, I retreated to my room with postcards of medieval art from the Cloisters on its four walls. And then I began to recall that all during my years in MRA I had longed for some way to transcend the sense of duty and the desperate race with time. I had felt there *must* be a space in which each individual could "live ideologically" while at the same time proceeding in sanctity according to God's intimate plan for him. I had known— instinctively, I think—that for me an integration of *being* and *doing* was the only hope for a life that made any sense at all. What was it, I wondered now, that had made the contemplative way of life seem like the answer to the old conflict? I had never subscribed to the idea of opening a book at random and taking the first sentence you see to be the Holy Ghost's answer to whatever your problem is, but that night I opened *The Seven Storey Mountain*, which was all marked up and coming apart at the seams, and I read a passage I hadn't noticed before. Merton was talking about Our Lady, and he said:

> . . . she comes bringing solitude and society, life and death, war and peace, that peace may come out of war and that my solitude may place me somewhere in the history of my society. It is clear to me that solitude is my vocation, not as a flight from the world but as my place in the world, because for me to find solitude is only to separate myself from all the forces that destroy me and destroy history, in order to be united with the Life and Peace that build the City of God in history and rescue the children of God from hell.

The more *organically* Catholic I felt, the more I felt I could trust my intuition that Catholics as a *genus* would instinctively feel something alien and foreign in the atmosphere of Moral Re-Armament. I could not put my finger on just what it was, but with each day in this new climate the past stood out in sharp relief. It was so natural, this new climate, that I wondered where I had been before. Everything now, in myself and in nature, seemed to have a natural gravitation toward a unified end. After I'd been in the Church for about six months, I felt I was sufficiently detached from the atmosphere in which I had grown up to be able to do some objective thinking about it. Many things had been resolved inside me, but I was not sure just where I stood in relation to MRA. I thought one key to the paradox might be the business of motivations.

What had motivated me in the past? What—as we used to say—had "made me tick?" I remembered going through phases of trying to coordinate what I had accepted as my "way of life" and "the real me." I struggled to "get this thing [MRA] into my bones." Now and then I would have a flash of perception about what went on below the surface, where I suspected the real me lived. I would almost touch the outline of some reality, but my hands never closed on anything solid.

Why was I in MRA? We were all encouraged to think this out for ourselves, so we could speak convincingly from the platform—sometimes at a minute's notice. There were some who always made a tremendous impression: the Marxists and communists who had found in MRA "the true meaning" of *The Internationale*: MRA was the *real* classless society in action. There were ex-Nazis who had changed and given up their hate and bitterness and apologized publicly on their country's behalf to the French people, and there were French people who had fought the Germans in the open or through the underground, who had lost members of their families in Hitler's gas chambers, now apologizing to the Germans for their bitterness. There were nuclear scientists who had come to see that the unspeakable dangers of advances in science and technology were outrunning moral growth; they apologized to Japan for their responsibility in dropping the bomb. There were agnostics who had found a faith; there were mothers who wanted a future for their children, and prodigals of many varieties who wanted an answer to the moral defeat in their own lives. There were "typical American" youths who were bursting with eagerness "to give everything for something great." There were bankers who apologized for their capitalistic mentality; there were labor leaders and workers who had found that if management is to change, labor must be willing to change first. All these people had a message, and they were all sincere.

But who or what was I? When I spoke on platforms, my *own* platform was that of an ordinary American girl "who wants to make her life count." But in those brief moments when I would catch a glimpse of the real me, I knew that I had no great passion to make my life count—nor did I have any real passion to see the new world. No doubt I lacked "vision." Emotionally, I was not the zealous, revolutionary American, but I clothed myself with all these patriotisms and loyalties as easily as the Europeans put on their national costumes to sing in the chorus. I had no way of knowing what I really wanted, but I had a half-blind instinct that there was *something* out there: some goal and purpose beyond all the things we talked about; something so absolute that it *included* all these things, and gathered them all up into one supreme end.

A friend, who was also twenty-four, wrote me a letter in which she expressed the same sort of groping:

> The thing that really started me thinking seriously about MRA for myself was when a Swedish girl said to me: "You do want to see a better world, don't you?" I had to admit that I did. Then I thought: "Am I willing to give all of my life all of the time to help build the kind of world I want to see?"
>
> I decided that I was willing. So I decided that as long as I felt in my heart that MRA was the most effective force meeting individual and world needs, then I would give one-hundred percent of myself to it and to the people who are dedicated to it. But I'm back home now in a world that is much different.... I'm finding it so hard to stick up for a decision ... when I can so easily be laughed at or thought "odd" by the girls with whom I work. I'm afraid I've slipped back an awful lot. I've still not found complete peace, joy, and contentment in my life. I still want to know why God put me here and what He wants me to do. I kind of know with my mind that I'm supposed to get closer to Him and to help others do the same, but with my heart I'm still not sure just what my purpose is. I'm probably making life much more difficult than it really is, and I think my self-will is keeping me from finding the thing I'm really looking for. You know what I really long to find (if there is such a thing) is God's over-all purpose for

my life: a main goal which will require the same intensity from every part of my being (not my mind plowing ahead because it feels it should and my heart lagging behind because it really wants to do something else). I'll bet I'm looking for something too big when the satisfaction of my heart really lies in the simple everyday decisions to be absolutely honest, pure, unselfish and loving.

How could I answer her? I could have written that letter myself. What seemed clear to me—as it did to many of my contemporaries in MRA—was that we had to accept our destiny. Somehow fate had put us here, in this ideology that was The Answer; and to know the answer and not to live it is treason, we said. And none of us wanted to think of ourselves as traitors. But of course simple acceptance of our "fate" and living by the four standards was not enough: we had to be infecting others, we had to be out life-changing—"If you're not winning, you're sinning." So far as "winning" was concerned, I wasn't very good at it: I lacked zeal. I think, now, that it was a problem of motive. If I set out to change someone, was it because of a desire to bring her to "God's fullest plan" for her or was it to justify my own existence in the movement? In contacts with outsiders, I had to rev myself up: rarely did I have my heart in propagating the message. I think this was partly because I am by nature not aggressive but also because I was not convinced, in the depths of my being, that God wanted them to be in MRA. *My* reasons for having accepted it could not be *theirs*. I could not expect them to choose freely and happily something which I had not chosen *freely* and was not always "happy" about. At times I wondered if it couldn't be a matter of vocation. Mine was to be in Moral Re-Armament: did that mean it was everybody's vocation? ("MRA is for all men, everywhere . . .")

To spread the spirit through plays and songs—that I *could* do happily. I could joyfully be a part of the working demonstration of the practicability of our ideology. But could I assume that everyone was destined to give their lives to God through MRA? It was not enough (we always said) to influence or to impress. We would smile wryly when well-meaning people would say to us: "You are doing such a good Work." The leadership frowned on financial gifts which were given as a "charitable contribution" because our job was to lead individuals to total commitment. (But we did not refuse non-committed contributions.)

So life-changing was not my starring role. Yet I remember that I did want to give people something. There really *were* hungry and wistful people who would come to us, and at times I was able to love them and forget myself and my self-consciousness. I may have helped some of them, but I was no good at "converting" them. My heart was simply not in it. I think I was aware of an underlying conflict in our whole philosophy of life-changing. Where were we to draw the line between helping an individual in real trouble, and changing lives on a scale which would affect the masses? I couldn't talk about this with anyone because I wasn't able to identify—to the point of articulation—the conflict within myself. Theoretically, there was no conflict. The new world would come through new people. But, realistically, it would come faster through *some* new people than through *others*—especially those who could be counted to *stay* "new." We had a big job to do, and every minute counted. We could for example spend much time rehabilitating drunks and saving marriages, but how much time and energy should we expend in getting individuals out of messes at the expense of changing "key" people? We were not social workers, yet we did not want to be seen as discriminatory. So there was always the conflict between our concern for the individual and our rush to save civilization.

IN THOSE MOMENTS of grace when I really cared about the individual I had "taken on," I did "fight" for her—but I was not fighting for her to make a decision about MRA. I think it was during those times that I was the *realest* me: I wanted something for that person over and beyond "ideology." I guess I wanted her to find God.

We had a song that we often sang at the very end of a play or an assembly. It had a catchy tune and a snappy rhythm, and the chorus began "Oh we're headin' right out to build a brand new world; are you comin' along, Mister?" I had good talks with people, but I could never seem to challenge them to "come along" with us. I made "spiritual friendships" but I didn't have any "scalps" to show. I consoled myself with the thought that maybe sometime, at some remote but decisive point in their lives, these people I had spoken with would remember something I had said and would drop everything and come along with us—

secretly hoping, of course, that they would credit me for having started the ball rolling. Yet with all my spiritual shortcomings I think I learned something in those days about working without looking for results—it was a kind of "holy detachment."

I think a lot of us found life-changing a strain, and this is significant because it's a fairly well-known fact that if people are confident about having truth, they do not hit people over the head with it. There is a peace and a calm confidence, and the best missionaries—whether in darkest Africa or sitting in a chair in front of their typewriters—do not spend their energy so much in pointing out truth as in creating an atmosphere in which its reality is inescapably obvious and naturally irresistible. "Out of the abundance of the heart the mouth speaketh." If you know you have the truth you do not push and pull people into acceptance: you have nothing to defend. And the more you love the truth you are serving, the more you will respect every individual's mind and free will—for God gave man free will. But He gave them something else as well: every man is born with the desire for truth just as he is born with the desire for food; and everyone has an undefeatable, even if unidentifiable, drive—almost like a homing instinct—to find that environment in which he can become the certain thing God created him to be.

All this reflecting about motivations clarified a number of things. I had not been "active" in MRA for many months; I had not gone to Dellwood on weekends, nor helped out at the office on Fifth Avenue when there were mailings to be got out. Still, MRA was a part of me. Even when something which has molded one's whole life has lost its exclusive claim to total assent, something has to happen to cut those last emotional strings. The bond would always be there, I knew, but the last fuzzy strings of security—a kind of umbilical cord—would have to go if there would be life and growth for anyone concerned.

There had been no specific moment in which I had said: "I will become a Catholic." There was just an awareness that the decision had been made; that the whole question had been resolved inside for a long time. I felt, now, that this conflict had been resolved in the same imperceptible and inevitable way. No one had *told* me there was a conflict: those in MRA who had anticipated one had only *hinted* about loyalties and the prime importance of being "free to do God's will." No one, either in the Church or in MRA, had said: "But the two are incompatible." I had not read any of the documents from the Holy Office about Catholics and MRA: nevertheless certain conclusions had worked themselves out in my mind even though I was not prepared to talk about them. But as had also been the case many times in the past, my interior convictions did not of themselves have enough impetus to break through my cautious nature with anything decisive. Something concrete had to happen in the external order of things that would merge my inarticulate convictions and my will together into a simple and defenseless acknowledgement of my position.

AND THEN, ONE DAY, I received two letters. One was from someone on the team, and it told about a recent series of meetings in all the team centers—yes, *all* of them. What had gone on might be described as a kind of self-imposed spiritual purge. Catholics might put it in the category of a "retreat," only in MRA it always happened suddenly; no one knew when it would start or how long it would last, and there was never anything systematic about it. As I read the letter, the whole picture came back, for I had been in on some of these cataclysmic sessions at Dellwood, at Mackinac and at the club. Everyone would be "drastically honest" about himself—his secret motives (of which he had just "become aware"): his costly mistakes, his inadequacies. Everyone would make drastic decisions to change and start all over. They were times of rededication. But they had often left me more shattered and bewildered than regenerated and inspired. People would get up on their feet and say "I have never really made this *my* fight; I have never really broken my will"—and most of these were people who had been in the movement from the start, who had sacrificed heroically. Now they were sharing sins they had "just seen"—though they had "just seen" them many times before this. It was like hearing the same record over and over.

It wasn't that I had expected perfection of these people, for our inadequacies and failings were our common bond: in our weakness was our strength. But it seemed to me that if the majority of our spiritual leaders periodically confessed to total failure, it was pretty hopeless for me to try to be "more changed." And if they periodically said they had not really had Frank Buchman's vision and had not been fighting "the right battle," how could any of us be sure we were "on the right beam"? People would share that what they'd had in the past wasn't "adequate." I was chronologically at the beginning of what had been their past, and it looked like a bleak future. Was it really so wrong, I wondered, to want to know you had truly begun and had got at least *somewhere*? Maybe it was supposed to be positive and inspiring to say "We haven't really begun to fight yet"—but wasn't it necessary to feel you had, to *some* extent, begun? Couldn't you go ahead without the probability that in five or ten years you would again be starting all over?

After these "overhaulings" we were all supposed to conclude that we didn't "know" anything: this was the needed "humility" that was the preparation for "the next thing God wants to give." Then there would emerge the Next Step for the team as a whole— the strategy, the line of action. But next week the focus was likely to shift. If you had been out of touch with the nucleus or with the full-time team your perspective might be way off. You might still be thinking in terms of your *own* change, when "the thing" was to get out of yourself and into the lives of others— to be creative and write plays and songs. Or you might be all set to go out life-changing and helping to create a renaissance when there was still "sin in the camp" and the thing was to spend more time getting the beam out of your *own* eye.

I tried to believe that these times of deep sharing and many tears were necessary, but they left me hopeless about ever "measuring up"—hopeless, in fact, on a deeper level that was beyond analysis. It was as if there was nothing I could do at all, for to worry about it was wrong, and to "try to do better" could be merely pride or a desire to avoid pain. There was nowhere to turn— least of all to God, for according to what everyone said, He could so easily be mistaken for one of the demons that disguised themselves to look like Him. It was for me, and perhaps for others, a nightmare of insecurity, because one never knew where one stood—with each other, or with God.

Some of these sessions drew the battleline very clearly and the sheep would be separated from the goats, and some people would leave. They were, we said, "not willing to pay the price." I was not unaware of the fight-or-flight instincts in myself, which

I know are common to every man and beast, but something was wrong with my adrenaline: I felt paralyzed. The fact of *knowing* I was afraid kept me anchored: I could not run. Nor could I fight. Before I could make any decision, didn't I have to "gain victory" over this fear? I had always thought that—no matter what the circumstances—"escape" was an Absolute Wrong. Perhaps I had to prove that I had overcome all my fears before I could take a stand. But then I wondered if that feeling wasn't after all a desire to claim a nature that was not mine and never would be. Perhaps I had the sort of psychological structure that would always threaten me and lead me into darkness and confusion when old patterns clashed with what I knew to be truth. Perhaps a realistic knowledge of one's own nature makes it *necessary* to escape certain things. And maybe it was not an unforgivable sin that those meetings always left me depressed and bewildered.

Catholics are sometimes criticized for avoiding certain movies and books, and even people and occasions that are considered a threat to their morals. Catholics, of all people (say those who criticize), should be beyond corruption. But Catholics who avoid "occasions of sin" do so usually not out of fear but because they know the plain cold facts of the weakness of human nature, and how emotions can do violence to the soundest minds and the strongest wills.

PERHAPS, THEN, I DID NOT have to prove that I was invulnerable.

All these thoughts unrolled themselves as I read the first letter, that evening. The other letter was a very different sort. It was from one of my best friends, and sometime roommate, who had always seemed to epitomize the integration of healthy young American and totally-committed revolutionary. She had very large brown eyes and an infectious giggle, and she was always losing her heart to one or another of the guys—and the attractions were mutual. But she also cared a lot about America, and God seemed to speak to her very clearly. At Mackinac in the summer of 1953 she told some of us that she had given up all thought and hope of marriage and a family of her own, because she felt that was what God demanded of her. She was as sincere as a nun taking a vow to consecrate herself to her Beloved. She was not dramatic about it; just simple, and radiant.

Now, in this short letter, she said that she had gone home for good, that she felt "sort of brainwashed," that all she wanted was peace and "a normal life." (We kept in touch: Betty Meskimen married her high-school sweetheart and they went on to have six children.)

The two letters and all the thought they provoked had brought a very large area into focus, and I said to myself: If people who have been in MRA from the beginning say they have never been "truly committed" and that they have never "really understood" MRA, how can they say that MRA has The Answer for everyone? How can they expect others with less intellect or less perseverance to grasp the whole message and change overnight, and stay changed long enough to make their experience count on a universal scale? And if some with the most potential in my generation suddenly find "it doesn't work" for them, how can it be true that MRA is for everyone, everywhere? By pragmatic reasoning, the test of the truth of something is that it *works*. Could MRA make the grade in the pragmatic sense? "The startling, the astonishing, the triumphant thing about MRA is—it works," exulted an editorial in the New York *Journal-American*. All my life I had seen MRA work: there were hundreds of specific instances of individual change with national and international reverberations. But what of the individuals who could not make it work? Was it their own fault, or was there some obstacle outside their own responsibility? And was it really meant to be such a struggle for some of the people who had persevered?

It seemed to me that 23 years of breathing the atmosphere, including four years of serving in many capacities in the heart of the movement, should have enabled me to think with maturity and objectivity about whether or not it could fully satisfy the whole person, with all his unfathomable longings.

I had implicitly acknowledged when I became a Catholic that I no longer believed MRA was God's fullest plan. However, if MRA were only a *program*, then anyone who had the same ideals could accept its shortcomings while continuing to work with and through it. Only conceit, or injured pride, would make one say "You are not all I once thought you were. I have been deceived and I will have nothing more to do with you." Or if the spirit of revolutionary Christianity were the only thing to be considered, there could be no incompatibility with the Catholic

Church. There would have been no conflict at all if I had not known that MRA was more than a program or a social movement: I had always known that it was "a way of life" and that one cannot live the life unless he is fully committed. But full commitment to MRA demanded winning others to it, or at least *wanting* to.

And so it seemed that those two letters had resolved the conflict—not on a sweeping emotional tide of disenchantment, but on the basis of the individual. No matter how wonderful and praiseworthy the goal of any movement, the important consideration is: What happens to the individuals involved in "the means to the end"?

John Henry Newman automatically ceased being an Anglican when he was received into the Roman communion: by choosing the one he rejected the other. If I had considered MRA to be a religion, just as automatically and abruptly my part in it would have terminated when I became a Catholic. Now, though I was still confused about the real identity of MRA, nevertheless if, according to my experience I felt there were elements—not just occasional sad accidents, but elements intrinsic in the way of life—that could be dangerous for the individual, then it would be against my conscience to win people to it. And in that moment when I knew I could no longer—even *theoretically*—want to win people to MRA, automatically I was disqualified, and ceased to be a part of it. An era was over—it had in fact been over for a long time, but now it was conscious. The last emotional ties simply dissolved.

THIS WOULD HAVE BEEN the time, in a parallel situation, to have issued a solemn statement of my position. But there wasn't really any parallel situation. I had never "joined" MRA in the first place; our slogan was "No one joins; no one resigns"—MRA was not a card-carrying organization. But I felt I owed some kind of statement to my family and friends who had restrained themselves from asking any direct questions. I could see myself through their eyes, and I remembered what I myself had thought about people who rejected MRA without giving any clues. Their very silence was an insinuation of some kind. If they felt we were persisting in error they had, I thought, a moral obligation to enlighten us. So how could I, in all conscience, sever the ties without issuing some sort of proclamation stating not just my experience and conclusion but giving all the answers as well? If I kept silence, would my best friends think I was abandoning them to whatever frightful consequences I had apparently foreseen? Others in the past had managed to fade quietly away. I knew that would be impossible for me, even if I'd wanted to; and I knew that eventually I would be put on the spot. My pride made me think that I could say nothing until I had all the paradoxes figured out—that it was not enough to see my *own* way; that if I could not deliver, in a neat package, a positive critique of the past and present of MRA and a vision for its future, my friends would think I was just another weakling who had chosen an easier, albeit respectable, life.

THEN THERE WAS the disturbing thought that they might think I was no longer operating as a free agent: I was a Catholic. What sinister notions would they get about the Church, because of me? But I knew that the Church had been exposed to misunderstanding before and somehow had always eventually made herself understood. All she asked of me in the way of loyalty was that I form a right conscience and live accordingly. All along, I had had to act according to whatever small lights were given me, without waiting to see the whole scene illuminated. That was part of faith: to take the next step, even when you can't see the whole staircase or even any landing. This was what I would have to do now. Whether I had the words or not, my decision was there.

And with the realization that because one was silent it didn't necessarily follow that one was on the defensive, all sorts of tensions relaxed; I felt liberated from the self-imposed role of Prophet. Who did I think *I* was, to present all the answers? I couldn't even untangle all the riddles. When you are brought up in the philosophy of "As I am, so is my nation" you come to feel that every personal decision is an expression of the course you advocate for everyone else. This time, I was not acting as anyone else's conscience. Certainly I had no desire to lure anyone away from MRA. And I wasn't even sure I *wanted* these people who had no possessions, no interests outside the movement, to see things the way I was seeing them. I couldn't imagine what

I would suggest they *do*. I could only act for myself. I had made my decision: people would have to think whatever they thought. I did not feel like a martyr, I did not feel like a traitor, and I no longer felt afraid.

Above all, I knew that anything I might say in a few short sentences would only bewilder, and would lead to more questions. If I tried to "state my case" I would fail completely to give these people the full explanation to which they had a right. I began to think that if I were to say anything at all, and perhaps I never would, I could say it in nothing short of a book.

Being silent, denying myself the consolation of an *apologia*—perhaps that was what God asked of me for the moment, and perhaps for a long time. And because of my pride, that kind of resignation could be a means of grace. I might suffer a little, and that would be a good thing.

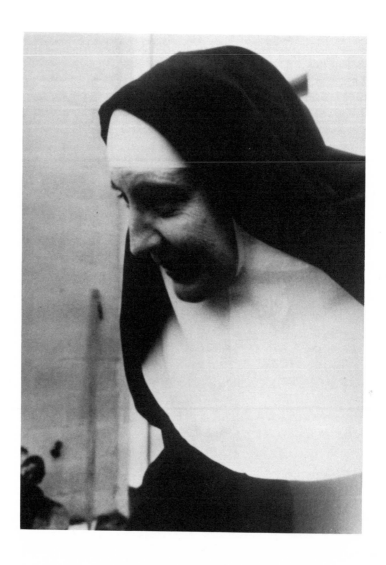

*Mother Assumpta was one of the Benedictine nuns Faith came to know
well at the Monastery (now Abbey) of Regina Laudis in Bethlehem,
Connecticut; she had come from the Mother House in Jouarre, France,
and spoke perfect English with an amusingly-lilting accent. She once
assured Faith that, if she wanted a husband, "We will pray you one"—
which, Faith believes, they did (in due course, her born-Catholic husband
Jim would declare Mother Assumpta his favorite nun). She died in 1979.*

My Dilemma

"What were you *before*?"

PATIENCE, AND SILENCE, were perhaps more of a "cross" for me than they would have been for someone else, because I had—as far back as I can remember—been enslaved by some inner compulsion to *write things down*. Not things I observed, but my thoughts and feelings. When I was ten I began a daily diary, which expanded—during high school—to include crushed corsages, photos, pencil sketches of boys I liked, clippings from the school paper, and all the ephemeral treasures that externalized what I thought of as "my life." I didn't "enjoy" writing the way one enjoys a hobby: writing was always more anguish than fun, for it brought me—more than did anything else—face to face with my own limitations. It walled me up in a false solitude that was a loneliness, and the only satisfaction it brought was a kind of sweet pain in feeling that I had some kind of obscure but special Destiny.

The feeling that my "destiny" was connected to *writing* had become intense when I was in Los Angeles in 1950. One of MRA's influential friends was the famous writer Adela Rogers St. Johns. Someone had got the inspired idea that we younger ones at the club would benefit from training in Public Relations, and who better to take us on than Mrs. St. Johns? Adela was more than willing, and a lot of us signed up for the course, and were immediately drawn into her area of expertise in journalism (as well as her personality). She seemed to know just about every important newspaper columnist and editor in the country, and VIPs in the movie industry, too. We had weekly sessions, and were given writing assignments, and I was thrilled when Adela took a special interest in *me*. She even had me delivered, one afternoon, to her spacious Hollywood home, for a private talk. She told me I had talent; she even confided in me about others in our group: one, she said, had "two left feet" when it came to writing.

OUTSPOKEN, CHAIN-SMOKING ADELA often brought prominent people to the club for the seminars. Once she brought the city editor of the *Herald Examiner* (and said I should sit next to him!) along with a well-known fiction writer, Harlan Ware, whose short stories regularly appeared in the *Saturday Evening Post*. He gave us an informal lecture on the power of fiction; that was a *four hour* seminar and I was enthralled, and afterwards dashed up to my room and gushed to my diary: "I long to know what part short stories (fiction) have in the revolution. I'd love to pioneer the work."

It wasn't until I had come to New York and was taking the writing course that I began to see just how naive I was. Presumably I had talent, and that I had Something to Say was a *given* (*everyone* in MRA had Something to Say). Therefore with those two requisites, talent and a Message, it was agreed that I needed some practical training: MRA was enthusiastic about this sort of thing. Especially when I explained that my ambition was not *personal*—that I wanted training in writing so that I could write for a hungry generation (which God would have all ready and waiting for my words). We all knew that writing was a weapon in the War of Ideas.

In New York, one of our first assignments in The Writing Laboratory was to write an essay about "Why you are taking this course." I thought this a Great Ideological Opportunity, and I ended my essay with:

> My hope is eventually to be able to use creative writing as a weapon in the fight to live and sell the real democracy the founders of our country fought for.

I have often wondered what our instructor thought of *that*.

Toward the end of the writing course, instructor Vance Bourjaily (who had written a novel and would write many more) had a conference, at his home, with each of us in turn. He told me that I could probably write a novel some day, that I should consider expanding the character sketch of my landlady, that he was impressed with my writing; but now, he said, I should do more reading—to get a sense of rhythm and other things that don't come from study or experimentation. And so I began to read, and that was the beginning of something far beyond learning to write.

As I began to discover literature, my idea of my own talent and ability was reduced to realistic proportions: it was a painful but healthy awakening to myself and to the demands of the art. I saw myself as a very small and trite someone, tongue-tied and pedestrian, and I was shorn of the illusion that I was unique even in my most secret and prized possession: a sense of mission. I found out that other people had things to say; that many of them were the same things I thought it was up to *me* to reveal to society, or posterity, or whatever. Oddly, I felt a kind of relief—as if I'd been delivered of a burden.

This, however, did not free me from the compulsion to wrestle with everything, on paper. I couldn't feel that any experience of mind or soul or senses was complete until I had hammered out, either in long terrible letters to friends or between the silent covers of my journal, the agonies and delights of everything I was "going through."

Later, in my job as secretary to the editor of a publishing company, I found that this inner compulsion was hardly unique. It was a depressing revelation to read the stream of manuscripts with thousands of words set down by people who felt the reality of their existence depended on seeing themselves in print. There were so many who were convinced that their beloved memories were destined to be cherished by mankind. As an editorial reader, I had to deaden myself to these pathetic efforts to dress up old bones in fabricated flesh. There were manuscripts from people who had written their autobiographies, or edited their grandparents' memoirs, or written travelogues, mainly because someone had kindly but stupidly told them "You should write about all this." There were "confessional" manuscripts disguised as "novels" and offerings from people who felt they'd been ordained to formulate a new myth for mankind. Some were typed in all-capital letters; some manuscripts had a comma after every single word; even some neatly typed and properly double-spaced ones were full of turgid prose and occult "revelations."

All this should have prevented me from yielding to the temptation to indulge in self-expression, or to resurrect a past which had outlived its value. I should have been aware of the pitfalls, and I thought I *was*; I even wrote about this in my journal:

> ... temptation disguises itself in all kinds of higher motives and there is always danger. But perhaps after all I am safe from some of the pitfalls, for I cannot read much that I have written in the past without feeling disgusted and humiliated. The cherished sorrows and joys; the bittersweet, the nostalgic; the ageless mementos, the vibrant experiences when expressed reveal themselves pathetically like old soggy ashes stuck to the floor of the fireplace. The things I wrote have a faintly decadent odor—gloomy and unreal. I read hopefully, but I do not discover any gems. I do not uncover any flashes of insight, I do not find myself at all. These words recreate the indistinct outline of a stranger. As a matter of fact, they *were* mostly other people's words and thoughts which I tried to express "in my own way" and which sound about as original as a high school student paraphrasing Hamlet's soliloquy ...

And so, after I'd been in the editorial milieu for two years, partly out of resignation and partly out of the fear of giving what I had found to be Truth an inferior rendering, I worked myself out of the somewhat obscure but ever-persistent notion that someday, somehow, I would be writing. My nature had not changed: more than ever, when I became a Catholic, I longed to communicate the incommunicable.

PERHAPS THIS ALMOST INORDINATE longing to *share* came from my earlier years when it was a joy beyond containing to have my friends meet my heroes in MRA. To bring my friends to Mackinac and to see them actually *present* in the atmosphere was the greatest elation I could imagine. I know that Catholics in some parts of this country suffered from a minority complex while they were growing up, but I think the minority feeling we MRA children had was even more acute and had more to do with the whole tone of our lives. If a child feels on the defensive because he is a Catholic, he knows that "they" at least know what he *is*: he is a Catholic. Others may not understand or approve, but they are aware of the *reality* of this thing Catholicism: they know it is *there*. It has a name. With us in MRA, there was very little concrete objectification of our way of life. It existed mainly as an "institution" in our minds: we could not point to something and say "See, that's it." Except of course when the plays came to our home towns. We wanted to take all our friends so they could "see for themselves." We wanted them to hear the chorus sing, to see the radiant faces of the people, to hear the foreign accents—all the little things that added up to "It." I would often have dreams at night about my friends meeting "the gang." That they would do so seemed the most mysteriously wonderful and magical thing in the world.

As I GOT OLDER, I learned to be more subtle and restrained about all this, but the longing to share was still there—almost like a pain, and very much a burden. Sometimes I asked *God* to take it away: *I* could never let it go.

But when I became a Catholic I understood that sacrificing something, "offering it up," was not merely a metaphorical concept with psychological value: one really could offer up a burden, not only of sins but of longings—the small pains, the whole confusing bundle of frustrations and ambitions, loves and fears. One *could* offer up this burden, and be delivered from it.

The Three Wise Men knew what specific gifts they brought to the infant King. But because of His Passion and Resurrection and Ascension, because He was a man and He was God, we can place on the altar things which are not neatly packaged and identified—those nameless things which make up ourselves—and we can know that Christ knows what they are and will take them to His Father.

And so, when I became a Catholic, I knew for the first time what it was to be free, and to be freed; and I also knew that what was offered up was not destroyed—that in God's mysterious and secret economy it would be used.

Where *writing* was concerned, there was nothing for me to do but offer up the compulsion and abandon myself to Divine Providence. But of course knowing for sure that it was God's will for me never to write another word would have been easier than this suspension which held just the tiniest hint that something would be demanded of me after all.

I remembered that Ronald Knox said the truth has a claim on us and that we are false to our own natures if we let it go untold. But I also remembered Thomas Merton's words:*

> If you write for God you will reach many men and bring them joy.
>
> If you write for men—you may make some money and you may make a noise in the world, for a little while.
>
> If you write for yourself you can read what you yourself have written and after ten minutes you will be so disgusted you will wish that you were dead.

IN THE MONTHS THAT FOLLOWED I learned more about silence, such as that there are two kinds: the mute silence a person is forced into because he doesn't have the words, and the elected silence of the person who has found the words but who knows that the time for those words has not come. And it not infrequently happens that the conviction "the time has come" intrudes just when the person has not only given up the idea of communicating, but also begun to feel a detachment from the whole business. He has finally gotten enough sense to know that some things can't— and some things shouldn't—be talked about, and he is content to leave them unsaid. It has taken him a long time to arrive at this inner serenity, and he does not want the tranquility disrupted.

The business of finding my tongue did not happen entirely according to the pattern of the word growing out of silence: I was forced into articulation. It was not from MRA that the pressure came, but from—oddly enough—other Catholics. By then I was meeting a lot of them, and when Catholics find out that someone is a convert they ask two questions: "How long?" and "What were you, before?"

If the convert had been an Episcopalian, or an agnostic, or a Jew, any further details about his background would be welcomed but not demanded, because though every individual's "convert story" is different, certain backgrounds are categorically understood. But to say that my background was Moral Re-Armament was only to invite more questions: "Oh, and what is that?"—a perfectly normal question, and a direct one for which I did not have a direct answer. When I tried to answer, I found I could not explain MRA in the old familiar terms: it was like trying to translate something familiar into a new language, or a new culture—the

*Seeds of Contemplation, page 71.

explanations I'd always given were a mixture of aphorisms and general moral "truths," non-objective statements inseparable from *conviction*. And these explanations were no longer valid, because they were expressions of a conviction and of a position I no longer held.

So before I could explain MRA in terms a Catholic could understand, *I* had to understand it, as a Catholic. What was MRA? Well, I could say it was a "movement." But then of course the next question would be: "What kind of movement?" The people who asked that would have assumed it was some kind of *religious* movement, because "background" implies *religious* background when one is speaking about being converted *from* it. (It dawned on me that, in that sense, *communism* was a religion, for if it were strictly political no one would talk about being converted from it any more than he would talk about having been a Democrat or a Republican before he became a Catholic.)

I could have avoided the whole issue simply by saying: "I was a Presbyterian." But that would have been (to borrow a term from the future) a "cop out." It was true, but it was not the *whole* truth: Presbyterianism was not what I had been converted from.

It was always easier to say what MRA was *not*. It was not a political, or a humanitarian, movement: it was not about Social Action. *Was* it a religious movement? And if so, what kind? The ambiguous nature of the "way of life" (we preferred that to "movement," actually) was the crux of the matter: identity was the stumbling block. Analytic thinking had never been my *forte*: my concept of MRA had had more to do with—in Walt Whitman's words—"that unspeakable something in my soul which makes me know without being able to tell how it is that I know." And that was clearly not adequate in these circumstances.

Once again, a book turned out to be providential. I had seen it advertised in a British catalogue we'd got at the office, I sent for it with an international money order, and when it arrived I read it almost in one sitting. Its rather formidable title was *The Right View of Moral Re-Armament* and its author was Msgr. Leon-Joseph Suenens, auxiliary bishop of Malines, Belgium. His intent was to explain the Belgian hierarchy's attitude toward MRA, and I was astonished by his skill in defining the *atmosphere* of the movement—something I had always thought no "outsider" could possibly grasp, much less communicate. The Bishop's book

was a calm and thorough study of MRA from the Catholic viewpoint.
It was objective in its presentation of the circumstances, completely
intelligible in its procedure, and logical in its deductions. It was
written with clarity and charity, and made me realize that I had
been privileged to grow up in Moral Re-Armament, and that
there were actual *words* for all the things I had felt. The book
didn't give me any fundamentally *new* thoughts, but it substantiated
my convictions and put them into a coherent framework.

After I had read the book several times, I felt that I could
explain the movement to people who didn't know about it, and
could clear up the misconceptions of those who did, but whose
knowledge was based on the half-lies and cloudy rumors that
had always been propagated by the press and through books
by some "former Buchmanite" who had a chip on his shoulder.
I could set the record straight, but that was not the main thing:
I had to address MRA itself. The book made me feel that I had
an obligation: that, among all the things I might be able to say
to MRA, the most important one was: "You must identify yourself."

SOMEBODY NEEDED TO SAY IT, and perhaps I was the one, for
I had always understood why we in MRA did not identify ourselves,
why we did not even like to be "pigeonholed" in the convenient
category of "movement." But if I were to try to explain the necessity
of identification, I would have to talk about the Church, and
about the Catholic concept of "faith" and a lot of other things,
and there would have to be a clarification of terminology on
both sides before there could be any exchange of ideas. Maybe
after all I was the one to explain why the basic ambiguity of
the movement was a stumbling block both psychologically, for
the individual, and objectively, in the eyes of the Church.

I knew full well that if I tried to put down on paper all these
things that had been ripening inside my head, and all the things
I felt about the Church, it would be the hardest thing I'd ever
tackled. I also knew what I had suspected before: there was too
much to communicate in any other way. And I knew that no
matter how well I might succeed in the labor and art of
communication, there would be some people who would be unhappy,
who would feel I had been "used" in some way. "He who is
not with us is against us"—we had often said that in MRA.

I made a few feeble attempts to escape from the conviction that the time had come to write, but all the signposts pointed inexorably in one direction, and there was nothing I could do about it. It was simply another case of the "next step," and I would have to take it, not knowing how to proceed and not demanding to know how it would all come out in the end.

And then certain people came into my mind—MRA friends who I suspected felt responsible for my departure, who were probably saying "It's *our* fault: we haven't been living the life *fully.*" I knew it would do no good to tell them that wasn't the point—I wanted them to understand the importance of identification, that I could not have broken the bonds had it been merely a matter of my own arbitrary choice. I also knew that these MRA people would say to me: "But if you only knew what it's like now; many things are different." And I would try to explain how that was not the point. What I wanted to tell them was that Yes, I'm sure there are many things different now, because you will never become complacent; you are always open to new ways of doing things, you are always ready to learn from your mistakes and to find better ways of living together and more positive ways of expressing your ideology. It will always be that way because you are of one heart and mind; you will bring all difficulties and dissentions into the heart of the family and together find the answer, so that there will be no opportunities for different schools of thought developing and splintering off. There will not be any kind of "schism" as long as you remain a family sensitive to the needs of all, open to the inspirations of the least among you, learn and experiment and change together. No, I would not be surprised to learn that "things are different now." They always will be.

I wanted to explain to these people that no one "joins" the Catholic Church because one of the current phases happens to interest him, and that no Catholic has a right to "leave" if—for instance—he disapproves of the "popular devotions" in his parish, or doesn't like the editorials in his diocesan newspaper, or disagrees with a speech some priest or bishop makes about censorship, or is disillusioned because some members of the clergy do not appear to be "living the life fully." These are not the things that make someone stay or leave. The Church has gone through all kinds of phases, from the days of the persecuted minority to the wealth of the imperial days to the militant days of the Counter-Reformation. But the basis remains the same, and—unless one goes along with something just for the ride and plans to transfer when the trip gets unpleasant—the basis on which one makes a decision has to do with the *nature* of the thing one is deciding about. If someone doesn't believe in the Divinity of Christ, he can't call himself a Catholic no matter how much conviction he may have about, say, the social encyclicals of Leo XIII or the Church's fight for racial integration.

And so I wanted to say to these MRA friends: When you say it is your fault that some of us are no longer with you, I would say that if there is any fault at all, it is in your trying too hard to be all things to all men—trying to fill a role you do not fully understand in a manner that will be understandable and acceptable to everyone.

When i was taking instructions, and found that I was not learning new things so much as learning the names of things I had always instinctively known, I thought that I might also find the real identity of MRA. But the more I looked, the more paradoxes I found, and the less I understood even what had seemed clear about our way of life. When people who had been in MRA from the beginning would share, with sincere remorse, that they had never lived it because they had never really understood it, I would wonder how any of us were expected to live it if even "they" couldn't, and how we could "change" other people when we didn't even understand what we were ourselves. I remember how we would give different definitions of MRA to different people according to what each inquirer's "deepest need" seemed to be; but we would admit to ourselves, and among ourselves in a kind of family way, that we didn't really know *what* MRA was. We weren't really *supposed* to know: that would have been *presumption*, and in a sense our security lay in our *not* knowing what we were; for if we did we could become slaves to "a program" and we could ossify into an "organization." No, we would remain unfettered, and undefined, so that the Holy Spirit could guide us in His inscrutable and mysterious ways. If a sense of failure was painful, a sense of success was often dangerous.

Nevertheless, this recurring conviction of failure was hard on the nervous system. It is one thing to know you have failed in something specific: human nature being what it is, this should come as no surprise, and you can start over again. This is what happens when a Catholic confesses his sins and failings and makes a "firm purpose of amendment." But it is another thing to try to live "fully" something whose claim to being "Spirit-led" is justified by the conviction that no one knows what it *is* or how to *live* it: this seems to be asking something beyond what God asks of people to whom He gave a mind and a will and specific laws, and a right to certainty. I could not live in that kind of ambiguity and I could not put my heart into trying to win other people to it.

I had learned about "fallen away" Catholics. Some blamed their falling away on a priest, or a grade-school nun, or on one or another Catholic—a role-model type—who didn't seem to be living the fullness of his faith. Or even parents, who didn't practice what they tried to preach. But I had also learned that "disedifying" Catholics were not the *Church*, which is defined in very specific terms.* That was one of the beauties of it, I thought: no matter where you thought you were, or weren't, in relation to *it*, you knew that it was *there* and if you didn't know what your standing *was*, you could easily find out: there were plenty of pamphlets and books available, for those who wanted to know the facts.

I had learned that, in the Church, one can aim for sainthood and one can also just get by, with the minimum requirements: attendance at Mass on Sundays and Holy Days, Communion once a year, and Confession if there's mortal sin. I knew that there were a lot of "mediocre" Catholics, along with the fallen-aways: I also knew that Catholics knew what was expected of them: it was perfectly clear. And so I found in the Church—after Truth—peace and stability. I knew what was what.

In Moral Re-Armament there was always—consciously or unconsciously—the problem of wondering whether we were "going off on tangents." There were to be no "limitations of the spirit" but at the same time one had to avoid being "carried away," soaring off on spiritual flights. However, if you were too cautious about the Spirit blowing you wherever it wanted to, you were

*I had scribbled these words from Father Clark in a margin of our instruction book: "If the local bishop had two heads and the Holy Father was always in a drunken stupor, it would still be the Church."

in danger of "living in a rut" and then you would have to go through the laborious process of "breaking old molds." Who was there to tell us what was the *norm*? Where was that straight, unwavering plumbline which by its very stability safeguarded the freedom to "live daringly?" If the four absolutes were the plumbline, to what was *it* connected? We depended on the guidance of God, but how did we know we had gotten the message right?

A friend wrote me a letter, which had this telling phrase (which was supposed to be *positive*): "Thank God MRA is not what I thought it was, or even now what I think it is." I thought: If no one knows what MRA is today, or what it is likely to be tomorrow, how is it going to be sold to anyone who has an analytical mind, or any sort of mind that will *count*, in the "ideological struggle"? Who will buy it? And if some do, will they find that they are constitutionally unfit to live on a spiritual roller coaster? Can they adjust to living in an atmosphere of surprises? If there was any truth in the conviction that "It is *our* fault: we have lost people because we have never really lived the life," perhaps the fault lay in setting an example of heroic flexibility which went way beyond the psychological powers of adjustment of the "ordinary man" Moral Re-Armament always wanted to win.

It is a cliché that life is full of risks, and I know that I will make plenty of mistakes, but they will not be a result of ambiguity about what I got myself into. When I became a Catholic it seemed to me that if MRA did not soon identify itself, it would find itself being identified.

AND SURE ENOUGH, that began to happen in the summer of 1955, when the Church put MRA in the category of "indifferentism." There was a statement from the Sacred Congregation of the Holy Office—actually a *re*-statement of a definitive judgement that had been released in 1951—and it included a summary of other documents that had been released in various parts of the world. Some warned the faithful not to take part in MRA; some *forbade* Catholics to do so.

"Indifferentism" was a word, or a term, that would have bewildered me when I was in MRA, because "indifferent" meant unconcerned, or nonchalant; our spirit was the very opposite of that. But what the Church meant by Indifferentism was something specific and difficult for Americans, especially, to understand.

When during instructions we had made a little side excursion into the subject of Catholicism in America, I began to understand America and democracy in a new way. They became *personal*, because I knew that if I became a Catholic I would be one of those Americans who (historically speaking) other Americans suspect of being *not* so very American. There was, in that August of 1954, an article in *Commonweal* magazine, about American pluralism. The author, Jesuit John Courtney Murray, wrote that the "American experience" is unique in the history of the world; that America has proved by experience that political unity and stability are possible without uniformity of religious belief and practice. A lot of anti-Catholicism was based on a misunderstanding of the Church as an "authoritarian institution," and there had been grim forebodings about the Church and Democracy.

When I became a Catholic, the Church in America was reaping the fruits of patient effort over the years, and in this new climate lots of books and articles were being published and Americans were coming to understand that one doesn't contradict democratic principles by following the religious dictates of his conscience: freedom of worship was a reality as well as a constitutional guarantee; America was gathering praise for her "religious tolerance."

A new ambiguity, however, came from "tolerance" being such a tricky word. It is often watered down to the popular maxim that it doesn't really matter what your faith is, so long as you live up to it. And if you don't have any particular faith, just be a good citizen. In a pluralistic society, the differences in belief between Catholics and the various Protestant denominations, and between Christians and Jews, are seen as less important than the "common ground," the search for which is bound to minimize and obscure differences in religious belief and practice. Diversity of belief is regarded as the normal way of life. This kind of "indifferentism" can destroy the very thing it hopes to establish: How can "tolerance" exist when no one knows exactly what he is tolerating? Brushing aside theology as unimportant or irrelevant is likely to foster, in the place of religion, merely a *feeling*: you could have no spiritual formation whatever and still consider yourself "a religious person." Sociologists were busily pointing out that this religiosity was already turning a secular structure, American democracy, into a religion—vesting The American Way of Life with a quasi-religious appeal.

In those days of the early 50s, in America and beyond, the prevailing idea among people of the liberal Protestant outlook was that when the need for unity was so urgent, religious convictions and the loyalties on which they rested were beside the point: the principal concern was to promote unity and goodwill among all men. That defined the *me* I had been: I was an American, a Protestant at least nominally, and a part of a movement which considered its God-given mission to be the uniting of all men of good will on a plane above dogma and doctrine. That was the "party line" but we had always been encouraged to think these things out for ourselves—to put them into our own words. An MRA friend, alarmed by my interest in Catholicism, did just that when she wrote that the important thing was "to get all the good people who think they are right, and are walking in the 'true way,' to pitch together for a much greater issue which is to rescue the world's people from disaster."

I had always known that Protestants were different from Catholics and Jews, but I couldn't have told anyone just *how* they were different. I knew that Catholics in MRA were encouraged to be Good Catholics: there were always available cars, in the team centers, to get them to Mass on Sundays. We understood that they had "an obligation." It was not considered important to be Good Protestants: we did go to church now and then, but not out of obligation. Mainly, we went (or so it seemed to me) to show outsiders, who might be wondering, that MRA was not a Religion.

I HAD ALWAYS HATED the word "religion," and the last thing in the world I wanted to be considered was "religious." When I was little, "religious" meant people with pious faces and excessive emotions that made me cringe. To me, *religion* was a poor substitute for *God*. As I grew up in the terminology and the training of MRA, I could speak comfortably about God and spiritual things, but "religion" was taboo. It was not ideological. "Spiritual" was sophisticated; "religion" was hokey.

Then at some point in my late teens, I became aware of the importance, to individuals, of religion—in the context of custom, ethnicity, habit, and loyalty—but that it had anything to do with *reason* did not occur to me.

About *loyalty*, though, I had gone through a brief stage of that, and it rather surprised me. I'd had a sense of outrage, in my pre-teen years in Chicago, when I found out that my mother and sisters and I were joining a Congregational church. I hadn't really known what was happening until I had to stand up and read some sort of creed, and by then it was too late. Wasn't this, I thought, being disloyal to my father? After all, he had been a Presbyterian minister. My loyalty phase was short-lived because I realized that Daddy in heaven was well aware of irrelevancies: ideology was the important thing. So whatever shade of difference there may have been between Presbyterians and Congregationalists shouldn't matter a whit.

Anyway, we became Presbyterians again when we moved to Richmond and Mother got a job at St. Giles church, whose pastor, J. Blanton Belk, was in MRA. He had sacrificed much for his convictions—had been driven out of one church, but most of his congregation left with him and together they built the new church. Dr. Belk was well known all over the state: he went on hunting trips with one of our senators, and Virginia's governor said that he had "the qualities of a true statesman." We all thought that a church which had an ideologically-aware statesman pastor was the only valid sort of church "for these times." There were not many ministers in this country like J. Blanton Belk. Nor had there been many like my father, in the Oxford Group days: he too had challenged his congregation and the opposition affected his health and very possibly hastened his death.

In most Protestant churches the congregation heard gentle, perhaps sanctimonious sermons (the sermon was of course the important thing) or they might hear—if they were Baptists— fire-and-brimstone orations. Sermons could touch on ethics and morals, but rarely did they illuminate anything about the nature of God and His way of revealing Himself. The duty imposed on Christians, because of God and His Son, was taken for granted rather than explored or explained.

All I knew about Episcopalians was that their churches frightened me: one was expected to kneel and do all those demonstrative things. Had I ever been obligated to go into an Anglo-Catholic church (such as St. Mary the Virgin in New York City, with its chapels and vigil lights and confessional boxes) I would have panicked. There was nothing scary about Presbyterian churches: you just sat, and listened, and stood up to sing hymns.

As for Catholics, I was beautifully unprejudiced and thoroughly ignorant. The few in MRA impressed me because they seemed to know what they believed—and in fact to know something I didn't. During the three years we lived in a Chicago settlement house (Mother was on the staff) I had some awareness of Catholicism: it was a Polish neighborhood, and the big Catholic school had very few unbroken window panes. I remember that one day I went to a school picnic with a neighborhood friend, and a Sister played softball with us, and broke her glasses. She seemed quite normal and not at all scary.

Looking back, I am appalled by my total lack of curiosity. I never questioned the notion that one religion was as good as another. I had heard that Catholics thought theirs was the *true* religion, but I had no curiosity about what that meant. If I had known anything at all about Judaism, I might have been curious about why, in my Chicago private school (where the great majority of students were Jewish), grades seven through twelve sang Handel's *Messiah* at the winter concert one year.

Religion as such never came up in MRA meetings, but sometimes "church" did. Whether "church" was generic or referred to a specific Church, I had no idea: I wasn't curious about that, either. I simply accepted the dictum that "the church"—capitalized or not—"did not live the answer." We (on the inside) had often heard the statement: "Christianity has failed." What the context clarified was not that God had failed but that Christians had forgotten their mission, and MRA, which was "for all men, everywhere," had as *its* mission to *remind* them.

If you don't know what something *is*, you can only guess at its purpose, and you judge its effectiveness by your own ideas of what it is *for*. A tool is successful if it does what its manufacturer guarantees it will do (or your money back). What was Christianity supposed to be, or to do? Had we read the Guarantee? That Christianity (the church or the Church) had "failed" was based on the premise that it was supposed to succeed in changing the world, and in 2,000 years "the ideology of the Cross of Christ" had not taken over. *Ergo*, Christianity had failed.

It is odd that a movement known for its spiritual values would be so empirical in its reasoning. I had never heard of empiricism, but I think that's what we used: we based our judgment on appearance and observation "without regard to system or theory." I guess you would call this "circumstantial evidence." We believed in the invisible working of grace in our own lives, but we did not connect that to the Church's divinely-ordained guarantee—which I also didn't know anything about.

Where secular things were concerned, our reasoning process was mainly *juridical*—"a practical system of placing moral judgment upon any issue as it currently appears." Thus our discussions about anything from politics to Broadway entertainment were automatically transposed into the *moral* sphere: we would be unanimous in our judgment about The Problem and The Answer.

Perhaps "Christianity has failed" wasn't meant to be taken literally, but that was "the thinking" as *I* perceived it. And of course I had no inkling that knowledge of historical facts would make any difference.

Sometimes, though, "historical" Christianity *would* be brought up in our team centers but always in an ideological context. In a study session at Dellwood, for instance, we were enlightened about how communism had resulted from the failure of Christianity. I scribbled down many notes, and here are some:

> Christianity failed . . . was never an *ideology* because it never became an *organism*. It became more and more organized because the priests themselves couldn't live up to their doctrines . . . they had no answer to temptation, no moral standards. Therefore rebellion came, in spite of the efforts of St. Francis and the others . . . if one pope was out for power, think what it did . . . everything failed because the idea became *organization* . . . too rigid to deal with human nature.

Within my narrow frame of reference, this was all logical; the right words were there, and of course "Francis" was our friend: we thought of him not as a "Catholic" saint but as a sort of MRA patron, because he had resisted becoming "organized" and was led by the Spirit—the same Spirit that led *us*. Francis was the patron of all Movements of the Spirit.

What is interesting about all this (in retrospect) is seeing how easily I accepted the stereotype of the Church as an institution, an organization vulnerable to all the evils that corrupt human societies, a repressive, reactionary monolith—and also realizing that all the things I wrote down and "shared" on the subject were never once challenged by people who surely knew more than I did. Evidently it was not considered essential to our training that we be equipped with an explanation of, for example, how and why the Church was an "organization." When I wrote in my notebook that Christianity had failed because it had never become an organism, I was implying that there had been the *possibility* of its becoming an organism. No one ever asked me to prove that it was *not* an organism, so I was left to go on thinking that (as I also wrote in my notebook) "Changing the world is not easy. That's why it hasn't happened in 2,000 years, and why God has created this force in the twentieth century."

I now recoil in horror at this presumption. If I had ever actually circulated a statement like that, our leaders would have accused me of misrepresenting MRA. But as long as "my thoughts" were "expressed" in "the heart of the family," they were OK: no one challenged my "reasoning."

SO MUCH FOR MY KNOWLEDGE OF CHRISTIANITY. One of Frank Buchman's early sayings was that we should "find out more about the way in which God works through history . . . to study the force of God as Holy Spirit." I don't think Frank was really advocating a group study; probably he just wanted the early Groupers to "have guidance" about this, during their morning quiet times. Every now and then I would come across that quote, in one or another of the MRA books, but I thought that although a "study" might be interesting, it wasn't essential because the *application* of Christian truths was the only important reason for studying the Holy Spirit, and of course we *were* applying these truths: that was our whole ideology. We were in a global effort to win the world to Christ, whereupon the great truths of the Gospel would once again become great, and Christ would be King. Moral Re-Armament, Frank said (and we believed) was "the whole message of the Gospel . . . the message in its entirety."

Therefore perhaps it wasn't strange that we felt an affinity with the early Quakers and others throughout history who felt such a *part* of the Gospel that they had never considered it objectively, as an historic document. For us in MRA, the Biblical "documentation" that counted was the experience of men through the centuries who had dared, under Divine Revelation, "to live experimentally with God;" we were part of that "creative minority" who from the Hebrew prophets through the early Church—if it was early, it was capital *C* Church—and its successors (especially St. Ignatius, St. Joan, and the Franciscan brotherhood) had created a striking example of Inspired Democracy. We in MRA were linked to the spiritual revolutionaries who, all down the ages, had been faithful to the vision of a world remade.

And so we talked about the Church having failed (without having defined Church even as "a conglomerate of Christians") as we analyzed Marxism in the light of its materialistic interpretation of Christian social principles. Christians had not lived the "communism" of the first disciples who held everything in common—when, as we said, because "everybody cared enough and everybody shared enough, everybody *had* enough"—and "neither was there any one needy among them." And we studied Inspired Democracy as exemplified in our American heritage: the Puritans, William Penn, the U.S. Constitution. We studied the *Communist Manifesto* and *Das Kapital* and agreed that there had been no Christian ideology adequate to meet the challenge of the industrial revolution. But there was no mention of certain documents that stated the fundamental Christian answer to communism and socialism in whatever forms, which was also the answer to the deepest needs in the soul of man. Apparently no one was doing anything about "dialectic and militant materialism"'but us in MRA: I thought *we* had coined the phrase.

Yet in my own lifetime there had lived a pope who spoke and wrote about all the things we were talking about and fighting for; and there had been popes before him, in the nineteenth century, who had spoken perceptively about the things that *were* and the things that were to *come*. Pope Pius IX's first encyclical pointed to the dangers of communism—that was in 1846—and there was the voice of Pope Leo XIII thundering ever more loudly as he recalled Christians to their mission. He was a giant in the field of the reconstruction of the social order, but I had never heard of him. As we studied the *Communist Manifesto* we didn't study the encyclical *Divini Redemptoris* (1937) in which Pius XI said a great deal about atheistic communism and totalitarian regimes and the struggle between good and evil. We studied the Labor Problem, but we did not read *Quadregesimo Anno* (On

Reconstructing the Social Order) which had been written the year I was born, and which restated the great encyclical *Rerum Novarum* by Leo XIII forty years previously.

People all over the world were studying those documents, while I was being indoctrinated with a lot of revolutionary truths which would have seemed far more revolutionary and even exciting had I known that they had not originated with Moral Re-Armament. But I didn't know that.

Frank Buchman had said we should learn more "about the way God works through history" but our access to history was limited. As for studying God "as the force of the Holy Spirit"— well, the Holy Spirit was presumably non-denominational and, in my mind, disconnected from the Father and the Son. It was often pointed out that John Wesley had not intended to found a new sect: he had said "It makes no difference whether one is a Protestant or a Papist, so long as he has the spirit of Christ." I accepted that without question, and my "convictions" of those days were later played back to me in a letter from a friend, who wrote: "MRA is the Holy Spirit in action . . . whatever form it takes and in whatever religion or creed it happens to occur."

There it is in a nutshell, I thought: that's what the Church means by "religious indifferentism." More formally explained, "indifferentism" is the belief—whether consciously arrived at or inherited—that the Church is a broad spiritual unity, with no visible earthly organization; that all who believe in Christ and have the Spirit of Christ are members of that invisible society, and that all religions are more or less relative and interchangeable.

And directly in opposition to this is the stubborn conviction of Catholics that the first requisite for the true following of Christ is to belong to the visible external organization which Christ founded.

If the term "indifferentism" baffles many people, Catholics are equally baffled by the fact that there are so many religions holding contradictory doctrines about God and man. The idea that they are all equally true, or can be held in varying degrees, strikes Catholics as absurd, and rather tragic.

Many of my friends in Moral Re-Armament were glad when they heard about my becoming a Catholic, and they told me so in letters. It made me feel very humble to know how sincerely happy they were for me. Later on, though, I got some letters which—by posing questions either directly or indirectly—seemed to substantiate many of the conclusions I'd been reaching about MRA. In one of those letters there was a short question: "Why did you stop halfway?"

That question seemed to vibrate with all kinds of assumptions and implications, such as that MRA is the highest and the greatest way of life, and anything less than total commitment to it is either a deliberate or an unwitting choice of second-best. I worked hard on my reply. I wanted to explain *why* the Church has this peculiar notion that *it* was God's "fullest plan" for the world; that for Catholics it was not simply a matter of "belief" or arrogant superiority or mob loyalty to "Holy Mother Church"—that Catholics were convinced of certain things upon which everything else depended; that they were convinced because these things were part of an ancient and ageless *organism* that entered into time when the Word became Flesh, when God put His knowledge into a human nature Who before He was crucified delivered to His special disciples the whole deposit of truth and told them to guard it and keep it intact; and because for the past 2000 years this organism which is both visible and invisible had fought without compromise to do just that.

I sent off the letter—which I feared sounded more like a theological exegesis—and eventually got a reply. My friend wrote: "You'd be a good Catholic, I have no objections—but the thing to do is to get all the good people who think theirs is the Right way fighting together . . ."

So there it is again, I thought: *indifferentism*. It doesn't matter what you believe: "Let's all unite above doctrinal differences and get on the Good Road together."

Then, in another sentence in that letter, came the question: "Do you still have guidance?" Meaning, of course, did I still listen to God in the MRA-ordained manner. The implication behind that question seemed more ominous: it could be grounds to prove that Moral Re-Armament is what it says it is *not*— a religious movement.

When I was taking instructions, and filling my notebooks with all sorts of quotes and material I didn't know what I ever expected to do with, I clipped a review which had a definition of religion. The quotation was from Erich Fromm: he said that religion is "Any system of thought and action, shared by a group, that gives the individual a cosmic frame of orientation and an object of devotion."

So now when my friend asked me "Do you have guidance?"
I began thinking about that system of thought and action, shared
by a group, known as "having guidance." Guidance from God
is nothing new, but a specific method for receiving guidance
which one man had found to be effective had been turned into
a tradition in MRA: the way in which one man found he could
"establish special contact with the power station" had come to
be regarded as The Method by which God communicates with
man—and that almost amounts, I thought, to a kind of dogma.

THAT WAS JUST ONE EXAMPLE, but it set me to thinking that any
group whose corporate viewpoint is that all religions are more
or less the same and the important thing is "the way of life"
may find itself saying, in the next breath, but Our Way is best
of all (which is of course what *I* had believed, but I'd never
put it into words). And it seemed to me that a movement which
thought of itself as *transcending* doctrinal differences had to
be very careful lest it turn into a doctrine itself, in the sense
of practicing a system of religious thought. I wondered if MRA
could be a "supra-confessional" movement when it defined such
things as "guidance" (and instructed how it should be had) and
when it gave, or implied, specific interpretations of Scripture.
It was one thing, I thought, for MRA to talk about "inspired
democracy"—a new pattern of democracy, designed by God and
"worked" by everyone, made available to everyone through the
coming of Christ. But wasn't it another thing for MRA to call
itself the *ideology* of that "inspired democracy"? In stressing
Christ's emphasis on "absolute moral standards" and the will
of God, wasn't there the implication that you, and *only* you,
were in possession of the full message of Jesus Christ?

MRA's Dilemma

Organism or Organization?

IT MUST HAVE COME as a shock to MRA's intelligentsia when in 1952 the American Catholic episcopate issued a statement saying it considered the movement to be "a non-Catholic sect in process of formation." On the other hand, MRA's leaders (who I suspect did not "share" this definition with the whole team) may have fluffed off the American bishops' findings: clearly "they" didn't understand the true nature of the movement. But then when the Holy Office levelled the charge of religious indifferentism, reminding the Catholic faithful that it is "a sin against Faith" to consider all religions interchangeable and relative, well—that was far more serious. In England and Wales, Germany, Belgium and Italy, the clergy had been forbidden and the faithful "discouraged" from taking any part in MRA.

However, warnings are not prohibitions, so there was still room for individual opinions and different convictions among Catholics; but it seemed to me that if certain tenets of MRA were not clarified, the Church might go still further. If MRA were to be defined, dogmatically, as a non-Catholic sect in process of formation, the Catholics I knew in MRA—who were good people following their consciences—would have a very large personal problem. And if a universal prohibition should come from the Holy Office, MRA itself—which insisted it was "for all men everywhere"— would have a *huge* problem.

We in Moral Re-Armament always talked about how we were "making history." We believed we *were* making history, but had it ever occurred to us that history might make *us* into something we didn't like? I didn't know, then, about the other movements

181

that had started out *not* to be "organizations." I had learned a little about them since coming into the Church, and although I did not have a historian's knowledge (and will never have a historian's mind) I had enough of a layman's comprehension of the historical pattern to understand that the logical necessity of history will calcify non-organizational movements into sects, because circumstances will not allow them to remain ambiguous. And I began to think that even within the first generation of MRA, history had modified the original vision of its founder.

In the very early days, Frank Buchman's followers had no name for themselves other than "the fellowship"—which I guess was an abbreviation for The First Century Christian Fellowship, which sounded rather too ancient. The press, lacking anything definitive, wrote about "Buchmanism" and unfriendly reporters wrote about "Buchmanites." In 1928 "the fellowship" became known as "The Oxford Group": this was because some of Frank Buchman's converts at Oxford University (some of them Rhodes scholars) had gone, on their "long vacation," to South Africa to spread the spirit there. A stationmaster (so the story goes) needed a name to put on their compartment: the only obvious thing these young men had in common was Oxford, so "the group from Oxford" became The Oxford Group. The *Pretoria News* and other papers picked this up, and the name stuck. Frank Buchman wasn't enthusiastic about this label, but he said: "If it's got to be called something, that's as good as anything." A year later Frank himself took a team to South Africa under its new Oxford Group label, and his followers all over the world could now talk about "the Group" rather than "the fellowship."

The Oxford Group became known as Moral Re-Armament some ten years later. When Frank Buchman was walking in the woods of the Black Forest near Freudenstadt, in 1938, the thought came to him: "Moral and spiritual re-armament. The next great movement in the world will be a movement of moral re-armament for all nations." At that time Europe was undergoing a war of nerves; Hitler's march into Austria had speeded up the military re-armament of the democracies. Armed conflict, thought Frank, could not finally decide the ideological issues in the world. So the *idea* of moral re-armament became the *name* and "Moral Re-Armament" was launched—a few days after that Black Forest walk—in London's East Ham Town Hall. That Hall—"a cradle of the British Labor Movement"—was having a reception for Dr. Buchman and there was an overflowing crowd of 3,000—including (on the platform with him) more than sixty East London Mayors, Aldermen and Councillors. Within a few days, press and radio had carried Frank Buchman's concept of Moral Re-Armament around the world.

During the early "fellowship" years, Frank Buchman saw as his God-given task the choosing and training of leadership. It was said that "Men came to him for help and stayed with him for life" and "Where other men founded organizations, he tended the growth of an organism." This organism had cells at scholarly universities like Penn State, Princeton, Cambridge and Oxford: students attracted to Buchman's New Idea felt that "here was something they wanted." It was not an organization: it was a spirit. It wasn't something you *joined*; it was a way of life you *lived*. "As I am, so is my nation." And so, during those early years, the core of a new "creative minority" was formed. As the years went by and Buchman's ideas took on global dimensions, emphasis on specifically Christian truths was gradually replaced by the rhetoric of ideology. What had been perceived as a new sort of Christian Evangelism evolved into something larger: the emphasis now was on a common denominator on which "everyone, everywhere" could unite.

As the number of full-time men and women grew, houseparties overflowed into hotel suites, team meetings grew into national and international assemblies; plays were written and produced, property was donated, and training centers established. Individuals and companies made gifts of money. Therefore, the movement had to yield to the demands of taxation legislation: even at the risk of misrepresentation, it had to allow itself to be incorporated as a "non-profit organization" in the United States, Canada, England, and elsewhere. So now it was Moral Re-Armament, Inc. (This helped with travel, too: there was a "clergy" discount for members of certain kinds of non-profit organizations. Even *I* had a "clergy card.")

And so Frank Buchman's organism became an organization—for *legal* purposes. The impersonal forces of necessity had led MRA into a situation that has been appearing and reappearing throughout history. On the one hand, here was a spiritual movement based on the simplicity of the Gospels. On the other hand, some kind of specific organization was needed so that those who had little or no contact with the Leaders of the Work could live the way of life and be a *bona fide* part of the team. When a "non-organizational movement" finds itself in this position, it must choose either to define itself or resist definition so as to remain Open to All regardless of race or religion or even class.

IN THE FIRST CASE, the movement must make clear that it is a concentration on one aspect of the whole picture, with an authority resting on known and acknowledged principles, and therefore open to people who share these basic principles and whose talents and inclinations draw them to the particular emphasis within the larger picture. In the second case, the movement will inevitably assume a kind of infallibility—an elitist, intransigent attitude of authority and superiority toward all who dissent from its claims or disapprove of its methods. Cut off from tradition, its authority is established by—and in—its leader: if it is a *spiritual* movement, its authority is grounded in the personal experiences of divine guidance, on direct contact with the Holy Spirit. The movement will speak in the tone of men who have an invincible assurance of truth. Those who do not accept this "truth" are considered blind, or prejudiced, or worse; therefore they are *morally* unqualified to criticize or to evaluate the movement. And eventually history will give this movement a name, and the name may not signify what the Founder had in mind.

There have been many movements and individuals throughout history whose aim was the restoration of the ancient and undefiled Christianity supposedly practiced in the time of the Apostles. Sometimes this spirit is "discerned" in existing organizations. The Oxford Movement (which was often confused with The Oxford Group) came about because John Henry Newman and others believed that the Church of England was still "the ancient Church," and that it needed revitalization. Perhaps if Newman had not become convinced that the "Roman communion" *was* the ancient church, the Oxford Movement would have become a sect outside the Church of England. But most of the individuals and movements whose ideas were based on *their* vision of the Church of the Apostles did not look to discover it in any *existing* institution, and they fought any tendency to institutionalize.

I was brought up in the MRA idea that organization, in the realm of the moral or spiritual, was something Bad. We did not want a label. We were a kind of leaven, a dynamic force in human affairs. Organization was an unfortunate result of the loss of the inner spirit. We said: MRA is an ideology. An ideology is Faith plus Force, the force being people who live it (live *what*?) intelligently. A superior force is an organism. Organizations have not been effective in history: they will break down on the inside and exclude some people. Organizations can be created by changing peoples' thinking: an *organism* is created through changing peoples' hearts and minds.

We were given examples of how, throughout history, organization hadn't worked. One such example was St. Francis of Assisi, the happy vagabond who was moved by the gentle breath of the Spirit, who—said Frank Buchman in a 1950 speech—"put aside fame and career and gave everything he had to change the world." The "tragedy" was that Francis was compelled to organize; therefore the inner, spontaneous spark was smothered under the blanket of rules, regulations and Orthodoxy. The rector of Bonn University had said that what St. Francis had done for the crisis of the thirteenth century, a similar movement, Moral Re-Armament, was doing for the yet greater crisis of today. We all memorized the exact quote because, we said, "it carries a lot of weight." But did we really think that St. Francis and his Friars Minor were the harbinger of MRA—that we were to carry on where they had left off? (And when *had* they "left off"?)

If I had used my mind to think logically about "organization" I might have seen St. Francis as a man whose ideas could not be exposed to the vagaries of history. Like Frank Buchman, he had an idea, and he lived it. It was an infectious idea. There were many who wanted to live as he did, but not everyone was able to wander about with him; it was simply not possible for everyone to catch his spirit by direct contact. Something more than personal contact with *il poverello* was needed if a movement that was growing so rapidly was to keep its momentum. If I'd thought about it, I might have realized that people are quick to respond to ideas, but if many people far away are to *live* by them, they must be defined and made specific. And if I had known anything about history, I might have seen that the need for organization as a framework for specific direction about living the full Christian life didn't begin with St. Francis, or St. Benedict long before him, or even with St. Pachomius, who did the first real bit of organizing with the desert hermits in the fourth century— it went back to the Apostles. Right after Pentecost, they got busy defining and organizing, not to *limit* man's freedom but to *protect* it; to safeguard the full truth. For even at the beginning, people preferred their own inner lights to the authority of these men to whom Christ had entrusted the meaning of His parables.

And so St. Francis turned out to be the founder of the Franciscans, and St. Benedict of the Benedictines, and St. Ignatius Loyola of the Jesuits; all of these organizations put special emphasis on a part of the *whole*, each springing forth unexpectedly in ages which needed to be reminded of the particular truths emphasized by the Franciscans, the Benedictines, the Jesuits. But they were all under one spiritual authority. And throughout the centuries their distinctive contribution *to* and influence *in* the Church, and on the world, is evermore understandable and "timely" in the light of *our* age.

The various "First Century Christianity" movements were begun by men and women of good will and much enthusiasm, who concentrated on being attentive to the direct guidance of the Holy Spirit. Some of these movements were essentially evangelical, some mystical; some sprang from a Reformation culture, and some began within the Catholic Church. None of them intended to become an organization; they did not want to be labeled. They were, however, not satisfied with a reformation of manners, so what eventually emerged was a whole different approach to religion. In outline and usually in detail, the pattern has been that movements which react against any form of institutional religion end up becoming institutionalized themselves. And, in the words of Monsignor Ronald Knox, in his classic study *Enthusiasm*, "A fresh name is added to the list of Christianities." Knox makes the point that there has been no such Christianity that, within a hundred years, has not become more or less institutionalized.

It is a curious part of the pattern that while these free-wheeling movements denied being something "new" they often implied that they *were* new. I think I had always sensed something paradoxical in the nature of MRA. I had written in my notebook "The principles of MRA are not new but the thoroughness in practicing them is. It is not an organization that puts a new spirit into existing organizations"—by which I think I meant it was not a "new religion" but a kind of ideological vitamin for existing religions. But I also found this in my notebook: "Frank Buchman has initiated a universal idea which the record shows is proving stronger than Marxism in its appeal to the human mind." Since "initiate" means to start something new, I had written down two contradictory evaluations—and had believed both of them.

In *Enthusiasm*, Knox wrote about George Fox and John Wesley and other men of vision and passion who had set out to restore, to reform, and to redeem, and described what history had made of them and their movements. In *Webster's* you can read that George Fox (1624-1691) was "Eng. preacher; Founder of Society of Friends (Quakers)" which was obviously better than "Foxism." And John Wesley (1703-1791) was "Eng. theol., evangelist, and Founder of Methodism." I wondered: Would Frank Buchman go down in history as "Founder of Buchmanism?" And were there *already* people who, for whatever reason, were making predictions about what history would do to Moral Re-Armament? If so, I thought, objective speculation is one thing, but anyone imbued with "the spirit of MRA" would find it psychologically impossible to scrutinize the movement with a detached, historical eye—would find it impossible even to *imagine* MRA going the way of other movements, or to view it in the light of two alternatives: calcification, or alignment with a traditional authority.

At this stage in my "evolving" I could be somewhat objective, but this wasn't pleasing because I knew the people involved and what they had sacrificed and how they were convinced that "there's never been anything like this in history." Who was *I* to "predict" or "advise"? All I could have said, had anyone in MRA asked me, was that it wouldn't be a bad idea for them to become informed (with as much objectivity as possible) about what had happened down the long avenue of history.

Maybe there *hadn't* been anything like MRA before. In his book *The World Rebuilt* (1951) Peter Howard had written "It is given to few men to be a full generation ahead of the time in which they live. Such men are centers of controversy to their contemporaries and a cause of thankfulness to succeeding generations. It has always been so in history. It is so with Frank Buchman." It is true that Frank talked about communism before most Americans knew what it was, and MRA used the word "ideology" before it became a common noun; perhaps MRA was a part of the "prophetic tradition." But if it would go *on* awakening people spiritually and ideologically, it would have to know about the heritage and character of that tradition.

Of course no one *did* ask for my views about what had happened down the long road of history, but now and then I got letters which seemed to pose questions obliquely and which I felt I had to answer—which in fact I *wanted* to answer. I welcomed letters, because I thought that in my replies I could clear up a lot of my own ambiguity. (I also think I had a secret notion that if I kept my carbons, someday someone might put them all together in an attractive, handy "definitive" volume—like Monsignor Knox's *Off The Record*, which had greatly helped me.) But I fear I had a depressing tendency to sound didactic and pontifical when I tried to make specific points. I had written some rather long, non-polemic (I thought) letters to a few special MRA friends about how I had been led to the Church, and these people had written back saying they were glad I had found a faith, and usually they went on to say that while "finding a faith" was fine, I must not forget my responsibility to all the *others* in the world who were Looking for An Answer. (In other words, finding a faith was a Good Thing if it helped you to live more ideologically.)

The implications behind the word "faith" in these letters made me realize that writing letters about identification and indifferentism and organization and authority (even if the letters managed to sound spontaneous and not like essays) would amount to little more than batting words through the air, because any clarification of issues or of terminology hinged on the *Catholic* concept of "faith." Catholics could not really understand MRA, from the outside looking in, without knowing the *spirit*; and my friends in MRA couldn't understand the Church unless they understood the underlying dynamic behind all the catechistical and theological works. What I really had to talk about *was* the Catholic *Faith*—which I felt I myself was just *beginning* to understand in all its totality.

Somewhere in the last few hundred years we have lost respect for the exact meaning of words: words that once had a precise ontological meaning are now used in a careless, vague sort of way, and certainly one such word is "faith."

Faith Fads of the '50s

Norman Vincent has a-Peale

IN THE EARLY 1950s, "faith" was considered a fashionable topic. No longer restricted to dark corners and intimate conversation, faith—as well as sex and psychoanalysis—was discussed at dinner parties and in magazine articles. Having "a faith" was back in vogue, as it had been back in Cardinal Newman's day when people talked and wrote a lot about "faith" and "religion." But they couldn't be too theological about it, because the stress was on *believing* rather than on the *object* of belief. In Newman's day too, "meditation" was *in*, but it had more to do with affections than with reason: when someone prayed, he didn't think so much about God as he did about whether or not he *felt* like he was praying. Cardinal Newman preached about how this led to self-contemplation, and C.S. Lewis' creature Screwtape delighted in this kind of "approach to God" when he wrote these instructions to his diabolic nephew Wormwood:

> . . . In all activities which favor our cause, encourage the patient to be un-selfconscious and to concentrate on the object, but in all activities favorable to the Enemy, bend his mind back on itself. . . . Let the reflection "my feelings are now growing more devout, or more charitable" so fix his attention inward that he no longer looks beyond himself to see our Enemy or his own neighbors.

In America, before the war, there was an assortment of religious leaders—mostly radicals and non-conformists—who echoed the "hard sayings" of the Gospel. Then these gloomy prophets were eclipsed by cheerful optimists who did not want to make anyone

189

mad. They were the first apostles and promoters of a new religious revival that just happened to coincide with the advent of home television. They sold their personalities on the TV screen, but since most Americans didn't yet have TV sets, they got their message across mainly through their books, many of which made the bestseller lists. These books were uplifting and inspirational; they offered the readers a program of prayer and Positive Thinking, through which could be found health, wealth, happiness and satisfaction. If the readers (the "seekers") would try the various easy-to-apply methods, then prayer and faith would be translated into health and wealth—"ideas into things." Prayer was depicted as a sort of magic potion which, if applied correctly ("using the Jesus Christ principle") would change your life from whatever it was into whatever you wanted it to be. There were Formulas of seven simple steps, ten workable rules, two fifteen-minute sessions of repetitious emphasis, and so on; the circulars advertising these books generously invited you to return them and get your money back if within a month you hadn't found the systems rewarding, if these Formulas had not increased the number of bright intervals until your whole outlook was one of optimism and hope. How comforting was the idea that if you kicked out all those gloomy old negative thoughts and concentrated on Confidence Concepts and Energy-Producing Thoughts, everything would be rosy. Simply (1) prayerize; (2) picturize; (3) actualize. The *world* will be different, and *you* will be that person you've always wanted to be.

For the depressed or neurotic, there was a book about "autoconditioning," which was "The New Way to a Successful Life." The ads said that with this book you would also receive a Mood-Meter which would teach you how to back up your faith and your prayers with deep-down positive thinking that would give you an unshakeable faith in YOURSELF.

Those who wanted their "religion" plain and comforting, devoid of any rational or theological elements, were no doubt relieved to hear that any serious thought about the nature of God and the mystery of suffering and evil belonged to the category of those dangerous, gloomy thoughts which were—once you got the Method down pat—so easy to dispel.

Of course there had to be a negative reaction to all this Positive Thinking business; soon there began to appear essays, book reviews and articles about the dangers of the "peace of mind" approach to God's truth: magazines such as *Saturday Review* and *The Reporter* ran articles titled "Pitchmen in the Pulpit" and "Some Negative Thinking about Norman Vincent Peale" conveying concern that the natural cravings for peace of mind and the Good Life were being reduced to the lowest common denominators of social acceptance, business success and self-confidence. The authors feared that in this new "religious revival" Christianity was being reduced to a system of "Successful Living."

Some of these writers were scholars in search of some undogmatic religion that would be the answer to atomic disaster. Arnold Toynbee was often quoted: the British historian had written a book based on arguments which he'd developed in his ten-volume "Study of History." Toynbee envisioned the emergence of a "broader faith" in which all "higher religions" would have a place. There would be, he hoped, a time when barriers of space and language would have been eliminated, and all the local heritages of nations and civilizations and religions would have coalesced into a common heritage of the whole human family.

If I had read about (and had been capable of grasping) Arnold Toynbee's analyses and predictions when I was full time with Moral Re-Armament, I would have thought it Very Sound (we used that phrase a lot) but I would have parroted the line that while Toynbee was busy working out the *philosophy*, we were busy working out the *answer*. (By which we meant "*living* the answer," but that sounded too presumptuous.) Toynbee had pointed out the common ground in the various religions of East and West and made a plea for "the highest ground of tolerance"— a synthesis of religions and cultures. MRA's vision was of a world community in which, through some kind of synthesis (all the best, from East and West?), a universal ideology would be forged: the point was *unity*.

Unity was also the theme of the early 50s ecumenicists: they argued that the division between constructive moral and spiritual forces was preventing the unity "for which everyone longs" and preached that men must unite on a level above all their "exclusivist" notions. That sounded a bit like MRA, but we would have left out "exclusivist" because we didn't want to exclude anybody and also because we didn't actually believe that Christian revelation and doctrine were merely human inventions, which is what the

ecumenicists implied. On the other hand, we *could* big-heartedly
sacrifice beloved traditions and customs in the interest of forging
a new unity—perhaps that's what God wanted of us. (That was
considered "ideological thinking.")

In any case, the New World we envisioned was not too dissimilar
from Arnold Toynbee's envisioned "Ecumenical Empire."

When Toynbee's book was being dismembered and appraised
by critics here and in England—in the Catholic press and the
New York *Times* and the *London Times* and *The New Republic*
and many others—and when Philip Wylie was speaking at the
University of Colorado Writers' Conference about the baleful
effects of religious dogma upon the course of human history
and the development of culture, yet another wave of "religious
books" was hitting the reviewers' columns. The authors were
also interested in man's destiny and the salvation of society:
the solution to modern man's dilemma, they said, lay in Mystical
Experience. Freedom from Orthodoxy was the thing: mystic insight,
not dogma. They were more concerned with man's soul than
with historical patterns and analogies: what was needed was some
kind of ethical system based on contemplation and interior spiritual
experience. The Positive Thinking concept of faith was an insult
to their aesthetic consciences and to their intellects. Their approach
was existential and metaphysical—brooding and speculative—
to some degree theological but exclusive of anything specifically
dogmatic. They said that all through the ages, an undercurrent
of mystical thought has continued "below the mainstream of
rationalism." It did not seem to occur to them that mystical
thought and rationalism could co-exist in the same philosophy.

When I became interested in Catholicism, I was warned about
that thing called "dogma." But even before I began taking
instructions, the specter of "dogma" had lost any terror it *might*
have had, because I had read Thomas Merton's book *Seeds of
Contemplation* and there was a chapter that impressed me so
much that I typed part of it in a letter to a friend who did not
have a sympathetic regard for dogma:

> The notion of dogma terrifies men who do not understand the
> Church. They cannot conceive that a religious doctrine may receive
> a clear and definite and authoritative statement without at once
> becoming static and rigid and inert and losing all its vitality.
> And in their frantic anxiety to escape from any such conception

they take refuge in a system of belief that is vague and fluid, a system in which truths pass like mists and waver and vary like shadows. They make their own personal selection of ghosts, in this pale, indefinite twilight of the mind, and take good care never to bring them out into the full brightness of the sun for fear of a full view of their insubstantiality.

They favor the Catholic mystics with a sort of sympathetic regard, for they believe that these rare men somehow reached the summit of contemplation in defiance of Catholic dogma. Their deep union with God is supposed to have been an escape from the teaching authority of His Church, and an implicit protest against it. . . . But the truth is that the saints arrived at the deepest and most vital and also the most individual and personal knowledge of God precisely because of the Church's teaching authority, precisely through the tradition that is guarded and fostered by that authority.

The dogmas of Catholic faith are not merely symbols or vague rationalizations which we accept as arbitrary points of stimulation around which good moral actions may form or develop—still less is it true that any idea would serve just as well as those that have been defined, any old pious thought would foment this vague moral life in our souls. The dogmas defined and taught by the Church have a very precise and positive and definitive meaning which those who have the gifts to do so must explore and penetrate if they would live an integral spiritual life . . .

And so, when I arrived at the rectory of St. Ignatius Loyola for my first instruction, "dogma" seemed like an old friend I'd not yet met, and I was eagerly awaiting an introduction.

Dogma would not be a surprise. What *would* be was learning how much the Church was involved with the world. Had I been searching for "a personal faith" as an escape from MRA, I would have been in for a shock when I realized that I was confronted with what I'd been trying to avoid—"eternal involvement in the lives and destinies of everyone," as I wrote in my journal. I blush when I read that now, but I wanted my MRA friends to know that the Church was not a refuge for ideological dropouts; that a conscientious and committed Catholic could not bury his head in the sand and forget about (as I wrote) "the suffering millions, the third of the world under communist domination, the instability and moral blindness of the West . . ." I wanted them to know that the Church has a world vision, that it was far more than a "personal

religion," that it had been about the business of Restoring All
Things to Christ long before MRA took on the job.

I came into the church at an auspicious time in its history.
In America, in the 50s, there was a kind of Catholic renaissance
going on. Catholic students were discovering the vitality of
Catholicism; they were devouring the works of Chesterton and
Belloc and Evelyn Waugh and Graham Greene, going on monastic
retreats (hoping to meet Merton at Gethsemani), reading *Jubilee*
magazine. Theology was discussed on campuses and at parties.
The genius of St. Thomas Aquinas was being rediscovered, along
with Scholastic Philosophy. There was a rediscovery of the Platonic
and Hellenistic influences on St. Paul, the early Fathers of the
Church, and St. Augustine. Even Protestant theologians were
saying that if Martin Luther were in the Church today, he would
not have left it.

And there was an exciting liturgical revival. Pope Pius X (who
died in 1914 and was canonized in 1954) had said that the liturgy—
the active participation by the faithful in the public and solemn
prayers of the Church—is "the primary and indispensable source
of the true Christian spirit." (His motto was *Instaurare omni
in Christo*—"to restore all things in Christ.") Our Pope, Pius
XII, had the revitalization of the liturgy on his agenda too, as
well as communism—MRA thought he had good ideological
credentials. (How nice it was to say "Our Pope" rather than
"the" pope.)

Above all, the early 50s seemed to usher in the Age of the
Layman. The layman, it was said, had too often been viewed
as a mere appendage to a hierarchical structure; now there were
so many books about "the role of the layman in the Church"
that one literary critic said it was time somebody wrote about
the role of the *priest* in the Church. Pius XII had said that
"The faithful, and more especially the laity, are in the front
lines of the Church; by them the Church is the vital principle
of human society."

In the United States, Catholicism had put down deep roots
and had begun to penetrate the life of the country. It was no
longer a matter of the Catholic, with a minority complex, holding
his own. The missionary era was over, and the Church was taking
every opportunity to let the faithful know that its responsibility
was a moral matter and not one of convenience or inclination—

that all of us, whether in government, education, science, or the arts—had to transcend nationalistic narrowness, partisan or racial commitments, in order to reunite human society. This Pope was reminding Catholics who were bricklayers, garment workers, movie and TV stars, writers and publishers, and employees of the Public Registry of Automobiles of our responsibility, saying things like this (how perfect for my MRA friends):

> It is not permissible to be a deserter ... that is the attitude of one who, either out of contempt or because he is discouraged, does not take part in the affairs of the nation but withdraws from the conflict while the country's fate is at stake. Abstention is to be condemned even if it is a result of indifference. Indifference to ruin into which one's own brothers or people are about to fall is even worse than contempt or discouragement. The just man is a Christian who will not be satisfied with standing idly amid the ruins; he will feel it is his duty to resist and prevent the catastrophe, or at least to lessen its impact. He will be there to rebuild.

In the long experience of the Church—in the centuries of treaties and documents and charters that often were little more than a great waste of paper—she certainly learned what Frank Buchman realized in 1921 when he was on his way to the Washington disarmament conference: you can plan a new world on paper, but you must build it out of men. "What is the use of making blueprints for a new society when the will to build is lacking, when behind the blueprints there lurks the old spirit of selfishness and competition?" No, that was not Frank Buchman—it was the English Dominican priest, Gerald Vann, in his book *The Heart of Man*. Right up MRA's alley, I thought, and wondered if my MRA friends would be surprised that it came from a Catholic priest. Gerald Vann goes on:

> You cannot live for the common good of the nations unless you can see the nations as a single family and will to treat them as a single family; and for that you must have the vision of the oneness of the world, the oneness of the world in God. ... You need the planning and the blueprints of the experts; but they, too, are helpless and will fail not only to put their plans into execution but even to plan aright, unless they have the clear vision of the end for which they ought to plan, the wholeness of the human family, and are supported by the strong will behind them of the people

to see the end realized. And that is where the ordinary man and woman have to help . . ."

It was a basic tenet in Moral Re-Armament that Christianity was (originally) revolutionary. Somehow the Catholic Church was never mentioned in this context—possibly because Catholicism had to do with tradition, and tradition couldn't be revolutionary— just old.

When I read the chapter on "Tradition and Revolution" in *Seeds of Contemplation*, I felt that Thomas Merton was speaking directly to me—to all of us in MRA—when he said: ". . . to those who have no personal experience of this thing, but who see only the outer crust of dead, human conservatism that tends to form around the Church the way barnacles gather on the hull of a ship, all this talk of revolution sounds foolish . . ." I had copied out other parts of that chapter and sent them off to the friends I'd been bombarding with Merton:

> The biggest paradox about the Church is that she is at the same time essentially traditional and essentially revolutionary. But that is not as much of a paradox as it seems, because Christian tradition, unlike all others, is a living and perpetual revolution.
>
> Human traditions all tend towards stagnation and lifelessness and decay. They try to perpetuate things that cannot be perpetuated. They cling to objects and values which time destroys without mercy. They are bound up with a contingent and material order of things— which inevitably change and give way to something else.
>
> The presence of a strong element of human conservatism in the Church should not obscure the fact that Christian tradition, supernatural in its source, is something absolutely opposed to human traditionalism.
>
> For the living tradition of Catholicism is like the breath of a physical body. It renews life by repelling stagnation. It is a constant, quiet, peaceful revolution against death. As the physical act of breathing keeps the spiritual soul united to a material body whose very matter tends always to corrupt and decay, so Catholic Tradition keeps the Church alive under the material and social and human elements which will be encrusted upon it as long as it is the world.
>
> The reason why Catholic tradition is a tradition is because there is only one living doctrine in Christianity: there is nothing new to be discovered. The life of the Church is the life of God Himself,

poured out into the Church by His Spirit, and there cannot be any other life to supersede and replace it . . .

. . . This tradition must always be a revolution because by its very nature it denies the values and standards to which human passion is so powerfully attached. To those who love money and pleasure and reputation and power this tradition says "Be poor, go down into the far end of society, take the last place among men, live with those who are despised, love other men and serve them instead of making them serve you. Do not resist them when they push you around, but pray for those that hurt you. Do not look for pleasure, but turn away from things that satisfy your senses and your mind and look for God in Hunger and thirst and darkness, through deserts of the spirit in which it seems to be madness to travel . . .

This is the most complete revolution that has ever been preached: in fact it is the only true revolution, because all the others demand the extermination of somebody else, but this one means the death of the man who, for all practical purposes, you have come to think of as your own self.

I had read somewhere that faith, in the original Christian sense, was the acceptance by the mind of what had been revealed by God. And it occurred to me that if people think dogma is something negative and ominous, it's because they don't know about revelation—"revealed truth," as Catholics put it. I typed this out in my notebook:

Christianity cannot but be dogmatic. I cannot enter into the idea of any other sort of religion; religion, as a mere sentiment, is to be a dream and a mockery. . . . The Latitudinarian doctrine is this: that every man's view of Revealed Religion is acceptable to God, if he acts up to it; that no one view is in itself better than another, or at least that we cannot tell which is the better. All that we have to do then is to act consistently with what they hold; that to be consistent constitutes sincerity. . . . Now, I can conceive such a view of the subject to be maintainable, supposing God had given us no Revelation . . . (but) Revelation implies a something revealed, and what is revealed is imperative on our faith, *because* it is revealed.

I wondered what MRA would think about *that.* Then I was amazed to find, in a book by Romano Guardini—*The Faith and Modern Man*—in the chapter "Revelation as History" a paragraph that exactly described the MRA concept of revelation:

> It would seem probable that God would speak to us men inwardly, to each one according to his nature. He would bear witness to Himself in the inmost recesses of our being so that each one would be aware that it was God who spoke. . . . He would have to illumine our intellects with His truth so that we could receive complete conviction. He would have to touch our hearts with His life-giving power so that we could learn to love Him; would have to instruct our wills concerning goodness and righteousness so that we could find the way without recourse to any other help. What one would learn in this way would be incommunicable.

And then:

> But, since every man would have been similarly illumined, all would share in the same deep, common understanding. . . . This might have been a possible and beautiful way for revelation to be given, but it was not the way which God chose. There are experiences of this kind; the mystics tell us about them. But the self-revelation of God upon which the salvation of all mankind depends did not come through the mystics, but through the Word . . .

So God revealed His ideas in the person of Christ, the Word made flesh. And people who believe that faith is a matter of deducing things from scripture according to each individual's own lights might be right, had there been *just* scripture; but there was also *tradition*. The word comes from the Latin *traditio*, "action of handing over." Says Webster's: "1. the handing down of information, beliefs, and customs by word of mouth or by example from one generation to another without written instruction." A Catholic dictionary defines tradition as "the sum of revealed doctrine which has not been committed to sacred Scripture . . . but which had been handed down by a series of legitimate shepherds of the Church from age to age. As revelation it must have come to the Apostles directly from the lips of Christ or been handed down by the Apostles at the dictation of the Holy Ghost. More broadly the term is used for the sum of doctrine revealed either in scripture or by word of mouth." (St. Paul said, in 2 Thess. 11, 14: "Hold by the traditions you have learned, in word or in writing, from us.")

AFTER MY INSTRUCTION BOOK had startled me with its calm statement about Christ having founded His Church as directly and immediately as General Booth had founded the Salvation Army (in the chapter "Why Organized Religion?"), it went on to explain how Christ, before He ascended into Heaven, had set up on earth a *visible* organization, with a central authority and properly constituted officials. We had received revelation at a specific time in history, and the Church continues to stand in a real, historical connection with Christ and His Apostles, because of the unbroken series of those Christ had authorized to teach in His name: He wanted the people of each succeeding age to have *certainty*. St. Paul had said that apostles, prophets, evangelists, pastors, and teachers are given us that "we may attain to unity of faith" so as not to be children "tossed to and fro, and carried about by every gale of doctrine." Christ had promised that the Church He founded would last until the end of time. Therefore, said the instruction book, "that visible, organized, Church is in the world today."

History, the book noted, is the study of differences—political, cultural, moral, ethnological, artistic, and geographical. Men have tried for unity of faith and philosophy and government and ethical conduct and political ideals, and so on, but they never achieve it because such unity is not a part of the natural order. Unity is something supernatural. That the Church is not only universal and apostolic but *one* in all matters of faith and morals—that she has existed throughout all the ages and has included all classes and races—that she is the same today as she was "when she set forth into the lanes of Jerusalem on that first Whitsun morning"—surely that is proof that she is more than a "natural" society, and *more* than the sum total of the great variety of saints and sinners who are her members.

WE IN MORAL RE-ARMAMENT knew that unity was not "in nature"—that it was *above* human nature—but we said that human nature could be "changed." We knew Christ had prayed "that all may be one" and that Frank Buchman had often said "Division is the mark of our age . . . unity is the grace of rebirth." (In our hearts, we believed that MRA was the *key* to that rebirth, though of course we wouldn't *say* that.) We did know that MRA was not unique in believing that a new spiritual unity was the only possible foundation for a rebuilding and rebirth of western civilization: Protestants, religious Jews, and Roman Catholics were talking and writing about the need for unity as a force against godless materialism; we thought of them as our allies, as positive forces that could join *us*.

Surely the Catholic Church, in particular, had an obligation to join with "all men of good will" in this time of global crisis, to help forge a unity on a plane above class or race or—no, we never added "creed," but there was a handy substitute: as the then-famous (and oft-quoted by MRA) Admiral Richard E. Byrd said, "MRA is above party, class, or *point of view*" [italics mine]. In 1946, the Admiral had told Frank Buchman that MRA "is America's answer," which inspired Frank to write that "If this is America's answer, then we are in a global effort to win the world to our Lord and Savior, Jesus Christ. Then the great truths of the Gospel will once more become great and Jesus Christ will be King. There is your ideology. It is the whole message of the Gospel. . . . The message in its entirety is the only last hope that will save the world. . . . Go forth with that message united and you will save the world."

In those days, lots of famous people were making statements about MRA being "the old truths with a new emphasis" and that the answer to the world's mess was "Christianity lived out." But did MRA have *all* "the old truths?" And how could Christianity be fully "lived out" if something had been *left* out?

I began to see that the Church, while it had an obligation to encourage all positive forces to unite against the common enemy, had a *higher* obligation, which was to the capital *T* Truth— the *whole* of it. (In a fervid moment, I wrote in my journal: "Absolute loyalty to the truth is the only condition for enduring action—only that could preserve us from the 'deceiving influence' St. Paul wrote about.") Even atheists, I thought, had to admit that the Catholic Church is the oldest continuous government in the world. What was the secret of the mystery of the unity in the Church? In MRA we often read the letters of St. Paul (only the Anglicans among us prefixed the "Saint": to most of us he was just plain Paul, our fellow-revolutionary). We knew that Paul had written a lot about unity: "Membership of the body binds us to one another" and "You are one body, with a single spirit . . ." That was *us*, of course. Or was it? Were we truly members of the Body, with Christ as Head? Or were we in reality members of an ideology with Frank Buchman as head?

That was unthinkable, but I began to think about it, and then I came across a speech Frank Buchman gave back in 1938, when the movement was still known as The Oxford Group. Hundreds (I read) in Sweden had been attracted to the movement but "had not, as yet, fully comprehended its aims and accepted from God the task of saving nations in a time of world danger." It was a challenging address which surely must have separated the sheep from the goats. "If you join in this great crusade," Buchman said, "you will get the way of the Cross. . . . I do not want you to come along just because I am here. . . . It is not I, but Christ. It is not I at the head, but Christ who leads." He wanted that made very clear. But then a few years later—in 1946, on the eve of sailing to Europe—Frank had said: "Great truths have been revealed to us. . . . It [MRA] is a great ideology. It is the full message of Jesus Christ. It is putting the message in a way that the world will understand."

How COULD IT BE the *full* message, though, if it wasn't all there? Had I put this question to friends on the MRA team, I would have got answers such as "But the full message *is* all there, really" and "But MRA isn't a *religion*, you know" or possibly "Well, but you see Frank's thinking has evolved into an *ideology* and that's what is so vitally important now." No fully-indoctrinated MRA trouper would have said that Frank hadn't really meant what he'd said; the Christian (and obviously Protestant) basis of MRA was just not the thing to be emphasized—not in these times of global crisis, when unity was so important.

I knew I would sound ridiculous (and "irrelevant") if I tried to tell my friends in MRA that the full message of the Gospels had to include the sacraments, and that the Eucharist was the unifying principle (we are all part of the one body); that the Mass was "social" as well as personal; that Communion wasn't just a pious remembrance of the Last Supper—it was the real thing, the Body and Blood of Christ. I didn't want to sound like a religious fanatic, and I was certainly not trying to convert anyone, but I did want my friends to know that the Church has a revolutionary agenda—that it had been committed to renewing the face of the earth since the days of the Apostles. My own words, I knew, were inadequate: someone, I thought, should speak to MRA people in terms they could understand and appreciate.

So when a new Thomas Merton book came out—*Bread in the Wilderness*—I thought: now here is language that will have a familiar ring; and I copied out these words and sent them to a few MRA friends:

> Mass and Communion do not make much sense unless we remember that the Eucharist is the great means which God has devised for gathering together and unifying mankind. ... Our life in Christ ... calls for ... a far-seeing and energetic action, based on prayer and interior union with God, which is able to transcend the limitations of class, and nation, and culture, and continue to build a new world upon the ruins of what is always falling into decay.

When the Sacred Congregation of the Holy Office issued another warning to the faithful, in 1955, it became clear that the Church had been watching the movement from its early years. MRA must surely have been aware of this, since it had used every opportunity to accentuate the positive. Catholic laymen (especially politicians and journalists and statesmen) and prelates who were enthusiastic about the Ideology of Moral Re-Armament were featured at world assemblies and their talks were printed and widely circulated. Among the many prestigious Catholics were Konrad Adenauer, Chancellor of West Germany, Robert Schuman, Foreign minister of France, and Karl Adam, Professor of Dogmatic Theology—he was also a priest, and author of *The Spirit of Catholicism.*

It was especially important for MRA to have good relations with the hierarchy in Switzerland, once the international conferences had begun in Caux, the new world headquarters. Bishop Francois Charrière, whose diocese included Lausanne, Geneva and Fribourg, had for a long time been maintaining "an attitude of vigilant caution"—he had not pronounced any definitive condemnation or prohibition, but he was now having certain misgivings, and in an effort to secure concrete safeguards against the perils to which MRA seemed to expose Catholic participants, he appointed (in 1955) a number of theologians to draft, with Peter Howard and other MRA leaders-of-the-work, a "gentlemen's agreement"—a "pact" aimed at eliminating some of the major obstacles that had prevented full Catholic confidence in MRA. (I wondered if MRA's faithful had been shaken by the idea that the leadership was actually considering a *compromise*, but perhaps the lower echelons didn't know about it?) An agreement was drawn up, with eight points. Among them were that MRA would avoid, in its official literature, the use of such Christian terms as "Church" and "Holy Spirit" and "Cross of Christ." Also that Catholics should not come under the moral jurisdiction of non-Catholics (MRA was not to substitute itself for the Church by giving religious instructions). "Quiet Time" and "Sharing" could give no absolute certainty about the will of God—they had a "relative" value and should therefore never be used as a means of pressure to change a decision or a life commitment; MRA should make a commitment not to infringe on the mission of the church—the goal of a Christian transcends all temporal ends, no matter how noble the goal of "remaking the world" might be. And also: that when participating in a world or continental (European) mission, Catholics would never be used as such for propaganda purposes; and in Catholic countries. MRA should never undertake any action without the approval of the local bishop.

Bishop Charrière said he hoped that, if these conditions were exactly followed, the cooperation of Catholics in MRA would develop in an increasingly fruitful way. After a "friendly and frank discussion" Peter Howard and his friends declared themselves ready, insofar as it lay in their power, to see that these eight points were put into effect.

Well, it couldn't have been much of a surprise that the "gentlemen's agreement" didn't work. Before long, there were press reports that MRA had "formally repudiated" the agreement; then it was reported that there had never been such an agreement in the first place. Presumably a source within the movement had informed the press that no person connected with MRA was in a position to have made any such pact, since MRA "is not an organization but an organism and, as such, cannot operate by way of human directive": no such commitment *could* have been made because what had not existed could not have been abrogated.

So all the old objections returned, with new evidence that MRA *was*, despite its insistence to the contrary, either already a religion or "rapidly evolving into one." Even if MRA deleted mention of the Holy Spirit, didn't the "cannot operate by way of human directive" imply some kind of *divine* authority?

So, I wondered, what would happen to Catholics in MRA, now that—as the saying goes—"the Church has spoken"? Since I was by now fairly distanced from MRA, I had no way of knowing whether the Holy Office directive had caused an upheaval— or even if the ordinary Catholic on the team *knew* about it. (The directive had been published in all the Catholic papers, but were those papers read?) And then I realized that I hadn't really known any Catholics *as such*: they were "teammates" who "just happened to be" Catholics. I *had* got to know, to some extent, Nancy Hawthorne—it was she who had put me in touch with Father Clark—but Nancy was almost as new to the Church as she was to MRA, and I thought it possible that her spiritual consciousness had been formed by *both*, so perhaps she would have no conflict about loyalty. The born-Catholics in MRA had been with the movement for a long time, and I imagined their reaction might be: "This too will pass," and "the Church just doesn't fully understand MRA yet."

The Holy Office directive had not prohibited lay Catholics from taking part in MRA, though it did specify that the faithful should not accept "posts of responsibility" in the movement, and that it was "especially not fitting" that they join the "policy team." Well, of course, in something that considers itself an "organism" there are no posts of responsibility and no policy committees: so an MRA Catholic could easily feel that the directive simply didn't apply to him or her. Yet here was another contradiction: if there are (theoretically) no posts of responsibility, and no policy-makers, then (theoretically) *every individual* identified with the movement is responsible. Which is, in fact, what Frank Buchman had always said. We were all in this thing together; we were all equally under the guidance of the Holy Spirit.

I knew there were some priests writing about how Catholics in MRA were *not* in danger of "indifferentism" and I thought some MRA Catholics might indeed be confused—but what it all came down to, I reasoned, was individual conscience, for I had learned that the Church is the guardian and defender of conscience—even an *erroneous* one. I had a Catholic Dictionary in which I read that "The clear voice of conscience, be it true or false, must always be obeyed." Conscience is "the norm of human action." For the Church, the formation of conscience is not arbitrary—it is bound by the objective laws of divine revelation—but the Church wants not merely external but *internal* assent. Even in the case of a lapsed Catholic, for example, though the judgment of his conscience be objectively false, and the working of his conscience not "ethically irreproachable," still he is bound to follow conscience "and it alone." When a person, according to his own genuine and invincible conviction of conscience, cannot give internal assent, the Church sets him free and leaves his conscience to the mercy of God. So therefore no Catholic, priest or lay, has a right to manipulate the conscience of an MRA Catholic. (Whereas, it occurred to me, MRA tended to have a manipulative effect on the consciences of everyone within its orbit.) The Catholic Church, for all its legendary intransigence, is against psychological manipulation of conscience: this, I thought, would probably surprise a lot of people.

I remembered Addie Johnson—an MRA old-timer—who had come to my baptism, and had stood there, beaming, rosary in hand, while I renounced Satan and all his pomps. I knew that her joyful presence helped legitimatize, for my mother and sisters, the step I had taken. I wondered if Addie was now having any problem with "Choose ye this day whom ye will serve" and I thought: probably not . . .

WHEN I BEGAN TO BREATHE the Catholic atmosphere, which was when I began to understand *from inside* the Catholic approach to many things, I began to understand why some Catholics were drawn to MRA while others were almost instinctively suspicious of it. From the early literature, one gets the impression that "the" Catholic reaction was overwhelmingly positive. And evidently it *was*, in the European countries where the threat of communism was real: here was this dynamic (non-sectarian) force through which they could help defeat the enemy. Here was a concrete way to be part of a revolution: here was the vehicle through which the ordinary man could do extra-ordinary things. It seemed that MRA was galvanizing Catholic youth in a way the Church *wasn't*. And "challenging" them, too. Karl Adam had said, at Caux, that "We Catholics . . . are at a moment of decision and of most serious reflection. For we must realize that the materialism of the East would never have found its way into the arteries of men and of whole nations if we Catholics had been sufficiently aware of our responsibilities." (His *Spirit of Catholicism*, published in 1932, was considered such a classic that it had recently been re-issued as a Doubleday *Image Book*, and I had read it.) He did mention, in his talk and article which appeared in a paper "of the Catholic party" in Lucerne, Switzerland, in 1952, "the religious subjectivism of Caux" but "behind" that there was "the most objective thing that exists on earth—the Christian revelation, the Christian doctrine, the Christian church." It was the Christian ideology, he wrote, that gives Moral Re-Armament "its great impact and its fighting force." He seemed almost to envision MRA as a great help to the Church, rather than the other way around, but since he said and wrote such good things he got maximum coverage. He spoke of MRA as "a Christian community" and said "The hour strikes in which all Christian communities in the face of the Russian danger stretch out the hand to each other and unite, if not in a union of faith yet in a union of love, for courageous defence against the barbarism of the East."

At this time there were a number of MRA plays on tour; one was given in the monastery schools of central Switzerland, and *Vaterland*, the leading Swiss Catholic newspaper, ran the headline: "Catholic Colleges Hail MRA Play." One rector was quoted as saying "We can all subscribe to the principles of MRA. To recognize absolutely the dominion of God, or to bow down under the domination of human tyrants, that is the alternative which should unite us all, whether we are Catholics, Christians, or non-Christians." Another college rector said: "Because you live what you believe, we can whole-heartedly accept this ideology."

Of course MRA had always welcomed Catholics, and now that *I* was one, I could understand why they felt "at home" at first. They would hear references to the saints (especially St. Francis of Assisi and Joan of Arc and Ignatius Loyola) and the apostles (especially Peter and Paul) and they would hear the familiar words such as God, Christ, the Holy Spirit. There would be fish on Fridays in the team centers, and transportation to the local church on Sundays and Holy Days. They would hear about the famous Catholic prelates and theologians and statesmen who had endorsed MRA, and they would be impressed by stories of French factory workers and British dock workers and Italian communists who, through MRA, had returned to the sacraments.

Catholics, like everyone else, would be swept off their feet by the dynamic plays and musicals and films. They would feel that this was a wonderful lay apostolate.

But after a while, some might begin to feel not quite so much at home. They would sense something alien in the atmosphere. Who *were* these people, they might wonder, who were so omniscient about things of the spirit—as if *they* had been entrusted with the whole deposit of the Faith as it was handed down from the Apostles? If Catholics began to ask specific questions, they would feel they just couldn't "get through." Which of course they couldn't, because theology was dangerous ground: it was not MRA's job to define doctrine, so enquirers would be cleverly diverted from objectivity. The thing was to answer a person's *needs*, not his questions. Should a young Catholic persist in seeking direct answers to direct questions, he would be made to feel he was just another "intellectual with a moral problem" whose theological questioning was really an attempt to avoid living the Four Standards. He would not be asked "When did you last go to Mass?" but "What has God been telling you, in your Quiet Times?"

Indeed, guilt is a great weapon.

IT IS SAID THAT there are no rules in Moral Re-Armament, but if you didn't begin each day with a quiet time—listening to God and writing down His thoughts for you as well as for the world— then you simply weren't a part of "the family." You hadn't really changed yet. If a Catholic had a serious reservation about the quiet time, he would be told that it was simply a form of meditation—and surely all good Catholics believe in meditation, and make time for it? (Guilt again, and a challenge.) But a closer look might lead him to suspect that there was more methodology than theology involved in meditation as quiet time, and that what theology *was* involved was in the Protestant tradition. Frank Buchman had said: "Divine guidance must become the normal experience of ordinary men and women. . . . Any man can pick up divine messages if he will put his receiving set in order." That was meditation, in a way. But Frank mentioned *rules* too: "Anyone can hear the words of the Lord. It is only necessary to obey the rules." The first rule is "that we listen honestly for everything that may come—and if we are wise we write it down."

(The writing-down part sounded more like recording prophecy than having meditation.) The second rule is "that we test the thoughts that come, to see which are from God." One test is the Bible, which is "steeped in the experience through the centuries of men who have dared, under Divine revelation, to live experimentally with God. There, culminating in the life of Jesus Christ, we find the highest moral and spiritual challenge—complete honesty, purity, unselfishness and love" (i.e., the Four Standards). Another "excellent test" is: "What do others say who also listen to God?" (That's where "sharing" comes in.) To listen to others who listen to God is "an unwritten law of fellowship" and "an acid test of one's commitment to God's plan." (Catholics wouldn't like the word "fellowship" and they might wonder about living "experimentally" with God.) Frank said: "When man listens, God speaks. When man obeys, God acts. . . . This is a daily possibility for everyone—to listen to God and get his program for the day." However, "No one can be wholly God-controlled who works alone" and "It is through God-controlled people that God must one day govern the world."

But who, the Catholic might well ask, *are* these "God-controlled people" of Buchman's vision? Was there more here than met the eye? Wasn't there more than an "organism" behind something that had produced such astonishing results and had achieved international fame? If there are no "posts of responsibility," how does the thing *work*? (And where *does* the money come from?)

If the enquiring Catholic dug back into Frank Buchman's early speeches, where he would read that MRA was "a direct production of the Holy Spirit," wouldn't he think that that implied a *religious* character? That there were, in fact, some definite doctrines, which were no less real because they were undefined? And doesn't anything that calls itself a "spiritual movement" (and "God's plan for the twentieth century") have to be based on some *kind* of spirituality?

It might be explained to the enquiring Catholic that whereas the Oxford Group did have a Protestant origin, it had evolved into an overarching ideology through which people of all faiths, or of none, could unite to defeat Godless militant communism. Was there a hint here of religious indifferentism? If the movement was "indifferent" about religions (which it *had* to be), wouldn't a Catholic, living in that atmosphere, be tainted by it?

Of course I didn't know whether any full-time MRA Catholic

had taken the Holy Office directive seriously—to the extent of seeking a spiritual director—but I felt sure that MRA, far from standing in the way, would encourage this, since it would show that its Catholics were not subjected to the spiritual guidance and moral jurisdiction of non-Catholics. But if there had been any lingering doubt in my mind about MRA's inherent assumption of infallibility in interpreting the Holy Spirit's directives, those doubts would have been dispelled that night in Rockefeller Center when I was subjected to the suggestion that I go to the MRA center at Mackinac to have guidance, "with some friends," about becoming a Catholic. I didn't know whether this was team strategy— to get me back into "the MRA family"—or whether it was a last-ditch effort on the part of my *own* family to save me from the clutches of the Catholic Church. Probably the latter, I thought: the team had left me pretty much alone. In either case, it was clear to me that what my mother and sisters and their teammates were incapable of understanding was that even if I didn't *want* to become a Catholic, I would *have* to, because I had learned the facts and was convinced that Catholicism was capital-T Truth; and that Truth had a claim on me.

I WONDER IF Frank Buchman hadn't unwittingly let his movement in for future charges of religious indifferentism and syncretism back in 1933, when he explained (in a letter to an English Jesuit) that for non-believers who had come to an experience of God through the Oxford Group, "Our whole policy is to let each individual decide to *what church he is guided to go*" [Italics mine]. That seemed to indicate that *belief* was a matter of "guided choice." I had no doubt that I had been guided to the Church: but that is very different from "having guidance to become a Catholic." The former has to do with the grace of God; the latter, with the team's current priorities.

I remember how often the team used the word "right," as in "We are wondering if this [idea, or decision, or inclination] is "right" for you, just now?" Which meant: "Is it right for Moral Re-Armament at this time?" Right was not the opposite of wrong; it was a synonym for "relevant." "Right" had to do with timing, not truth. If something wasn't "right" now, it *might* be, later, if it was seen to be ideologically expedient. And this of course was the secret of unity in the movement. Every individual decision affected the whole of the "organism." If a full-timer had notions of doing something on his own, without clearance, he would be reminded of what Frank had said about how no one can be fully guided if he acts alone.

While I was still taking instructions, I had some contact with an MRA full-timer who said that she, too, was attracted to Catholicism, but she felt it just wasn't the right time, yet. Whether or not her attraction had got to the point of having guidance about it, I don't know—I didn't know her that well. But I could understand her position—that if you were fully committed to a superior ideology, then a superior spiritual obligation would be totally foreign to your comprehension. One's individual spirituality was subject to the dictates of the Holy Spirit as interpreted by the mystical body of Moral Re-Armament.

FRANK BUCHMAN NEVER CLAIMED to be a prophet or a saint, but he drew inspiration from both; and at times he had said things which led unkind critics (who no doubt had moral problems) to accuse him of messianic assumptions. They could have used, as an example, this (from a speech in 1938): "What is the particular genius of presenting truth that has made the Oxford Group so effective in so many countries? . . . The odds are seemingly against us, but just as individuals are delivered from their prison cells of doubt and defeat, so it is possible for nations to be delivered from their prison cells of fear, resentment, jealously and depression, and oftentimes through one illumined man, one masterful prophet. How often this has been true in history!" Or they might have used this, from 1939: "Moral Re-Armament is recapturing, re-vitalising, re-living the message of the prophets. It is tried. It is true. It is tested." All mean-spirited critics aside, what is undeniable is that Frank Buchman did indeed seem to feel that he had been especially commissioned by God to spearhead a new spiritual revolution for the twentieth century, and that this new revolution was God's last hope for the world.

Saint Benedict

. . . and Nuns of the Above

IT SEEMS THAT EACH AGE has its saints and its prophets. And in every age the one thing all the wonderful variety of saints had in common (besides their sanctity) was this: they did not analyze themselves. Someone famous (I don't remember who, but I have this written down) once said: "He who interprets himself sinks beneath his own level." Down through the ages the prophet and the saint have said startling things, but one thing they did not say was: "I am a prophet and a saint."

Saints did not ordinarily have a Program, or a Project: they merely surrendered themselves to their destiny, which was usually beyond their comprehension.

Saints have sprung from unlikely places. They have come from all ranks of society—there have been gentlemen saints and soldier saints; saints in robes and saints in rags. There have been statesmen saints (some of whom lost their heads), saints of gigantic intellect, and saints who were illiterate. There have been saints who travelled widely, having romantic and chivalrous adventures (which often ended in martyrdom) and saints who never went anywhere; there are saints who had been great sinners and saints who had never done anything very bad at all.

They have been born in a variety of circumstances: creatures of their environment, like everyone else, but somehow managing to transcend their natural limitations and the restrictions and conventions of class and culture and time. Saints go in and out of fashion. Some were suspected of sanctity in their own lifetimes, and revered; others were reviled because to their contemporaries they were unintelligible or even repellent. G.K. Chesterton, in

211

his book about St. Thomas Aquinas, *The Dumb Ox*, wrote:

> The saint is a medicine. Sometimes he is mistaken for a poison
> because he is an antidote: he will generally be found restoring
> the world to sanity by exaggerating whatever the world in his
> time is neglecting. Each generation is converted by the saint who
> contradicts it most.

They were non-conformists, the saints, because they were busy
conforming themselves to Christ and in that way reconciling
the world to Him. Quietly, not calculating their effects on society
and not measuring their progress, because they knew that their
own sanctity was a matter of grace rather than a promethean
human effort. The saints went on sowing the seeds of the greatest
revolution the world has ever known, against which all the forms
of tyranny look like counter-revolutions. They knew they were
already living in the new world; that the history of the Kingdom
of Christ was working itself out, but was hidden from "the wise
of this world" in the mystery of faith: they knew that the final
day of its manifestation is reserved for the future, for the end
of time, when Christ will come this time in majesty and power.

The saints had the answer to their age: and their answer was
first of all their own existence. Man is a creature prisoned in
time but made for eternity, and therefore usually a confusion
between being and purpose: in saints, being and purpose are
the same. Saints are at the disposal of the Holy Spirit—not like
speaking tubes, as were the prophets of the old dispensation,
but as an existence.

Some of them indeed had a peculiar existence, like St. Simon
Stylites who sat on top of a pole, and St. Philip Neri who—
in order to divert attention from his visions and ecstasies and
all the mystical phenomena which embarrassed him—acted like
a clown and became renowned in the sixteenth century as a humorist.
Some were almost scandalously notorious, like Catherine of Siena
who hardly knew how to read or write but was involved in the
politics of thirteenth-century Italy and bossed around clergy and
popes, and kept secretaries working day and night: "illiterate"
St. Catherine left four hundred letters and a book, and history
has placed her beside Boccaccio as the most notable Italian writer
of her day.

There was the cheerful little barefoot beggar of Assisi, singing
about his Lady Poverty in an age when people shuddered at

the idea of poverty. And there was one of the most obscure saints, Thérèse of Lisieux, hidden from the world in a Carmelite monastery. She wanted only to become little and helpless, but within a decade after her death at twenty-four, her sanctity was no longer a secret: she was famous to the ends of Europe. Even in America, she— who was at first thought of as a kind of pastel "saint of the itsy-bitsy"—came to tower over the more "heroic" saints. Through her hidden microscopic acts of charity, her "little way of the Cross," she has shown the way to sanctity for the humblest, least-gifted person. Although she never left her monastery, she was universally chosen as Patroness of missions; she is also co-Patron of France, for it is perceived that in her hidden acts of self-denial and charity she was as heroic as St. Joan of Arc.

There were the Ancients: St. Anthony, for one, who succeeded in keeping his sanctity hidden for awhile, but soon the mobs were rushing into the desert and beating a path to his cave. And there was St. Benedict, in the sixth century: more about him, later.

In these saints and in many more whose existences could not be summarized even in all the 2,565 entries in the volumes of Butler's *Lives of the Saints*, there is a balance and a sanity and a reckless kind of humility and detachment that mark the difference between saints and fanatics. Saints allow themselves to be used by the Holy Spirit; religious fanatics try to *use* the Holy Spirit, claiming a direct line with Him and setting about interpreting His message to the world.

CATHOLICS IN PARTICULAR are suspicious of people who talk with intimacy about the Holy Spirit, who try to comprehend all dimensions at once, looking through God's eyes, evaluating and analyzing and consciously "making history." Long ago St. Paul warned the flock about false prophets; Catholics hearing authoritative statements about God's will tend to ask: "What is your authority? Where are your credentials?" When they hear statements like "God means to bring renaissance into the world *now*" and "God has chosen Mackinac" (or Caux, or Dellwood) "as the spot in the whole world to manifest His glorious plan for mankind" they may ask: What makes you so sure?

Many saints have had visions and revelations (St. Joan and her voices); children claim to have seen and heard the Virgin

Mary (Fatima, La Sallette, Lourdes) and all of these things are subjected to rigorous tests to establish whether they *may* be a part of Catholic belief and devotion: it is up to the individual Catholic how much attention he wants to pay to these miracles. The point is: it's *okay* to believe these things really happened. When the proofs have been established, and the messages have been translated into all languages, St. Paul's words still hold true: "Friends, though it were we ourselves, though it were an angel from heaven that should preach to you a gospel other than the gospel we preached to you, a curse upon him!" For the real prophet's job was over when Christ was born, and since the death of the last Apostle, when the full body of revelation was complete, God has shown different ways to speak to men. He may speak to a special nation at a special time through one of His saints. But even then the saint is only stressing something already revealed and perhaps forgotten; anything else the saint may say must be taken seriously but cannot be accepted *infallibly* as God's words.

If you look back to the long list of post-apostolic (and official) saints, to find out what predictions have come true, you will find not prophecies but lives; because it is the saints' *presence* that is prophetic. As the saint lived his daily life, he may have felt that he was somehow part of God's overall plan; but he knew that it was not up to him to interpret or even to understand this plan. It was not his business to know the meaning of his life.

The world is fond of discovering new mystics, who are not really mystics because if they *were*, they would have a hard time being discovered: least of all would they discover themselves to the world. The true mystics warned about visions and ecstasies and any kind of "sensible" feeling of devotion, for—they say— these things may be illusions or even tricks of the Devil. One of the greatest (and most balanced and sane) of the mystics, St. John of the Cross, wrote about the danger of ascribing to the spectacular experiences of the mystics and about not making contemplative prayer a matter of publicity.

And so when people speak intimately, or publicly from the platforms of Moral Re-Armament, about what God told them and how God is using them, they are liable to send Catholics gathering up, like skirts, the advice of St. John, and running in the other direction. And when these people predict God's actions in the world, and interpret their existence and their mission, Catholics are likely to be afflicted with instinctive suspicions: for deep in the collective Catholic consciousness are the words of St. Paul: "Stand firm . . . and hold by the traditions you have learned in word or in writing from us."

Yet this is no excuse, for those who are running in the other direction, to run away from sanctity, which is the normal vocation of every Christian: it is the Christian ideal, as the Perfect Man, the Hero, was the ideal of the Greeks, and as the Knight was the ideal of the Middle Ages.

I remember Father Clark saying, during instruction, that the saint—basically—is the successful Christian; saints are friends of God, and the ordinary Christian can become a saint by leading an ordinary life in a supernatural manner. (And I remember how we in MRA always talked about "the ordinary man doing the extraordinary thing.") But sanctification doesn't necessarily come through ferocious activity or athletic feats of asceticism— it comes more often through obscurity, by usual skills and common tasks and routine. Of course you could become an official saint through martyrdom, if it could be proved that you had indeed died for Christ and had done so willingly; but there were plenty of ways you could "die for Christ" in the course of a very ordinary day, while continuing to be a whole and healthy Christian. (I was interested to learn that "holy" comes from an Anglo-Saxon word, "halig," which means just that—whole and healthy.) Being a saint means saving your soul, which sounds selfish and easy; but it isn't easy and it's not a private thing, either, because of that mysterious, imperceptible but definite interrelation between your own life and the lives of many others you know and do not know. If you are a friend of God, you will inevitably make other friends for God—just by *being*.

My concept of saints (or angels: I never quite knew the distinction) had always been more Christmas-card than theological. But I began to grasp what sanctity was all about when I was reading *The Seven Storey Mountain*, and got to 1939, the year of the Second World War. "By this time," Merton wrote, "I should have acquired enough sense to realize that the cause of wars is sin." (That was something Frank Buchman had certainly realized, and said often enough.) Merton goes on: "If I had accepted the gift of sanctity that had been put in my hands when I stood by the font in November 1938, what might have happened in the world? People have no idea what one saint can do: for sanctity is stronger than the whole of hell. The saints are full of Christ . . . and they are conscious of it, and they give themselves to Him, that He may exercise His power through their smallest and seemingly most insignificant acts, for the salvation of the world."

WHEN I WAS CONFIRMED, in the spring of 1955, I was once again (as at my First Communion) one of just a few adults in a church full of children. The boys and girls were all dressed in red (for the Holy Spirit) gowns and we adults were not, but we all had our saint's name written on little slips of paper. Our sponsors would give these to the presiding bishop, who would pronounce our saint's name as he slapped us (gently) on the cheek and reminded us that we were now soldiers of Christ.

In every Confirmation Class, there are many Johns and Joans, Patricks and Teresas, Marys and Elizabeths. I chose Benedict. I thought that St. Benedict had had a great deal to do with bringing me to the Church, and would have a great deal to do with my being the right sort of Catholic; and so I put myself in his care.

In July of that year I wrote Father Clark a long letter. I wanted him to know my reasons for choosing Benedict as my patron saint, and that I felt my affinity for the liturgical life was, in some mysterious way, the key to my integration both personally and "as a part of the social unit." I went into some detail about what had led me to this realization, and then I asked him for advice: "What do I *do* with all this?" I had no passion to rush into the Lay Apostolate, to join one or another Catholic organization, though of course I had to be *willing* to. "But," I asked, "if there is a particular place for one with a love for the liturgical life in all its manifestations, I'd like to know about it." (And I made it clear that I felt no "call" to a religious vocation.) I told him I didn't expect him to answer immediately with a list of ideas, names and addresses—I doubted if there *were* any—but I wanted him at least to know "the bent of my mind."

In just a few weeks, I got a reply to my letter:

I was more than delighted to hear from you and to read all that you managed to squeeze into that letter. It is a very valuable gift to be able to discern the direction of one's own thought and

to see beneath them the disposition that inclines us in one direction
rather than in another. Once you have decided that there really
isn't anything quite as valuable and real as closeness to God,
one has the less pressing but more complicated decision (or is
it an evolution) to consider what will lead you along the path
that, somewhere, God has designed for each one. Even putting
it in those words makes it seem more shaped and definitive than
it really is. And who will ever tell us—beyond our sense of "fitting"—
that we are _surely_ in the right groove? No one. We just follow
our best inclination, knowing that our temperaments and inclinations
ought to be used and not fought, trusting very practically and
fully that God, in His love and in our trust, will never lead us
down an unprofitable and dead road. He just doesn't.

You made a very keen observation I think when you wrote of
your thoughts in the kitchen and the genuine satisfaction you
felt there as a problem in identification, mainly. It ought to underline
how very gently God leads us; and how much sounder and safer
evolution in thought is than sudden leaps and sensational decisions.

In Benedict you found the right name and in your thoughts, if
I may say so, I think you are on the path to the richest and most
serene juncture with God that Christianity has found. The combination
of deep liturgical worship (such a joy in itself!) and simple devotion
to the work at hand, intellectual and manual, allowed St. Benedict
and those who developed his rule to produce a mind (and way
of life) that can develop, at once, a tremendous elevation and
refinement of spirit and a balance of mind that comes from staying
close to reality and human beings and common sense. For someone
of your gifts and temperament, the Benedictine way of life could,
under God, lead you to the happiness of being close to Him for
the rest of your life.

And you must not neglect what a need there is among so many
people today for the Benedictine way. If it appealed first to Christians
weary of barbarism and terror, I think today it has an enormous
appeal to the Christians who are weary of the inane and neurotic.
Benedictine beauty and sanity ought to seem like a great protection
on the road to God in the twentieth century. I mention this because
I know that some of the very finest people in my acquaintance
are devoted to that ideal personally and socially.

I should like to recommend to you the Benedictine Oblates. Whether
or not you care to link yourself to them in their very praiseworthy
group, I should like very much to introduce you to a few of them.
They are all lay people . . . solidly devoted to the liturgy, living

it as fully as circumstances allow. I think you may find them stimulating to your own thinking and possibly find in them the companions of thought that everyone really ought to have, in some form, for the long haul. And besides, they are very nice and kind people . . .

These people are, incidentally, very interested in the Benedictine foundation (ladies) at Bethlehem, Connecticut. I am sure you would enjoy a visit there sometime when the humidity drops . . .

So of course I followed up on this, and Father Clark arranged for me to meet one of these Oblates, and I was invited to go with the Oblate group the next time they went to the Monastery of Regina Laudis. And of course I *did*.

In his Holy Rule, St. Benedict wrote: "Let all guests be received as Christ." We were certainly received graciously—almost as members of the Benedictine family. Our meals were served on the ground floor of St. Joseph's, an old factory building that had been turned into the men's guest house. At my first meal with the New York Oblates, I was seated next to Father Jerome d'Souza, an Indian Jesuit who was currently stationed at the United Nations. He seemed about eight feet tall, and he regaled us with an explanation of the Indian Rope Trick. The nuns who served us were cheerful and glowing with health; they enjoyed our conversations, too. I learned that they were "extern oblates," which meant that they were not strictly cloistered and could do "outside" things. The cloistered "choir nuns" were separated from us, in the chapel and in the "parlors," by the prescribed "grille" which was actually just a wooden lattice that didn't seem at all like a barrier.

I realized almost at once that this monastery of Benedictine nuns was a magnet, drawing people from all over and from all walks of life. The men-guests slept in "cells" upstairs at St. Joseph's: the women were comfortably put up at "St. Gregory's," a 200-year-old house with wooden ceiling beams. Every bedroom had a saint's name, and there were "PAX" signs everywhere (*pax*, Latin for *peace*, is the Benedictine motto). "Pax, St. Gregory" announced the bath mat in the second floor bathroom: "Pax, clean linen" (hand-lettered in monastic script) was on one cupboard; on another there was "Pax, dirty linen."

I sat with some of the other guests on the sunny front lawn of St. Gregory's. There had been a serious drought in Connecticut, and people from all over the state had written to the nuns, asking them please to pray for rain. But I took a secret delight in the sun which smiled down on the wide expanse of hilly meadows, woodlands, country roads, and the small pond where in the evenings vociferous bullfrogs would offer their dissonant supplications. In the afternoons, everything was very still; the songbirds, the drone of locusts and the occasional rumble of a tractor, the trees with branches moving in the wind seemed to blend together in a great peace.

It seemed that on these acres, human beings had settled in to live with God's creatures in a mutual understanding of why they were all on earth together. "That in all things God may be glorified"—that Benedictine phrase was reflected from every corner of the barn-red New England monastery buildings, the guest houses, the Little Art Shop up on the hill by the large parking lot. There was a balance and harmony, an order and rhythm in all created things that are true to their nature. I remembered Merton's sentence: "A tree gives glory to God by being a tree." The trees here were certainly giving glory to God.

As I sat under the glorifying trees on St. Gregory's lawn, I thought about the contemplative life: about the nuns up the road in the monastery kitchen, in the chapel, and on the farm. I thought about all the books that had been coming from the silent Trappists and Carmelites and Poor Clares and even the hermit Carthusians, who had their first American foundation in Vermont. Everyone seems a little astonished by the way Americans are reading these books. Europeans have long been familiar with monasticism, at least as a part of their culture and history: most Americans are not, but some are beginning to wonder if the contemplative life might not have something to offer in the way of *wholeness*— for individuals and for the nation.

Yet there are Catholics who do not see why intelligent and gifted sons and daughters are justified in disappearing behind enclosure walls. They simply don't comprehend that, for instance, a scholarly head of the departments of psychiatry and psychology at a large university, who had a medical degree from Johns Hopkins and had been a Paulist priest *and* a Benedictine, had—at the age of seventy—"disappeared" into the new Carthusian hermitage in Vermont. Surely all these people who have degrees and training are needed in the world, where there is so much to be *done*?

I have read that today "when there is so much to be done" the world is witnessing the greatest contemplative revival since the Middle Ages. And it seems that Americans who are reading the books of these silent ones are beginning to grasp that they "left the world" not because they hate it but because they love it. These books do not say much about what contemplatives are accomplishing: that's best left to God, and to outside observers. And sometimes outside observers who are members of the active and visible clergy manage to evaluate the contemplative life with a perception surprising even to the contemplative himself: Bishop Fulton Sheen was one of these.

I REMEMBER HOW we in Moral Re-Armament admired Bishop Sheen. Whenever possible, we would watch his popular weekly television program; we read and studied and discussed his book *Communism and the Conscience of the West*; we respected him because he was, we said, "ideologically straight." He was dynamic and revolutionary and "on fire for a new world." You could see it in his eyes, we said. Surely Bishop Sheen understood the need for practical action to save civilization? Here is what he wrote (in his 1949 book *Peace of Soul*) about contemplatives:

> Why are there monasteries and convents? Why do so many young souls leave the lights and glamour of the world for the shades and shadows of the Cross where saints are made? . . . These hidden dynamos of prayer, the cloistered men and women, are doing more for our country than all its politicians, its labor leaders, its army and navy put together; they are atoning from the sins of us all. They are averting the just wrath of God, repairing the broken fences of those who sin and pray not, rebel and atone not. As ten just men could have saved Sodom and Gomorrah, so ten just saints can save a nation now. But so long as a citizenry is more impressed by what its cabinet does than by its chosen souls who are doing penance, the rebirth of the nation has not yet begun. The cloistered are the purest of patriots. They have not become less interested in the world since leaving it; indeed, they have become more interested in the world than ever before. But they are not concerned with whether it will buy and sell more; they care—and desperately care—whether it will be more virtuous and love God more.

Americans are an active lot. We like to know we are accomplishing something. We like to see results. In times of war we have surprised the world by our eagerness to tackle the enemy on every front; in times of peace we organize charity and welcome refugees and immerse ourselves in Good Works. We hope to see the fruits of our activities reflected in the appreciation of others. It is almost as if we are afraid to be silent—as if we cannot really be sure we exist unless we see our "good works" producing tangible results. We do not think it is much fun to work for something that does not guarantee satisfaction. Americans like proof—with figures, and statistics. Who could make a mathematical survey about how many prayer-hours are required of monks and nuns to stay God's wrath and keep Him from wiping us all off the face of the earth? Bishop Sheen wrote:

> There is no mathematical equality—no tit for tat—in the work of redemption. Ten just men could have saved Sodom and Gomorrah. In the Divine reckoning, it is Carmelite nuns and Trappist monks who are doing more to save the world than the politicians and the generals. The alien spirit which preempts civilization can be driven out only by prayers and fasting.

Here is a pithy definition of prayer: it is the highest activity of the soul, for it is the concentration of the highest faculties of the soul, the mind and the will, on its greatest object, which is God.

There was a popular writer and speaker who preceded Bishop Sheen by a good many years: he was not a bishop or even a Catholic, and he had a reputation as an intellectual agitator; but he thought there was something sensible about prayer. He was George Bernard Shaw. Somehow he had become a good friend of Dame Laurentia, the superior of a Benedictine abbey in England, and to one of his many letters to her (October 25, 1931) he added this P.S.:

> I don't mind being prayed for. When I play with my wireless set I realize that all the sounds in the world are in my room; for I catch them as I alter the wave-length receiver—German, French, Italian and unknown tongues. The ether is full of prayers too; and I suppose that if I were God I could tune in to them all. Nobody can tell what influence these prayers have. If the ether is full of impulses of good will to me so much the better

for me: it would be shockingly unscientific to doubt it. So let
the sisters give me all the prayers they can spare; and don't forget
me in yours.

There are those in the Church who grudgingly accept the *fact*
of the contemplative orders, because after all the contemplatives
are at least *Catholics*. They see the importance of nuns who
teach and who nurse; they understand the mission of monks and
nuns who go off into jungles. But they see the contemplative
life as a waste. It was perhaps for these "actives" among the
faithful that St. John of the Cross wrote:

> Let those that are great actives and think to girdle the world
> with their outward works take note that they would bring far
> more profit to the Church and be far more pleasing to God if
> they spent even half this time in abiding with God in prayer. . . . Of
> a surety they would accomplish more with one piece of work
> than they now do with a thousand and that with far less labor.
> (*Spiritual Canticle*, xxxix 3.)

Yet St. John, and his contemporary St. Teresa of Avila, who
are considered the greatest mystics of their time, were also extremely
active in laboring for the reform of the Carmelite Order. St.
John was not saying that we should all go off into monasteries
or repudiate the active life: just that if our minds and wills are
perfectly united and absorbed in God, we will be free of the
activities that are prompted by our tastes and ideas, and God
will use us as instruments of His love; to communicate His love
to other men—the great work of His love which (I read in a
little booklet by Thomas Merton) "is designed to overthrow the
powers of the world in the moment of their seeming triumph."

IF YOU ARE A CONVERT to Catholicism, you have probably got
used to questions about what you were before, and what brought
you to the Church. The impossible question sometimes asked
by fellow-Catholics is: When and where did your conversion
begin? Since conversion is a process, an awareness that leads
to affirmation, only God knows the answer. For all I know, He
may have planted the first seeds in my unconscious when I was
five and went with my friend Jeannie Noto to light a candle
in her Catholic church. God is outside time and place, but He

operates within both; so the best you can do to answer the "beginning" question is to make a stab at it—to try to remember a time and a place when and where you became conscious of something like a new dimension in which all your ragged parts would be gathered together into a wholeness.

If I could pinpoint a time when and where this consciousness happened to me, I would say it was in the spring of 1953, at Dellwood in Mount Kisco, during what turned out to be the last months of my full-time work in MRA. I was spending most of my time in the kitchen there, in MRA's Eastern headquarters, and I became aware of something I couldn't identify until later, when I began reading about contemplation.

At that time there were not many of us cooks, but lots of hungry people. There was a scarcity of men, too: some of the few guys were busy with pigs and cows on Dellwood's farm and some, dressed in business suits, commuted daily to the New York office where they were busy getting people on planes to Mackinac or Caux and visiting important delegates at the United Nations. So we women who cooked the meals at Dellwood also had to wash the pots and pans afterwards. Very *large* pots and pans.

For some reason, I rather enjoyed the physically demanding job of scrubbing five-gallon soup pots and greasy black roasting pans in the two deep sinks. And for some reason, I no longer had guilt-feelings about my lack of desire to be "on the front line." I was no longer trying to prove even to myself that I was a "born revolutionary" and I wasn't even trying to *feel* like one. Nor did I feel I was "hiding" in the kitchen—if God dictated that I should go out and establish contacts with significant people and speak in meetings, I could probably manage to do these things; but God seemed to want me in the kitchen, and that was fine with me.

The kitchen had, after all, been my novitiate when I went full time with MRA at seventeen. My fellow high-school graduates had gone off to colleges and universities to improve their minds (and their social lives) and eventually to acquire degrees: I had gone to Los Angeles for intensified training in Moral Re-Armament, in which the only "degree" that mattered was the degree of commitment to the revolution. We were often reminded that a revolution demands blood, sweat, and tears. In the kitchen, it often *did*: literally, not metaphorically. We sweat over the hot stoves, we cut our fingers and bled profusely, and we shed tears—not just over the onion-peeling but also over our small sins of self-will which, if unchecked, would cause small errors in formulas and timing, which would in turn result in large problems—deflated cheese souffles or curdled custard sauce or four gallons of gravy when all you needed was one. (My sin was that I tended to put too much salt in sauces and too much vinegar in salad dressings: I was thinking of *myself*, not "the family.")

Even in my first days in the kitchen at the Los Angeles headquarters, I could see how the kitchen was a workshop for "Inspired Democracy." It was a proving-ground, in a very real and practical way, for MRA's theories about remaking the world. We of the kitchen stated publicly, to assembled dignitaries, that "If democracy can work in the kitchen, it can work anywhere." Meaning that if a lot of *women* from different backgrounds and classes and nationalities (and even differing "degrees of commitment") could work together to produce a meal, why, there you have a blueprint for world unity. If you couldn't make democracy work on your cook shift, then our whole ideology was shot. So we always made sure that democracy worked in the kitchen and actually it *had* to, because—unlike some of the other MRA teams—we always had a *deadline*. In a sense we were like journalists: meals, like newspapers, had to be *out* at a specific time. You couldn't sit around having guidance about when to put on the water for the potatoes or when roasts should go into the ovens.

So the kitchen was, every day, the proving-ground of our whole philosophy. And it was in the kitchen that you learned the importance of working with your hands—something we said Society needed to rediscover the dignity *of*—and it was there that you learned about the standard of perfection: the food had to look and taste absolutely right; everything had to be "up to MRA standards." The kitchen was a microcosm of the new world.

There was all that heavy ideological significance, but there was also a *social* ambience about the MRA kitchen (and the kitchen is the very heart of every MRA center). People working *in* it or just walking through and chatting for a while, as they helped themselves to warmed-over coffee or brewed-fresh tea, seemed able to relax and take a few minutes' respite from the intensity of changing the world. It seemed that revolutionaries were the most *human* when they dropped by the kitchen.

One of the more "devotional" books we in MRA were encouraged to read was Brother Lawrence's little book of letters: *The Practice of the Presence of God.* He was a 17th century lay brother who spent much time among the pots and pans of his monastery in Paris, and he had a lot of good things to say about what all that had to do with serving God. And at Dellwood a lot of us were reading Henry Morton Robinson's best-selling novel, *The Cardinal,* in which there was one phrase we cooks all loved, about Brother Alphonsus in the kitchen who went about his duties "with great inner serenity and much exterior banging." There was plenty of banging in our kitchens, but there was an inner serenity, too, which probably came from a sense of security in knowing *precisely* what our job demanded. There was always the temptation to put our security in "knowing how to do a job" and therefore the kitchen could be "an escape" from the other things in which we did not have expertise. And there were some who were sure they would be successful in more glamorous settings, who were doing kitchen work as a kind of penance. You could always tell which cooks *these* were, because they went about their work silently and with an "ECM" demeanor: ECM was our acronym for Early Christian Martyr. There they were, grimly laboring behind the scenes, as it were, as they tried to gain victory over their pride.

I didn't feel at all isolated in the kitchen. Perhaps I was an incipient socialist: I enjoyed working with my hands, and had a "brotherhood" sort of feeling about humanity—a sense of kinship with all those who live by the labor of their hands—who are, we said, historically and actually "the backbone of America and the strength of any sound social order." As I labored in that huge, institutional kitchen which had been that of the Ladies' Athletic Club in L.A., before MRA took it over, I was not especially aware of inner serenity, and I did plenty of exterior banging (in the kitchen you could vent your frustrations noisily and usually no one would notice) but perhaps all this kitchen activity was even then planting seeds of contemplation in my soul: for later, in those last months in the Dellwood kitchen, when I had that strange inner serenity, it was like meeting an old friend whose name you hadn't quite caught before. And when I began to learn, from reading, that there was a *specific* way of life known as the "contemplative," I was able to understand it, to some extent, because of those days in the kitchen when I half-consciously realized that doing things as a kind of prayer, an offering and consecration of the most mundane activities to God, raised these activities above their immediate concern and gave them an eternal value.

I BEGAN GOING to the monastery of Regina Laudis often, with the New York Oblate group and sometimes on my own: I even spent a vacation week there. This was somewhat alarming to my boss and his wife—were they going to "lose" me to "a nunnery"? I assured them this was not going to happen—that lots of laypeople were drawn to the Benedictine way of life *as* laypeople—that they were part of the extended Benedictine family.

And I realized that I had felt at home at Regina Laudis from the very first visit: perhaps because "communal life" is not an alien concept to anyone who had been full time in Moral Re-Armament and stationed in team centers—especially at Dellwood, which to us "behind the scenes" often seemed more like a farm than an ideological training center. We were close to nature there. I remember being behind the scenes in Dellwood's kitchen as, at the monastery, I walk down the road from the chapel and pass by the kitchen. You can tell it is a kitchen because of the unmistakable sounds that come through the unbleached muslin curtains—the rattle of dishes, the whirl of an egg beater, the closing of a refrigerator door. In the small room, called a parlor, where women guests have their meals, we sit on wooden stools around a refectory table, and the food comes through a drawer beneath the wooden lattice which separates the Inside from the Outside—the enclosure from the world. Behind the lattice there is a happy nun, working that side of the drawer: she greets us by name, asks how we've been, and tells those who have asked for "parlors" with one or another nun when and in which of the parlors they are expected.

In the food there is reflected the same care we put into our cooking at team centers. One of the Benedictine Mottoes is: *Ut in omnibus glorificetur Deus*: That in all things God may be glorified. God was certainly glorified in the monastery fruits and vegetables, in the golden-brown corn fritters, in the (perfect) cheese souffles; even in the delicate herb seasoning in the stuffed tomatoes. And always there is the monastery bread and the preserves, and honey supplied by a nun's father, who keeps bees. Benedictine monasteries are traditionally self-supporting, and guests know that if, for instance, the salad is a bit meager, it's because there hasn't been much rain; what isn't available serves as an implicit request for our prayers, and makes us feel more a part of the community. And I realize again how much of MRA'a communal life was based—however unconsciously—on the monastic ideal.

FRANK BUCHMAN HAD SAID, in a speech in Washington in 1939, that "MRA is the triumph of a God-given thought. It came as the answer to a crisis that threatened civilization." Like all the others brought up in MRA, I believed that we were living "in crucial times" and, when full time in the movement, I stated this publicly, to audiences, as we *all* did. But I didn't know much about *other* crucial times in history: St. Benedict's, for instance. It is not known that he ever thought he was the answer to the crisis that was threatening *his* civilization, or that he knew the extent of the crisis. What he *did* know, as a student in Rome, was that the city was pretty corrupt, so he fled (actually, he ran away from school) and settled in with a loose-knit congregation some thirty miles away. There he unwittingly performed a miracle, and when word of this got around he had to flee again, this time into the wilderness near Subiaco, where the lived as a hermit in a cave for three years—known only to a monk of a nearby monastery, who supplied him with food. Then he got discovered by shepherds, and reports of his holiness drew so many men to him that he built twelve monasteries and put twelve monks, with one abbot, in each. They were all under his own care and direction. My *Manual for Oblates* says that "The increasing fame of his sanctity encouraged even Roman nobles to place their sons under his direction; but it also excited jealousy and persecution." So, to protect his monks, he had to flee yet again: this time to Monte Cassino—a mountain about half way between Rome and Naples. There he built a monastery, right on top of the mountain, and there, in about the year 529, he wrote his Holy Rule, which would become known as "a code for Gospel living."

One of the first things I had read about St. Benedict was the essay by Whittaker Chambers in the 1952 book *Saints for Now*,

edited by Clare Boothe Luce. Chambers tells how St. Benedict
had saved Europe from total eclipse during the Dark Ages—
turning Christianity back to its roots, laying down a concrete
way of life against a background of intellectual confusion and
moral chaos. "What was there in this little book that changed
the world?" he asks about the Holy Rule, which "at first
glance . . . seems prosaic enough, even fairly obvious." And that,
says Chambers is the heart of its inspiration: "In an age of pillar
saints and furiously competing athletes of the spirit, when men
plunged by thousands into the desert, in a lunge towards God,
and in revulsion from man, St. Benedict's Rule brought a saving
and creative sanity. Its temper was that of moderation as against
excesses of zeal, of fruitful labor as against austerities pushed
to the point of fruitlessness, of discipline as against enthusiasm,
of continence of spirit and conduct as against incontinence."

Chambers says there are three great alienations of the spirit
which are "perhaps among the little-known reasons why men
turn to Communism: these are the alienation of the spirit of
man from traditional authority; his alienation from the idea of
traditional order, and a crippling alienation that he feels at the
point where civilization has deprived him of the joy of simple
productive labor." And:

> These alienations St. Benedict fused into a new surge of the human
> spirit by directing the frustrations that informed them into the
> disciplined service of God. At the touch of his mild inspiration,
> the bones of a new order stirred and clothed themselves with
> life, drawing to itself much of what was best and most vigorous
> among the ruins of man and his work in the Dark Ages, and
> conserving and shaping its energy for that unparalleled outburst
> of mind and spirit in the Middle Ages. For about the Benedictine
> monasteries what we, having casually lost the Christian East, now
> casually call the West, once more regrouped and saved itself.

> So bald a summary can do little more than indicate the dimensions
> of the Benedictine achievement and plead for its constant re-
> examination. Seldom has the need been greater. For we sense,
> in the year 1952, that we may stand closer to the year 410 than
> at any time in the centuries since . . .

By the time Benedict settled in at Monte Cassino (from whence
he did *not* flee) he must have known that he was living in a
time of crisis. Yet in his "little book" there is nothing about

the temporal and immediate: it's all rooted in the spiritual and eternal. The world then had gone quite mad: there was almost constant warfare, book and art collections were being vandalized, as were cities and large towns. He stayed put but sent his monks out across Italy and into France where they established new monasteries on hillsides or in remote valleys; as the Dark ages extinguished intellectual activity, these monasteries became the centers of tranquility and order, of learning and literature in Western Europe. St. Benedict died at Monte Cassino in about the year 547: within two hundred years, his Holy Rule had been adopted in Italy, Spain, France, England and Germany. By the thirteenth century it had superceded all other monastic Rules. There *was* something about "this little book" that changed the world. Arnold Toynbee, who knows a lot about the rise and fall of civilizations, looks upon the sons and daughters of St. Benedict as the greatest civilizing influence in the western world.

It is unlikely that St. Benedict's contemporaries could have foreseen any of this. He did not appear to be setting the world on fire, pioneering a new social order, spearheading a moral offensive against the enemy, or "meeting the need of the age." The Holy Rule was not a manual for Remaking the World. Who could have predicted that he was preserving Christianity for future generations—that through the centuries his children would carry on their patient anonymous labor, turning swamps into meadows and deserts into fields, copying whole libraries—that at each crisis in history, when all the lights seemed nearly out, there would be these Benedictines in their black habits keeping the light on so that humanity could see its way back to sanity?

THE POPE HAS SAID that the decisive remedy for the universal crisis which is agitating the world is a return to Jesus Christ, the Church, and the Christian way of life: a complete restoration of the spirit of the Gospel. That was Frank Buchman's idea, too, with the exception of Church with a capital C. And there have been (as I learned while reading Ronald Knox's book *Enthusiasm*) groups of people, all down the ages, who banded together in the belief that the salvation of the world (or the answer to the current crisis) was a matter of getting back to simple, basic (*very* early) Christianity. Sometimes they formed communities modeled after First Century Christians. Some of these groups produced "good fruit" but, I wondered, mightn't their fruits have been more abundant if they hadn't thought their way of life was so *original*? If they had drawn from *tradition*, rather than scripture alone? There is no indication that St. Benedict thought he was original. There had been St. Pachomius and St. Basil and others before him; he mentioned them often, in his Rule. What if he had *not* built on their wisdom and experience— and what if he *hadn't* written his "little book"? If he had not made the Christian way of life practicable and concrete in the sixth century, crystallizing it in a simple and wise and specific Rule, it might not be possible today for anyone to even *visualize* a life in which every action, every material object, and all of nature, could be consecrated to God; in which all of us, in the twentieth century, could help change the world.

*   *   *   *   *

(Author's Note: *In the years following the first draft of this manuscript, there have been many changes in the world, in the Church, in Moral Re-Armament, and of course in my own life. The monastery of Regina Laudis is now an Abbey and there have been changes there, too, which it is not my business to go into here. In order to remain within the limits of my purpose in writing this book, I have decided to leave these last pages as they were originally written, in the present tense, because what was present to me in the 1950s belongs to the eternal present.*)

WE COME TO THIS MONASTERY, where the Rule of St. Benedict is being lived for the same reasons and in the same manner as it was fourteen centuries ago; we come with noisy imaginations and untidy wills and with all sorts of ideas about the renovation of our interior lives. We come from our jobs in the dusty cities, with lists of Things to Think About and Decisions to be Made. But each time we come, we are surprised. Pressing concerns fade into irrelevance. We will forget our lists. Mostly, we are surprised by the silence.

The visitors who are probably the most surprised are those

who come expecting and anticipating a "spiritual experience." They wait with relish for interior delights and revelations; they go to the knotty-pine chapel and the pure, thin thread of the nuns' chant will not excite their liturgical emotions nearly as much as the chant records they have at home, since the acoustics aren't those of Solesmes, for instance, and the singers are not monks. The most startling phenomenon they will experience will be that of silence. And if they (and we) can keep silent, the Holy Spirit will have a chance to break through our fog.

Many of us who come here have read a lot of good books written by those who not only know about the contemplative life but who have put it into comprehensible English, and we find it hard to nourish the illusion that we could add anything. Strangely enough, when I am at the monastery I am free even of the *desire* to write or talk about the contemplative life—and perhaps this is because everyone here breathes the same atmosphere, so no one gets all wound up and grabs someone and says: "You see! This is what I mean." (The sort of thing we did in Moral Re-Armament—we wanted to make *sure* that new people caught the infectious life-changing bug.) Here, an attempt to communicate the obvious would be as silly as though you were at the North Pole and pulled your friends aside and said: Isn't it *cold* here? Even if this monastery incarnates all that you feel most deeply about, it is simply not necessary to tell everyone how it all makes sense. There is no need to analyze the peace and the joy, or to relate it all to Modern Society. It is not even necessary to talk to *yourself* about it. You may have spent months holding discourses with yourself about the significance of the contemplative life in the technological age; now your voice is silenced in the obviousness of it all.

I liked what Whittaker Chambers had said about St. Benedict's Rule—the part about "moderation as against zeal" and "discipline as against enthusiasm." Here, whatever inarticulate enthusiasm you may still feel is no longer your private burden; your poverty of language is a part of everyone else's solitude, and you find expression for it in the words of the Psalms which are intimately personal and at the same time full of "we" and "us" and addressed to the "Thou" of a common Father. Your solitude is a part of the solitude of the nuns here and the monks elsewhere, waiting in expectation, officially praising God on behalf of the Church and the whole of creation. "It is good to give praise to the Lord; and to sing to Thy name, O most High."

Everything is its own reason for being. All of us—people, trees, buildings, cattle and sheep, are collected and gathered up in a single focus and offered to God from Whom we also came. The bells for each of the canonical hours the nuns sing remind us that we were created to praise God, and we are kept true to our natures each day by the rhythm of body and soul in prayer and work. Every minute God is knowing us and loving us and showing us our identity.

Language is not necessary.

Here I can be myself. I do not have to "find myself" through laborious introspective scrutiny. There is nothing to do except to be silent, to enter into a solitude that is a withdrawal not from other people but from the artificial and fictional level of my being, and let God discover me to myself in a secret and lucid clarity. And then, if I can let God go on doing it, I will be fulfilling His purpose for my life in the lives of others.

God Himself is the only justification for the cloistered life. It is not justified by its intellectual, cultural, or agricultural contribution to society, nor even by its social function in the Mystical Body, doing the work of intercession for the rest of us. That one's life should be wholly given to God is the Christian ideal, but only the cloistered nuns and monks are free from the distractions which are inevitable for the rest of us; only they can fulfill the ideal in a literal way. Yet their purpose is not that of being inspiring examples or embodiments of ideals, for whether anyone pays any attention to them or not, they are the supreme testimony to the absolute transcendence and absolute sovereignty of the One Who alone is "I am Who am."

The essence of the monastic is one thing: love. It is love that draws the contemplatives to their vocation, and the love of all these monks and nuns makes it possible for the rest of us to become children again. They preserve the relationship with God the Father so that we may all enter in to that love. The early desert Fathers and all who followed them down through the ages had great minds and great hearts and also that simplicity which is the wisdom of the essential. Because of them it is possible for the children of this world to find out how the Father is loving us every minute: no longer as the formidable God of the Old Testament but as the Good Shepherd who leaves his whole sheepfold to descend into the valley and find the sheep that has gotten lost. Because of them it is possible for us to return to the source of our creation and to become children of the light, running and leaping with the freedom of the children of God who will inherit the earth. And the Lord has already overcome the world.

An Appendix

In "NEW YORK, NEW YORK" *(Chapter 6), there is a description of the "Creative Writing" course I took at New York University. The instructor, Vance Bourjaily, was on his way to becoming a well-known novelist; I was fortunate to have got into his course, and flattered when he showed an interest in my writing. Among our assignments was a "character sketch" of someone we knew. My choice was obvious: my Landlady, a formidable woman given to sometimes hilarious, sometimes frightening, mood swings. Bourjaily did indeed like my piece; he encouraged me to re-write it—to make it better than merely "good." I did re-write the sketch, several times, but didn't consider it* finished *until long after the course was over, so Bourjaily never saw the result. But it remains a fond* memoir *of what many young girls who "went to business" in the Manhattan of those days lived through in the various "women's residences" that dotted the City. So I decided to include it here, as a fitting* finale *(or so I hope) to my story, which also took place long ago, in a much different time and place.*

THE LOVELY GIRLS

"THEY DON'T COME ANY BETTA"

T HE VOICE AT THE OTHER END of the phone was neither warm
nor inviting. It was heavy and coarse, and each syllable was
like a muted hammer blow.

I was calling to inquire about a furnished-room ad in the New
York *Times*. The voice asked many questions and I had to repeat
the answers more than once, each time louder: What was my name,
where was I working, where had I been living? Finally the voice
instructed me to wait on a certain corner at a certain time that
very evening after work, whereupon the voice would meet me
and take me to see its "apahtment foah young business girls."

I assumed the voice to be that of a woman, and I waited for
her at the appointed time, on the corner of Lexington Avenue
and 34th Street, wondering what sort of woman belonged to
the voice. And then she appeared. She did not introduce herself;
she didn't say anything at all, but somehow I knew she was
the voice.

In silence, I followed her across 34th Street and into a large
building and through the lobby (which smelled of cats) and into
the elevator.

There were two young-business-girl types already in the elevator,
and I supposed them to be inmates of the apartment—which,
as it turned out, they were. There was no communication between
them and the woman. I smiled pleasantly, expecting an introduction.
There was none.

The woman definitely belonged to the voice on the phone.
She was probably in her forties; she was rather short—compactly
but generously built and, somehow, symmetrical. If an abstract

237

or an impressionist artist had captured her on board or canvas, I thought, the work might have been called "Square on Solid" or "Solid on Square with Moveable Parts" or, simply, "A Study in Symmetry."

Her face seemed especially square, framed as it was by straight, short shiny black hair with a fringe of bangs strung evenly across the top. A rather long (and also shiny) nose extended from palish eyes to a small mouth. All her features had a downward trend, except for the eyebrows which were like straight lines heading slightly upward until they almost met in the middle, thus giving the face a curious mixture of surprise, skepticism, and wariness: a ready-for-anything expression.

There was total silence during the slow ascent to the fifth floor. The woman unlocked the door to the apartment. The two girls disappeared behind their doors, and I followed the woman down to almost the end of a long, dark, narrow hall. The woman rattled a great many keys, selected one, opened the door and showed me the available room.

It was clean and large enough for my immediate needs, and my needs *were* immediate; so I paid the deposit and said that I would move in on the following Saturday, if that would be all right. And then, to be polite and friendly, I began to ask questions about the apartment, such as how many girls live here, how long have they been here, and where do they work? Quite normal, affable, questions, I thought. The woman responded by asking me, in a manner not merely *un*friendly but almost menacing, why I wanted to know these things. Which was, I thought, rather like greeting someone with the standard "Hi, how are you?" and being answered not by "Fine, and you?" but by: "None of your damn business and why the hell do you want to probe?" Here, she stated militantly, was the room. I could take it or leave it. If I didn't find it satisfactory, I could move.

Obviously, I had somehow put her on the defensive and this had made her belligerent. And with what I then considered to be profound insight, I deduced that she was either trying to impress me by her indifference or to convince *herself* that she didn't give a damn one way or the other; and that her facial expression was "superiority superimposed on insecurity." *I* was not going to be put on the defensive, though, so I gave her a nice reassuring (I hoped) smile and said that I was very pleased with the room.

I was indeed pleased about the rent: only $10.50 a week plus Kitchen Privileges. These had been mentioned in the ad, and I hoped this woman would not take offense if I asked her what they were. Kitchen privileges, she explained (calmer, now) meant that she provided breakfast Mondays through Fridays, that each girl could keep, in the refrigerator, a bag (with your name on it) of snacks or food you wanted to cook for supper or for meals on weekends; we could eat in the kitchen, nights and weekends, as long as we didn't make a mess.

(What she did *not* mention was that the refrigerator was unreliable; it was very old and one's groceries—as I would find out later—alternated daily between soggy and limp, or frozen stiff.)

On the following Saturday I moved into my room. *My room*: that had a nice sound to it. I was, I thought, at last "on my own."

THERE WERE, IN THIS APARTMENT, six or seven rooms strung along one side of the hall: whether they were singles or doubles (or closets) I couldn't know, since all the doors were closed. Later on I learned that the first room was a large bedroom with a bay window on the 34th Street side: five girls shared that room, or so I was told—I never saw the inside, nor did I know which girls lived there. That was obviously the corner room, so maybe it had a window on the Lexington Avenue side, too.

Then, before the other bedrooms began, there was a kind of utility room or "pantry" which had two deep laundry tubs and clotheslines strung across the top. Next to that there was a sliver of storage and closet space (which I don't remember ever using) and then came the kitchen, and then—set back a bit—a bathroom; and then there were the remaining bedrooms. Mine was next to last. I'd thought, at first, that my room was at the very end of the hall, but there was another door sort of angled against mine, and this door opened into the final room, a double. This room would prove to be very important.

On the opposite side of the long dark narrow hall there was, mostly, just *wall*, but on this wall there was a telephone (*the* telephone) and near the phone there was a door, which was the door to the Lavatory. In this lavatory there was a toilet situated atop a raised platform, and the toilet had a chain for flushing. There was another chain dangling from the ceiling, and that was to pull the light on and off. I don't remember any basin or sink: I think there wasn't any. The real *bathroom* had one of those old-fashioned bathtubs on legs, and a floor which tried to look like tile but which was actually warped linoleum, probably vintage-depression.

The presence of, or the *fact* of, the lavatory and bathroom, kitchen and pantry, established this place as an "apartment" rather than merely "rooms."

I didn't know my landlady's name, since she had not introduced herself; and she never did. There were, however, notes Scotch-taped here and there, such as the one in the bathroom warning one not to wash one's hair in the sink, and these were signed: "G. Woods." She signed the rent receipts that way, too. Therefore we all thought of her as G. Woods or, simply, "Woods."

We were expected to keep our rooms neat and to do our personal laundry, but we did have a luxury of sorts: G. Woods employed a mousey cleaning lady, a Mrs. Peterson, and a laundry man. Mrs. Peterson would appear, in fear and trembling, once or twice a week; the laundry man was large and gruff and seemed to have a permanent scowl, as he collected the dirty sheets and towels and delivered the clean ones. G. Woods always hollered and bellowed at them both (this would begin before most of us had left for our jobs) and the laundry man would usually bellow back. They seemed to be perpetually engaged in some battle, and there was never any truce. Whatever threats and insults and recriminations passed between this odd trio were mostly unintelligible to us, as we'd listen, snickering, with our ears pressed to our doors.

Since I had moved in on a Saturday, my first communal breakfast was on Monday. It was—as I wrote in my diary—an Experience. (Later I would watch with some compassion but more amusement the bewildered newcomers at *their* First Breakfasts.) It was dingy and musty in that old-fashioned (even for those days) kitchen. Odd pots and pans hung on nails or hooks; there were some plates and glasses on a shelf above the porcelain sink, and there was a fascinating jumble of knives, forks and spoons in an enormous cardboard carton which had its own special place on the floor. There was a table with four chairs. Rows of empty bottles stood dustily on a high-up shelf. On a rack near the sink there hung a damp towel and a dish-cloth which was full of coffee grounds.

As I entered the kitchen, I had to pass by G. Woods, who was standing—as if at attention—by the door, a tall glass of coffee in her hand. Several girls were already sitting at the table, and they glanced up at me, dully. Again, there were no introductions. The only sounds were the chewing of toast, the stirring of coffee, and the heavy, deliberate movements of G. Woods as she left her post at the door and, with an air of martyrdom, set about fixing my breakfast. The House Breakfast was a glass of juice (canned); anemic toast and weak coffee with grounds floating around in the chipped cup. Paper napkins doubled as place mats.

I began to take a knife out of the pile of rusty utensils which were on the drainboard; for some reason they had escaped the cardboard carton (into which I had visions of falling head-first) and G. Woods said: "Pohdon me Sweethaht but do me a favuh—rinse that off unda hot wautah. You don't wanta get soahs on youah lip." She had, I thought, the kind of accent one would hear, in those days, on the radio, when people would be trying to imitate New Yorkers.

I did as I was told, and we ate in silence—a silence broken only by an occasional long sigh of "Oh, hell," which seemed to emanate from the very depths of G. Woods. The kitchen had a large window with ample sill, upon which she would sit once she had completed her kitchen duty. The window looked down on the Bickford Cafeteria on the southeast corner of Lexington Avenue and 34th Street. She would glance down at Bickfords as she sipped her coffee (she *always* had her coffee in a glass) and then she would glance at us: nothing escaped her vigilance. She seemed to take in everything and everyone, like a cat ready to pounce on its prey. How eagerly she waited for the chance to remind us to wipe off the table and to rinse our dishes unda hot wautah.

I noticed with not a little surprise and with much pleasure that there was real butter for our toast; here, I thought, was perhaps a new opportunity to begin a friendly conversation, so I expressed my delight about the butter.

This was clearly a mistake: how could I have been so naive? G. Woods' eyebrows rose, her eyes widened, and she said: "What do you usually have, that Marjorol-or-whatever you cohl it?" For days she harped on this. "Anyone who uses that Marjorol-or-whatever it is don't know what good food is." She had the same contempt for instant coffee—ours being the real thing, of course, grounds and all.

Thereafter, I avoided the topic of food, for any reference to food would launch her into a lengthy speech about the importance of Good Food to Healthy (by which I think she meant Moral) Life. It was one of her favorite tirades. . . . And every morning I stared at my cold, real-butter-saturated, limp toast.

FROM THE VERY BEGINNING, an aura of mystery seemed to enshroud G. Woods. No one seemed to know where she went, when she left to "go to business." No one seemed to know her full name, whether she was Miss or Mrs., what sort of past had brought her to this present. Whenever she *did* happen to mention anything that might have given us clues, these would be merely fragmentary bits and pieces of allusions to things vague and depressing, which would inevitably lead her to the Preamble of her Creed: You can't trust nobody; the only way to stay outta trouble is to mind your own business. She'd been brought up to believe that Honesty was the Best Policy and it wasn't (but *she* was honest, even if it didn't pay), and so on. Eventually I learned (or *heard*, for I never "learned" anything first-hand) that G. Woods had been married when she was quite young and that it hadn't worked out; that she had worked during the days and had gone to college at night; and that she was an accountant.

As the weeks passed, my first impression of G. Woods as a tyrannical, domineering virago began to change: I perceived hints of warmth and benevolence under her tough and brittle veneer, or so I thought. Although she frequently and dogmatically extolled the virtues of Keeping yourself to yourself, at times she fantasized that we were "family" and that her place was real nice and homey. One evening, for example, she came in with ice cream for whoever happened to be "home" and we congregated around the kitchen table, laughing and chatting almost normally, while *she* of course sat on her beloved windowsill, keeping her distance. When she was at her most gregarious, she'd come into the kitchen while some of us were trying to deal with our refrigerated brown bags, and she'd have a beer or two; and then she'd begin telling jokes and teasing us (about what, I can't remember) and her laugh would become loud and raucous and would go on and on, expanding in volume, and we would force ourselves to laugh along with her, till our faces froze. But even when she was at the peak of this unpredictable effervescence, she would never let down her guard. Her eyes never lost that wary, suspicious look; she could change in a flash and become vitriolic.

Now and then she would "go out of her way" for us (always making sure we *knew* that's what she was doing). She would make a special trip out to mail a letter or buy a bottle of aspirin; she'd take a pocketbook to be mended—and whether these selfless gestures were attempts to fan the smouldering embers of her own picture of herself as a generous, responsible and nice landlady or whether they were cold, calculating acts to make us indebted to her, so that when the time came she could accuse us of Ingratitude, possibly even *she* didn't know. Nevertheless it was inevitable that we *would* all turn out to be Ungrateful: the script had been written and there could be no changes, except in the cast of characters.

G. Wood kept lots of keys to all sorts of mysterious closets, and she would rattle them importantly—rather like a prison guard, I thought. She had a sort of uniform, too—a dark skirt, a sporty, long, mannish jacket, and flat shoes. In the mornings, as she fixed our breakfasts, she wore an oldish blue bathrobe; when she went out at night she'd wear high heels and bright red lipstick. She must have been going out to dinner most of those nights, in fact, for I never saw her cooking for herself in the kitchen. She was always secretive, about everything, and therefore to prepare food for herself openly would constitute an invasion of her privacy. (I never saw her using the laundry tub or ironing her clothes, either). We knew she *had* dinner, because she would often inform us that she allowed herself two luxuries in life: good food and taxis.

No matter what she did or where she went in the evenings, she always returned just before eleven. I would hear her coming down the long hall, her keys clanking in rhythm with her footsteps. Her key would turn in her lock; the door would squeak open and close quickly. Then there would be the rustle of newspaper pages turning, and the grating sound of her rasping, choking cough, and then Kenneth Banghardt and The Eleventh Hour News would blare forth: we didn't need our own radios to keep up with world events. Although her actions were slow, deliberate, and plodding, her ears were as alert as were her eyes. She would

pounce on any carelessly-dropped word or phrase, or she would
detect a sinister meaning underlying some innocent sentence,
and detect an Issue: then she would begin a debate, which of
course wasn't a debate at all since there was only one side—
hers. In her opinionated crescendo of conviction, about whatever
it happened to be at the moment, she always had the last word—
if only because she had the greater endurance. It was rarely possible
to have a normal conversation with her, for to begin a conversation
was like turning on the radio and getting a stream of propaganda
which would go on and on, beamed to whoever might be within
earshot. There was no way to turn the dial so as to change the
station: the only thing to do was to get far away quickly and
as unobtrusively as possible.

No: there was nothing remotely timid or taciturn about G.
Woods. She did however have a profound (and ostentatious)
respect for Privacy. Our rooms were off limits, to her. When
it was in her line of duty to knock on one's door—perhaps one
had had a phonecall, or something—she would carefully—
monkishly—avert her eyes, when the door was opened. She would
not look at the person, nor beyond the person into the room.
When we paid our rents, she would make out the receipts and
hand them to us through a crack in the door. Apparently a wide
open door was somehow obscene, so we all got into the habit
of opening our doors just a wee crack.

Indeed, privacy was sacred to G. Woods: she was as protective
about our privacy as she was diligent about her own "duties."
Whatever her own unspoken rules may have been, she was as
fanatically conscientious about her part as she was dictatorial
about ours. So conscientious about her obligations was she that
one Thursday morning, when she had overslept and had therefore
not fixed our breakfasts, she was so filled with remorse that
she insisted on giving us extra bread "for the weekend"—*that
night*. Breakfast was as usual on Friday morning. By Saturday
of course our weekend bread had turned to stone.

There was one frequent source of entertainment for us young-
business-women in the G. Woods' ménage: we would listen, behind
our closed doors, when G. Woods answered the phone, because
these phonecalls were almost always from girls who had seen
her ad in the paper. Snickering, within the security of our rooms,
we would hear the following:

"Hell*ew*?" (Her voice always became refined, when she answered the phone.) There would be a short silence, and then: "Well, heah's something . . . May I ask how old you are? Oh . . . well, these are mostly *young* girls. You wouldn't want to share a room or an apahtment with a young girl at *your* age, would you?" Another silence. Then: "Well, heah's something . . . uh, let me ask you, what kind of place did you have befoah? Oh . . . well, I mean, wouldn't you find this difficult, aftah that?"

And then the usual—about the rent, and breakfast five days a week, and kitchen privileges. If the hopeful on the other end of the line had survived all this, the final sentences would be: "Well, now look: theah's a drugstoah right across the street, it's a *Rex*ohl Drugstoah, R, E, X, A, L, L, *Rexohl.* You cohl me from theah and I'll come and meet you and show you the place."

Then she would repeat the name of the drugstore, and would tell the caller not to get *that* drugstore mixed up with the one on the *next* corner.

At first, G. Woods' attitude toward her tenants seemed paradoxical, but each new inmate would eventually come to understand that this landlady had a Good List and a Bad List. If you were on the Good List, you were a Lovely-Girl-They-Don't-Come-Any-Better. How long one stayed on the Good List before being transferred to the Bad List seemed to depend entirely on G. Woods' own peculiar whim. We had no insight into her rationale or her methodology: there were no clues about the inner workings of her mysterious clock, or whatever it was.

For a while I was one of her stars: one of the lovely-girls-I-wish-they-were-ohl-like-you. Apparently I had passed the first test, whatever *that* was; now that my tenancy had been firmly established, I was taken into her confidence. These confidences were always preceded by a ritual: "Listen, Sweethaht, come heah." She would go into the kitchen: I would follow. She would then exit kitchen, peer down the hall, re-enter kitchen and shut the door. And then her eyes would gleam as she would launch into defamatory revelations about this or that girl (who probably didn't live there anymore, although one could never be quite sure since it was difficult to put names with faces). I would listen and would respond with the sort of expressions and noises she seemed to expect. It wasn't exactly *gossip* that G. Woods was indulging in, because there was never anything very specific.

Or perhaps she *was* more specific than I can remember: possibly her hushed tone of voice and the drama she created around herself were sufficiently awesome so as to airbrush all details from the mind of the listener.

I do remember that whatever specific theme may have begun each of these revelations, these True Life Stories, they were all more or less the same; G. Woods' mouth would spew forth examples of virtues and vices in a series of unrelated stories which always had the same moral: *trust no one.* A form-letter type of Shocking Revelation would go like this: "Ninety puhcent of the girls heah are Problem Cases. Their parents won't have them. So I take them in, they have lots of freedom, low rent; but are they grateful? No. They're ohl alike. They don't appreciate what they got heah. . . . Now, if they was all like you and Vivian—lovely girls, they don't come any betta."

There was one specific example given, nameless and faceless and so therefore probably representative of the many; and this was The Case of The Girl Who Got Sick. "I cohled the doctah, I gave her food and took care of her. And what did I get but a kick in the pants. I nevah should have taken this place. If I had known what I was getting in foah, I nevah woulda taken it. It's moah trouble than it's worth."

There was, in fact, another girl who always seemed to be sick— or so I was told, some years later. This girl could not hold down a job and was apparently in the protective custody of G. Woods, who always let her rent slide and never yelled at her. I seem to remember seeing her shadow now and then. She lived on the other side of G. Woods' room, I think; but I have a vague memory that she was *in* G. Woods' room, most of the time. Of course G. Woods never mentioned *her* . . .

And there was a girl named Jean: she had been a lovely-girl- they-don't-come-any-better. Jean was from a Lovely Family: "It was a pleashuh to have a girl like her." (Alas, the girls on the Good List could fall from grace and find themselves on the Bad List almost overnight, it seemed). It seemed that Jean began to "spread malicious gossip." That was one of G. Woods' favorite phrases: she loved the sound of *malicious gossip.* "Listen, Sweethaht, don't get me stahted about her . . ." For Jean was, she said, an Agitator; and agitators are Communists so therefore it followed that Jean was a Communist. And G. Woods hated Communists.

Quite possibly G. Woods had good reason to distrust some of the inmates of apartment 5A: there *were* some rather odd characters who would eye me curiously at the breakfast table and whom I would eye even more curiously when their backs were turned: girls who would appear and then would disappear—the only proof of their brief tenancy being a trail of empty beer cans.

When G. Woods first began to confide in me, I thought it would be easy to avoid the pitfalls of Those Who Had Erred. I was a good listener and had, I thought, a "knack" for "bringing out the best in people." Perhaps I could help G. Woods to be more "positive" about these girls: perhaps I could help G. Woods, herself. But as time went on, reality began to sink in. I realized that I hadn't actually *known* how these various girls had erred. And so, becoming wiser in the ways of the world, I figured the obvious sane thing to do was to keep listening, to continue being generally sympathetic and to have nothing to do with malicious gossip. Not that I had anything malicious to gossip about, and I wouldn't, if I *did*, but clearly the safe thing would be to make it absolutely clear that I was above this sort of thing.

It is true that the girls in the next-door room and I would sometimes joke a bit about malicious gossip, because we heard the phrase so often. But we were very careful never to be overheard for we knew it was in our best interests to please and appease our landlady. We were never quite sure exactly *how* to do this, though, because one night G. Woods might be complaining vociferously about the last group of girls—they had been loud and obnoxious, they'd had phone calls at 5:30 in the morning, and she didn't like that, no Sir, and the next night she would be saying that she didn't want a bunch of old maids who just sat around every night. Why, she'd had the *nicest* girls last year: they used to have pahties and take each other out when one had a birthday and oh-yes, they all had a lovely time togethah.

Although I had been, I thought, securely established on the Good List, I began to have an eerie feeling that there were insidious forces at work: forces about which I could do nothing. A force, or forces, plotting my imminent and inevitable fall from grace.

And the rest of this story is about my decline.

There were several incidents which led to my excommunication. One had to do with an ironing board.

I had been doing my ironing on my two ancient suitcases,

pushed together with newspaper and tissue paper spread over the tops. The other girls may have done the same, or maybe they ironed their clothes on their beds. By this time I had become quite friendly with the two girls who lived next door, Vivian and Beula. Our rooms had a connecting door, which we were more or less aware of but for all practical purposes it was just a part of the wall, and we had furniture against it, for we had little enough wall space as it was. One morning we got talking about the ironing problem, and decided that a real ironing board would be a great convenience; so one night after work we met and went to Macy's basement and bought a respectable, full-sized ironing board, the kind with wooden legs, and we brought it back with us on the subway. We were very pleased, and did not mind sharing it with the other girls in the apartment.

But very early, one rainy, gloomy Saturday, I awoke to shouts and threats coming from the hall. G. Woods was actually *maligning* Vivian, whom she accused of having lent the ironing board to someone who had not helped pay for it and who had left a (minor) scorch on top. G. Woods was *ordering* Vivian to make "all the girls" who *had* helped pay for the ironing board give the money back; and she warned Vivian not to lend out the ironing board, *ever*: "I don't want anyone borrowing anything from anybody! This isn't no Girls' Residence Club!" Vivian, she roared, was to keep the ironing board locked in her room.

We knew that G. Woods was being totally irrational; we also knew that the thorn in her flesh was much sharper and deeper and broader than a mere ironing board, so there was no point in making an issue of it. And Vivian and Beula and I went on sharing the ironing board; only now we passed it through our "secret door" so as not to expose it in the hall.

By now it was obvious that Vivian and Beula and I, the three Lovely-Girls-They-Don't-Come-Any-Better, had become good friends: and this was the beginning of the end. G. Woods was convinced that we had formed an alliance. The ironing board was merely symbolic, and was not mentioned again: the alliance, however, was a fact. Almost overnight G. Woods turned against us. She accused us of having formed a "clique" so that we could gossip about her and turn everyone else in the apartment against her, and she would not leave us alone. When we three would congregate in my room or in their room, she would be listening. We didn't try to *prove* this, but since she had always closed and locked her door immediately upon entry each evening, and *now* she was keeping her door open a wee crack (through our keyholes we could see a sliver of light in the dark hall) there was little doubt about what she was up to.

FOR WHATEVER REASON, G. Woods had turned especially on Vivian, the quiet, rather shy young woman from Colorado, who had come to New York to study voice and was hoping for an operatic career. It was not enough that Vivian keep the ironing board in her room: now she demanded that Vivian keep her door closed *at all times*. Vivian, stated G. Woods, had been keeping her door open so that she could eavesdrop on all conversations. Vivian had "degraded" all the girls who had roomed with her before, in that double room. She had filled them with Malicious Gossip. And she, G. Woods, didn't want no moah of that, no sir: if there was anything she couldn't stand, it was Malicious Tongues.

Ridiculously enough, we three began to feel guilty whenever we were seen together in the apartment, so we began meeting on the sly. It was rather fun, this cloak-and-dagger business. One at a time we would sneak, undetected, down the long hall, into the elevator, to have breakfast out. Sometimes we would meet at night at something called Tyme Letter Shop—a direct mail operation, where anyone who could type reasonably well could pound away on ancient typewriters with faded ribbons and get paid according to how many envelopes you had addressed or how many inside-addresses you had typed. I think one hundred envelopes netted one dollar, at a penny apiece; inside addresses and "Dear So-and-So:" paid more. The people in charge at Tyme knew the exact weight of envelopes and sheets of paper, so we were paid according to scale—*literally*: Tyme Letter Shop's own metal scale. In those days, every penny counted.

That cliche "every penny counts" had become a reality for me one day when I left the office, at Madison Avenue and 52nd Street, and discovered that I had exactly nine cents. Bus fare was ten cents. So I walked to my building at Lexington and 34th, faintly amused by the irony of the situation: here I was secretary to the Managing Editor of Harper's Bazaar magazine, and I literally didn't have a dime. It seemed that all the secretaries at Harper's Bazaar were paid notoriously low salaries: presumably this was because ours were considered "glamour jobs," which meant that you were so grateful for the privilege of working for that prestigious, exciting, slick fashion magazine, that money didn't matter. I suspect that my fellow-secretaries were subsidized by their parents, and lived at home—in Queens or somewhere. I was determined to be self-supporting, which was not exactly a matter of choice, anyway. So G. Woods' low rent, and Tyme Letter Shop, and another occasional night job—typing up bills and reports for two dentists, a husband and wife, in their posh apartment/office—made it just barely possible to afford my Glamour Job, and to go to a movie now and then.

By this time, it had become clear to Vivian, Beula and me that G. Woods was more than a "character": we decided she was either psychotic or paranoid, or both. And if at times I thought I was over-dramatizing the situation in apartment 5A, my *mother* didn't, and she urged me to take precautions. So every night I locked my door and piled my suitcases against it, just in case G. Woods might have one of her rages and turn into a Lady Macbeth sort of creature, with a knife.

As winter approached, a cold and sinister atmosphere pervaded the apartment. All conversation between inmates was hushed: telephone conversations ceased abruptly when *her* footsteps echoed in the hall. There was much shouting about Malicious Gossip—directed to us at large, and somehow including the hapless cleaning lady and the laundryman. And no one new came to see the apartment.

Nevertheless, despite all this, or perhaps *because* of it, G. Woods decided to give a going-away "pahty" for two of the girls who would be leaving to get married. Beula was one. This event was announced one morning to all who were within hearing distance: not as a novel idea, don't-you-think-so?, nor as a "duty" but purely as a matter of fact, or of routine. There would be, she said, a few cans of beer, some coffee and ice-cream: she, G. Woods, would buy a wedding cake, and would we all be willing to donate a dollah? Yes, we said: *of course* we would.

As the day for the party approached, G. Woods seemed indeed to have had a change of heart. She became almost cheerful and at times bordered on the euphoric. She bought a china Bride and Groom for the top of the wedding cake, and she showed this decoration to all of us: she was rather like a small child with a new toy.

And then came the night I shall never forget. About an hour before the party was to begin, I was in the kitchen, frying a solitary hamburger. Suddenly the front door slammed and G. Woods strode into the kitchen and wordlessly handed me a crumpled dollar bill. I didn't take it: all I could do was stare at her. Then she said: "Heah, I owe you a dollah." "No you don't," I said, having recovered my voice: "What for?" And she replied: "The pahty's off."

Her voice had actually been shaky and there was a moistness around her eyes. I clutched the dollar and she stalked down the hall to her room and slammed her door with a reverberating bang.

BY THE TIME VIVIAN GOT HOME the tension had become palpable; and before I could say a word to Vivian, G. Woods stormed out of her room, gave Vivian back *her* dollar, and stormed back into her room, Vivian was equally dumbfounded. There were a few moments of ominous silence and then suddenly G. Woods appeared again; and now she was acting like a raging maniac (this was, as I later wrote in my diary, "no laughing matter"). She began screaming insults at Vivian, accusing her of vague but presumably dreadful things, and screaming things about Beula, too. It seemed that Beula and a girl named Barbara had been together the night before and had been indulging in Malicious Gossip; but somehow this was all *Vivian's* fault because, she screeched at Vivian, "Beula was all right till she moved in with *you* and I'm not gonna let anyone move in with you aftah Beula leaves! You'll hafta move in with someone down the hall so you can't poison any *new* girl!" As she continued hurling abuses and insults and threats at Vivian, her volume arose alarmingly, and as her decibels increased, so did my adrenaline: something new and alarming was happening to *me*. Part of me was thinking: G. Woods is to be pitied—she's a mental case. But suddenly my well-balanced control of pity-over-anger went haywire. I couldn't stand it any more: I literally saw red. I hated G. Woods. I wanted to destroy her. In one split-second she symbolized all the stupid prejudice and injustice in the whole world. Then, without premeditation but in a surge of blazing anger, I did something terrible: I slammed my door. I slammed it, *loud*.

There was a moment of stunned silence. My radio was on

and instinctively I turned up the volume, whereupon G. Woods increased *hers* again: "Anyone," she shrieked, "Anyone who slams the door in my face, I'll slam their head in!" And she thundered out of the apartment.

I waited for a few minutes, to make sure the coast was really clear, and then crept into Vivian's room—this time through the regular door, not the secret one. We stared at each other in disbelief and shock, but I suspect we both felt rather victorious. We agreed that it was most unwise to hang around *there*, so we headed out to a movie. And as we might have expected, when we went out through the lobby, there *she* was, coming in. But without a word or a glance, we continued in our opposite directions. And this time her suspicions were justified: we certainly *were* going to have a delicious time indulging in Malicious Gossip.

It was with some trepidation, though, that Vivian and I returned to the apartment after the movie. We had visions of murderous threats smeared on our doors, in red paint or maybe even blood. Or would G. Woods be waiting for me, behind my door, knife in hand? (I can't remember what movie we had seen: perhaps it was a horror film.) But all was dark and deathly quiet in the apartment. We proceeded as quietly as possible to our rooms, put the keys in our locks, and I slowly pushed my door open, with one foot, till I heard it connect with the wall: no, she was not there.

The next morning, there were no sounds from G. Woods' room; there was no smell of coffee from the kitchen. As I crept stealthily past her room and down the hall to the front door and the liberating elevator, I could not sense her presence anywhere. No one else seemed to be around, either.

But during that day I began to wonder and even to worry a bit. I had visions of G. Woods lying, dead, across her bed, clutching an empty pill bottle or maybe there would be an open container of rat poison near her lifeless body. I even contemplated finding a ladder and climbing it so as to peer into her room through the transom, should there turn out to be any grounds for suspecting that she'd done herself in. But we found out from the superintendent (possibly this was the first time we knew of *his* existence) that G. Woods had gone out very early that morning. Obviously there had been no breakfast for anyone.

About the door-slamming: I didn't regret the incident, even

though my conscience told me that I had stooped to G. Woods' own methods. Anyway, it wasn't true that I had slammed the door in her face, since her face hadn't been anywhere near the door. The door-slamming, though, was symbolic: it had been a *statement*. I had been pleased with, and proud of, what I thought was my new "independence." I had got, on my own, a job and a place to live. What I hadn't yet got, though, was my own *self*. All along I'd had an *idea* of myself: in the G. Woods' context I was a Peacemaker and/or innocent martyr, and basically I'd always been a Nice Person who, in trying situations (of which there had never been any remotely like this) felt compassion and tried reasoning, rather than feeling anger and using violence. I was above childish outbursts. I was, somehow, superior, but possessed of that true Christian "humility" which always lets the adversary know that you have The Answer to his or her Problem.

And so that idea of myself got slammed away when I slammed the door. And I felt, for the first time, truly independent.

. . . I realize now, and wonder why I wasn't more aware of it then, that G. Woods' outburst had taken place on Holy Thursday, so Good Friday was the day she hadn't appeared. Harper's Bazaar let us off at noon that day, and I went away for the weekend.

THE EASTER WEEKEND HAD BEEN restorative to some extent, but on the train back to the city my new self-confidence began to dissolve. At Grand Central Station my knees were rather gelatinous, as I de-trained; I wondered if I was near panic, but decided I wasn't, since along with mounting apprehension there was this curious detachment, or a detached and very real *curiosity*. It was as though I were a character in some gothic novel, wondering what would happen to me in the next chapter. I could not imagine how the chapter would end; nor had I any idea of how, if I were the author, I'd *want* the whole story to end.

There had been times when the outbursts of G. Woods had rebounded in a way which turned her, for a while, into the opposite sort of person—servile and placating. Would this scenario be repeated, I wondered?

No, not this time. The proverbial die had been cast; the pendulum had swung and stuck. I was now most definitely on the Black List. There were hushed reports, from Beula and the other girls who had survived the weekend in 5A, that G. Woods had been impossible: had shouted and cursed and blasphemed for three days, and one of the girls had left for her honeymoon under a shower not of rice but of insults and rebukes.

Beula would soon be leaving too, for Florida and her fiance; Vivian, as it turned out, would be leaving even sooner. She had been so disgusted about the ironing board incident ("This is no Girls' Residence Club!") that she'd got herself on the waiting list at a Girls' Residence Club—The Evangeline, on 14th Street, owned and run by The Salvation Army. She was at the end of a very long list, but after that last G. Woods' explosion she gave the admitting lady such a sad and desperate tale of woe that the Salvation Army apparently decided she was a needy case and moved her up to the Urgent List; within a few days she got accepted. Beula and I helped her move. And so, shortly after that, of the three notorious malicious-tongued trouble-makers, I alone remained.

My courage had returned, and with a vengeance. But my mother was worried. She had phoned once or twice when G. Woods had been riding her broomstick; by now she was seriously concerned for my safety. She thought my days were numbered, and urged me to give immediate notice, in which case God would most certainly provide a new place to live. I knew that my days in that apartment were numbered, but I was determined to take the days one at a time. I had no doubt about God providing, but I knew that that would demand something on my part, too, and I wasn't up to it. I was nearly penniless, was once again in the throes of job-hunting, and had a lingering virus, so I was determined to stay on, for the time being. I refused to be intimidated. I could cope.

But I dared not speak to anyone else in the apartment. I had heard that various girls were spreading lies about various other girls, and I didn't know which tongues were malicious and which were just inexperienced, or who was spreading what about whom, so I kept myself to myself, just as G. Woods had said—very long ago, it seemed—that that was what one should always do.

By tacit agreement I took breakfast alone in my room: toast and coffee were shoved in to me through a crack in my door. If I happened to be walking down the hall and G. Woods was coming up the hall, she would disappear into a closet or flatten herself against the wall, to let me pass. She never looked at me; she never spoke to me. It was an uneasy truce, I thought. And now she always left her door open, just a crack.

ONE NIGHT WHEN we passed each other, I risked a "hello." She didn't acknowledge my greeting but said, as she went into her room, that she wanted me to give her a week's notice before I moved out. I tried to look surprised and nonplussed (maybe I *was* surprised: she hadn't actually *mentioned* my moving, before) and told her that I wasn't planning to leave. She said nothing more, then, but next morning, next evening, and so on for several days the scenario would be repeated.

If G. Woods had, unwittingly, made me truly independent, she had—by way of this latest turn of events—made me very stubborn, too. The more obvious she made it that she wanted me out, the more determined I was to stay—not so much out of necessity as of spite. Her constant nagging about my giving her a week's notice, synchronized now with the ever-present dripping of water from somewhere in the apartment, began to take on a plaintive, pleading tone: "Listen," she'd begin—and I would remember how in the early days it had been "Listen, Sweethaht . . ."—"Listen, you *gotta* give me a week's notice."

I began giving *her* the silent treatment. It was rather perversely fun, my being impervious to the new note I detected in her voice. It was obvious that she was most eager to get the rotten apple out before it could infect the bunch: there were some girls waiting to get into the double room next door, she said, and there was in fact "Someone interested in youah room" who was all ready to move in as soon as I moved out.

When she realized that I was not taking immediate action for removal, she regrouped her demons and used another strategy: every day, twice a day and even three times a day, she would warn me about Malicious Gossip: "Now listen heah, I don't want no moah of this malicious gossip. I can't stand these malicious tongues." I'm not sure what this "strategy" would be *called*, but eventually it began to work on me, or anyway it began to wear me down, and I decided to let her think that she had won this cold war. (Besides, my mother was making noises about removing me bodily and putting all my belongings in a locker in Grand Central Station.)

My mother hadn't given up on God's Providence, however, and she didn't seem very surprised when, within the week, I had found refuge in the girls' residence directly across from The Evangeline (whose waiting list I was on) and this was called Katherine House. This happened so fast that I was unable to give G. Woods' her famous Week's Notice: therefore I had to pay her an extra week's rent. I did not complain; nor did I complain when she refused, in angry tones, to give me a refund for the extra key I had bought.

When I was all packed and ready to leave, she spoke nicely to me for the first time in many weeks. How did I like my new job, she asked, and how was my family, how was I feeling, and could she help me load my things onto the elevatuh?

Perhaps she was just relieved to be rid of me at last, but she seemed *so* different that I wondered if she might be one of those multiple personalities: was this a new face emerging? I needn't have wondered long, though, because there was one final episode which seemed to portray the whole enigma of G. Woods, whoever/ whatever she was. Again, it had to do with the ironing board.

The other partners of the by now famous, or infamous, ironing board had moved out, leaving me its sole heir. After much debating with myself I had decided that the thing to do was to ask G. Woods if she knew of anyone who might like it, since I wouldn't be needing it. Her reaction was surprising. I expected something like: "Listen, that's youah problem and I don't give a damn what you do with it." But what she said was that she would try to sell it "to one of the girls heah" and then she became earnest: "You won't believe me, but if I can sell it I'll send the check to you in the mail. You don't think I'll send it, but I will— you'll see. I'm honest—*too* honest. It's terrible to have an obsession like that."

I thought: It sure is awful to have obsessions, and you sure have a lot, but if honesty is one of them I'd hate to know about the others. . . . Not that I doubted her sincerity. She'd send me the check, I was convinced, as a lasting reprimand: a final proof of her misunderstood nature . . .

She never sent a check. Perhaps she couldn't find any buyers for the ironing board.

I went back to Apartment 5A just once, after I had moved, to pick up some mail. By this time I was indeed well into a much happier chapter; my sense of balance and well-being had been restored, I had no lingering resentment about G. Woods and in fact felt a small pang of sympathy for her. So it was not a strain to greet her in a friendly fashion.

The place was just as dismal, just as gloomy. The same notes were on the walls: the same month was on the calendar. G. Woods was in her same old blue bathrobe, rattling the same bunch of keys. She did not meet my gaze, but said: "Look heah, I wanta show you something."

Down the long dark hall she marched and I followed her obediently. She opened the door to what had been Vivian and Beula's room and showed me the dingy room trying to hide behind a coat of fresh paint.

"See! The new girls heah decided they wanted to paint the room and make it real nice. See, isn't this nice? I just wanted to show you how *lovely* it is to have two girls who appreciate what they got heah."

And then she added: "I don't want no moah like that Vivian and all the rest of them . . ."

And across the platform of my mind marched white lines of Lovely Girls—pale ghostly girls turning darker and darker. Forever there would be new girls: inevitably there would be Black Lists.